HOW TO LOOK AFTER YOUR HORSE

HOW TO LOOK AFTER YOUR HORSE

ESSENTIAL SKILLS AND PROFESSIONAL TIPS

PETER BROOKESMITH

TECHNICAL CONTRIBUTOR: LIZZIE HOPKINSON

amber
BOOKS

This Amber edition first published in 2018

Copyright © Amber Books Ltd 2018

All rights reserved. No part of this publication may be reproduced, stored in a retrieval system or transmitted in any form or by any means, electronic, mechanical, photocopying, recording or otherwise, without prior permission in writing from the publishers.

First published in 2004 as *Taking Care of Your Horse & Pony*

Published by
Amber Books Ltd
United House
London N7 9DP
United Kingdom
www.amberbooks.co.uk
Appstore: itunes.com/apps/amberbooksltd
Facebook: www.facebook.com/amberbooks
Twitter: @amberbooks

ISBN 978-1-78274-591-4

Printed in the United Kingdom

Picture credits
Artworks: Amber Books Ltd

Publisher's note
Neither the author nor the publishers can accept any responsibility for any loss, injury or damage, caused as a result of the use of techniques described in this book. Nor for any prosecutions or proceedings brought or instigated against any person or body that may result from using these techniques.

This book is dedicated to the memory of
YORKIN CYRUS 2001–2003
and
RED 1994–2002
(who started it all)

Contents

Introduction 6

1
Sports and Pastimes 12

2
The Nature of the Horse 46

3
Stables, Fields and Food 80

4
Partners 116

5
Choosing a Horse 150

Glossary and Directory of Resources 186

Index 190

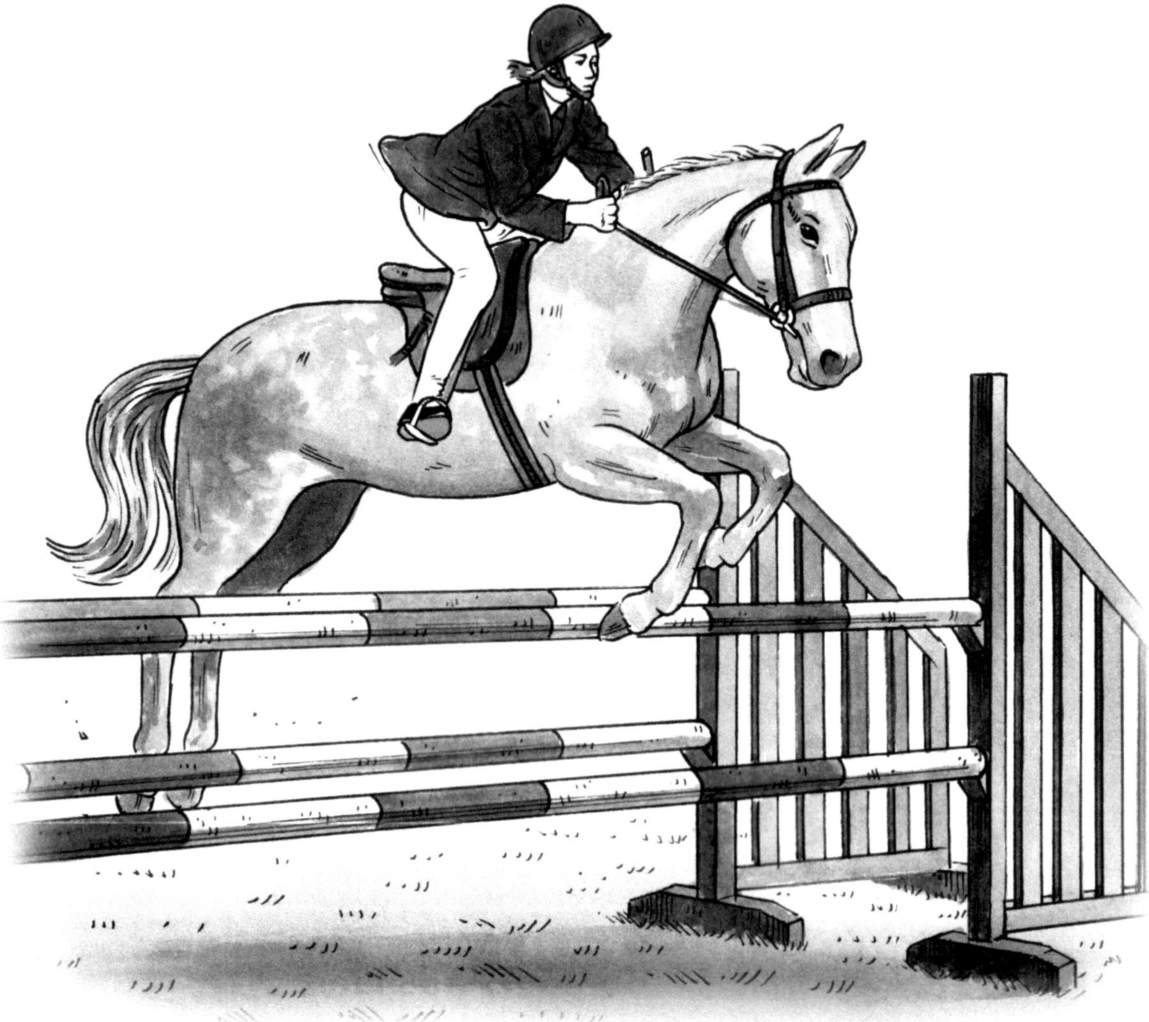

Introduction

Looking after a horse means more than knowing what he likes to eat and making his coat gleam. To keep him contented and cooperative and have a truly enjoyable ride, you need to understand how his mind works.

Comparing the virtues of various sporting pursuits, nursing pioneer Florence Nightingale wrote to a friend in 1900: 'Drat hockey and long live the horse! Them's my sentiments!'

She was in good company. 'A canter is the cure for all evil,' nineteenth-century British prime minister Benjamin Disraeli once proclaimed, while an ancient Arabian proverb declares: 'The wind that blows between a horse's ears is the air of heaven.' Monty Roberts, probably the most famous horseman of recent years, has said: 'I cannot imagine my life without horses. They have been my teachers, my friends, my business partners and my entertainers. Their message to me has been so strong that I have dedicated my life to interpreting what they are trying to tell us.'

Perhaps the greatest tribute to these warm, emotional and supremely intelligent creatures is the modern Greek word for a horse – *á logos*. The term literally means 'wordless' – reflecting a notion that the only difference between humans' and horses' intelligence is the human ability to speak.

However – even if horses cannot use words, there's no question that they do communicate, in many other ways, both among themselves and to any human in their company. They have a very limited vocal vocabulary, but use their bodies – often voting with their feet – in dozens of ways to 'say' what they are thinking. One of the magic keys to unlocking the secrets of looking after a horse or pony properly is to learn how horses convey their messages, to spot when a horse is trying to tell you something, and to understand what he is trying to say. Once one has unlocked the code of the horse's language – and all horses speak the same one – it's usually crystal clear what he wants to tell you. Monty Roberts's great achievement was to bring the essentials of this equine language to a wide public; in this book we delve into the reasons why it arose, and how to read it, in a wide variety of contexts and situations.

introduction

Horses are indeed great communicators, but they are not at all like humans in other respects and, even among real horse lovers, a passionate appreciation for them has not always gone hand in hand with true kindness to them. This is because, for one reason or another, people who would truly do anything for the sake of their horses have often failed to understand their horses' true nature.

One of the most common errors in keeping horses has been to assume that, because they are so intelligent, they think like humans. The truth is that they do not even sense things as we do. Their eyes are constructed differently from ours, their noses are thousands of times more sensitive than ours, and their hearing is far more acute. Humans are predators by nature, but horses are prey animals – and, for all their amazing individuality, they are also creatures of the herd – and they compute the information they receive from the world entirely differently from the way we do. As a result, the same event will mean one thing to us, and something entirely dissimilar to a horse. It's crucial to take these differences in the ways the world is seen and understood into account, when dealing with horses. At the risk of sounding pompous, it's actually our duty to do so: for while humans have the ability to interpret the horse's language, he can understand ours – especially our body language – only in his own terms. A wave to us is friendly: to him it's a threat. We ask so much of our horses, and they strive so generously to give us what we want, that the least we should do is to learn to make our requests in ways that they will understand, so that they accept them because they want to – and enjoy carrying them out.

Tradition has much to answer for in the odd ways horses are handled. The 'way it's always been done' accounts for a vast amount of unwitting mistreatment of horses, whether in the way they have been stabled, or fed or ridden. But since the 1980s, a mass of research into horses' psychology and behaviour, and fresh thinking about how to get them to accept a rider, how to train them and how best to feed and keep them, has begun to filter into the public domain. This book is based on that new – or sometimes rediscovered – knowledge. This is, then, not a traditional horse book in the way it approaches looking after equines and riding them. Rather, it belongs with that 'new wave' of thinking that takes trying to understand how horses see themselves and the world – whether they're in the warmth of the stable, on winter pasture, or out on a rainy trek – as the starting-point for all one's dealings with them.

After all, there is no reason why, as rational, sentient and sympathetic humans, we cannot at least imagine our way to a useful extent into horses' apprehension of things, and take account of how they have evolved – from what best suits their stomachs, through their pleasures and fears, to their mechanical structure.

A fine instance of how people fail to take the equine outlook into account is the way some approach training horses on a system of rewards and punishments. There are times when a horse needs to be told off, but the kind of training that may work on a dog won't make much sense to a horse, any more than it does to a cat. And why should it? They are entirely different kinds of animal.

For example: if a horse refuses to load into a trailer or horsebox, you won't make the process any easier the next time if you whip him into going on board. By then he will simply associate the trailer with a beating, and do his best to make off. At this point he's not refusing to load – he's trying to escape the beating he thinks is inevitable. The original reason he didn't want to load wasn't stubbornness, cussedness or disobedience, but because dark enclosed spaces are the last places horses want to be.

Predators lurk in places like that, and there's nowhere to run once he's inside. And just as bad, he can't see where his friends – his herd – are.

Understanding such things, we can make a start on treating horses according to their idea of what is meaningful, safe, fearful or terminally frustrating, to keep them content in as many aspects of their lives as we can. For the simple truth is that a happy horse will do more, and more willingly, for you, than an unhappy horse. There's nothing sentimental about this. Let's be blunt: horses are dangerous creatures. Not because they mean to be – they are naturally the most affable of animals – but just because they are very large, immensely powerful, and usually react instinctively and very fast indeed to anything that in their minds is suspicious or threatening. Only a fool walks up close behind a horse that she doesn't know intimately and knows to be safe, since a horse's natural response to anything strange coming up behind him (even his best equine friend) is to send it packing with a well-directed hoof.

A miserable or misunderstood horse can buck you off his back, or trample you to death underfoot – simply because he's more concerned about extricating himself from an unbearable, man-made confusion or from some imagined danger, than he is about your welfare. Horses are prey animals, and flight in the face of danger or agitation is instinctive to them: it means self-preservation. Disasters like this, that occur because of human misunderstanding, won't happen with a horse that's managed, fed or ridden with his way of thinking uppermost in your mind. In other words, looking after a horse in a way that accords with his inner nature will result in your having a safer horse, one who will trust you, take pleasure in your company and, given luck and good judgement on your part, will go that extra distance for you.

introduction

English and American riding terms

There are some differences between English and American horse riding and horsekeeping terminology. English terms are generally used throughout this book. Not all those below are used, but they are useful to know when reading other books by British or American authors. Most words are explained in the text, as well as in the main glossary following Chapter 5.

English riding terms	US equivalent
Brushing	Interfering
Bad doer	Unthrifty horse
Bandage	Leg wrap
Blaze	Stripe
Corn or hard food	Grain
Cubes	Nuts or pellets
Dishing	Paddling
Draw rein	Check rein
Fetlock	Ankle or joint
Field shelter	Run-in shed
Girth	Cinch
Good doer	Easy keeper, thrifty horse
Hogging	Roaching
Horsebox	Van
Lead rope	Lead shank
Livery stable	Boarding stable
At livery	Kept at a boarding stable
Loose box	Stable
Numnah	Saddle pad
Over-reach boot	Bell boot
Plait	Braid
Roughing off	Letting down
Rug	Blanket
Skewbald	Pinto
Stable yard	Barn
Surcingle	Overgirth
Trotting or running up in hand	Jogging up in hand

introduction

Or will not go anywhere at all, if you don't want him to. In the late 16th century the distinguished English judge Sir William Fleetwood became renowned for his vigorous campaign to rid the roads of highwaymen. Feeling their livelihood threatened, a gang of villains waylaid Fleetwood, who was on his horse, near London's gallows at Tyburn.

They tied his hands, strung a rope around his neck, and fixed it to the scaffold. Then they rode off, imagining his horse would follow theirs, and their adversary would be hanged. But the thieves had foolishly not thought to gag Fleetwood, who simply said to his horse: 'Stand.' The horse stood patiently for half an hour, until honest citizens saw Fleetwood's plight and released him from the noose.

Fleetwood and his steed, it hardly needs saying, had complete faith in one another. It's the aim of this book to help you achieve that kind of relationship with horses. But if you're going to ride well, enjoy riding, and do justice to the horse, you also have to know your own talents and capabilities. So, first, there's a guide to equestrian activities, to help you choose the pursuit that's best for your physique and temperament, and give you an idea of the kind of horse that's suited to each. Next comes a close look at the horse's outlook on existence and his essential character. Everything that follows in the book about the practical, day-to-day matters of looking after a horse – be it the best ways to house and pasture, feed, groom, ride or even say hello to him – all flow from this basic understanding of the horse's nature. Finally, there's a selection of the world's favourite breeds of riding horse. Some are rare, some are numerous, some less famous than they ought to be, but each one is unique in its way.

The points of a horse

The words used for the various parts of the horse's body are highly specialized. But you need to be familiar with them, because everyone who has anything to do with horses uses them all the time. Many of them come from Old English and Old French – a small indication of how long people have taken a keen interest in every aspect of the horse.

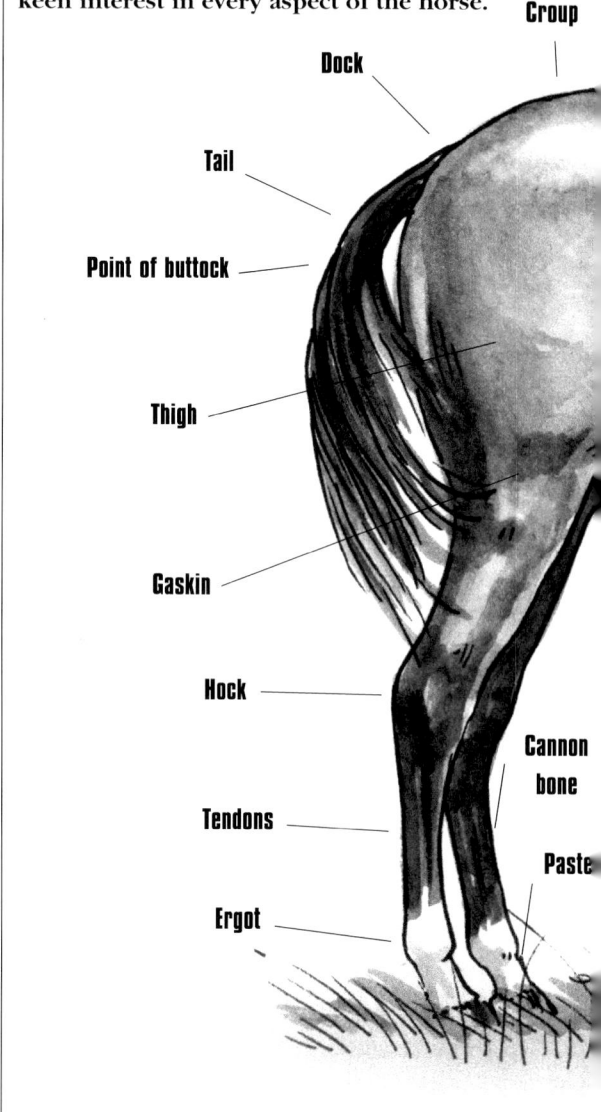

- Croup
- Dock
- Tail
- Point of buttock
- Thigh
- Gaskin
- Hock
- Cannon bone
- Tendons
- Paste[rn]
- Ergot

introduction

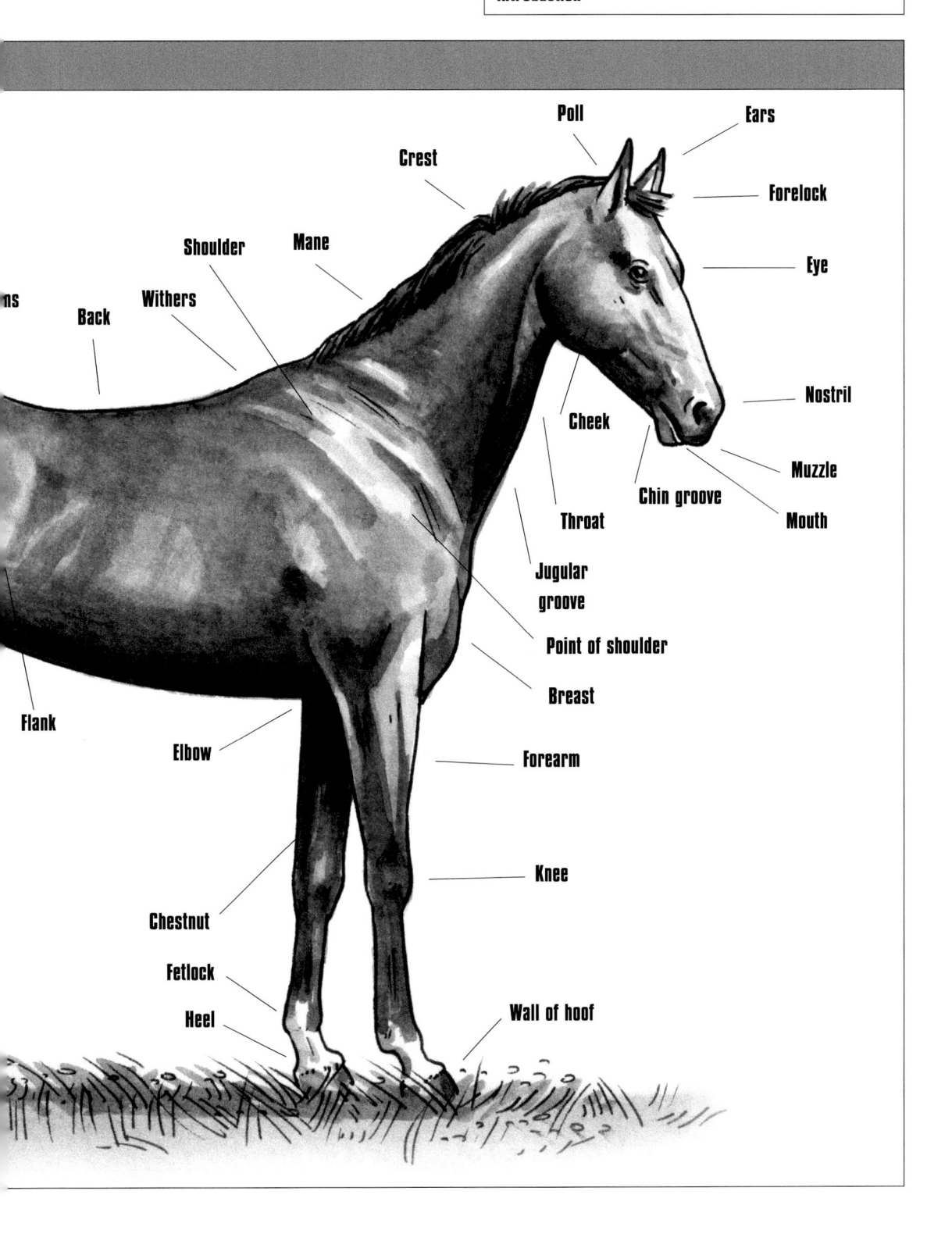

- Poll
- Ears
- Crest
- Forelock
- Mane
- Shoulder
- Eye
- Withers
- Back
- Nostril
- Cheek
- Muzzle
- Chin groove
- Throat
- Mouth
- Jugular groove
- Point of shoulder
- Breast
- Flank
- Elbow
- Forearm
- Knee
- Chestnut
- Fetlock
- Heel
- Wall of hoof

12

CHAPTER ONE

Sports and Pastimes

A guide to a wide range of horse sports, activities and disciplines, designed to help you to find the equestrian pursuit that suits you best, and to direct you towards the best kind of horse to choose for the task.

If you are new to horses, it is as well to know something about the major sports, disciplines and activities that you can enjoy with a horse, and have some idea of the qualities in both human and animal that each demands. True, there are some breeds that can do almost anything, but even these are better at some things than others, and you don't want to find yourself with a horse that is entirely unsuited to what has become your favourite occupation. Similarly, it doesn't make much sense to set your heart on an equestrian pursuit that's going to make a wreck out of you, the rider, because it conflicts with the grain of your being. You can't be dishonest with a horse - he will always see through your self-deception - but above all, in dealing with horses, you cannot afford to be dishonest with yourself. Think carefully about your own physical and psychological talents, potentials and limitations, and the kinds of challenge you want to meet, and listen to what your instructor has to say about your strengths and weaknesses.

To begin with, if you're not excited at the thought of always having to expect the unexpected, you should find another hobby! But if (for example) you don't have lightning reflexes, really excellent eye–limb coordination, and considerable reserves of physical courage, don't set your heart on taking up polo or polocrosse or stock-handling sports. If you don't have bags of stamina or enjoy living rough, trail riding and endurance will soon become a misery. If you're not that sensitive to the subtlety of a horse's mood and movements, or aren't prepared to put in endless hours of detailed schooling, dressage probably won't give you much pleasure either.

Besides the tax on you, your mount will soon pick up on your frustration or discomfort and become at worst fractious and disobedient, and at best depressed, making things even less like fun. On the other hand, most horses enjoy a challenge, even if, like many humans, some have to be reminded of the fact from time to time – and they have to know they can trust you absolutely.

SHOWING

One way of dipping your toe into competitive waters is showing. You can show horses at any level, and in about as many ways as there are of riding or driving. The basic level is the annual village show or county fair, where there are classes for everything from Best Child's Pony shown in hand, through riding and jumping and driving, to The Horse The Judges Would Most Like To Take Home. At the opposite end of the scale are state fairs and other large regional shows, often held over a number of days. The great thing about the local shows is that with a little extra effort almost anyone can win at something.

This may not sound like very much in the abstract, but it does give you the chance to judge your progress against very heterogeneous competition, some of which, by the law of averages, will be at your own level. Very few horsey folk are too proud to turn up at their local show. And the grandest, the kind who might expect to be placed in international competition, often do so with no particular expectation of winning, bringing along their younger or less experienced horses to get them used to being out in public.

Taking part in a local show, like any public exposure, puts pressure on you, but not out of proportion to the amount of fun you can have. It gives an additional purpose to what you've been doing with your horse the rest of the year. And, of course, you may also find that this is the way you want your equestrian life to develop, and go in for showing seriously. Besides that, you get to meet a lot of horses and, what may or may not be more fascinating, their owners, riders and trainers.

It's not easy to give firm guidelines on the kind of horse most suited for showing – that really depends on the classes in which you decide to compete. But very nervous horses won't enjoy going to a show. And any horse you show has to be good at the class you have chosen to enter, or at least be happy and responsive when taking part.

Having said all that, it's not compulsory to compete in any way at all, to enjoy riding. Indeed for most people, the insight gained into an entirely different sentient being, getting to know another kind of intelligence and warmth, and the pleasure of mastering the basic skills of riding, are enough for a lifetime – and wouldn't be exhausted in several. Hacking (riding out) in the countryside a couple of times a week or doing a few jumps at a local riding centre once a month can be entirely fulfilling, certainly don't lack challenge, and are eminently respectable ways of stretching yourself and your horse.

HACKING

Psychologically, horses probably need to hack even more than people do, perhaps even as much as they need to be out grazing with other horses for at least a few hours a day. They might get exercise and mental stimulation in the schooling arena or on the gallops, or with their equine friends in the field, but they have limits, just as we do, for how much they can absorb in lessons or at play without getting bored. Riding out is a change that's as good as a rest – offering something new to look at, obstacles to negotiate, new people, animals and traffic to meet, and a variety of terrain

sports and pastimes

Showing in hand

Showing in hand is a good way to get the feel of competing without too much stress – and to meet loads of other horses and the people who are addicted to them. It's good for the horse, too, to get used to the bustle and learn to stay quiet and obedient in front of a crowd. At small local shows, there are often so many classes almost everyone can win something.

and gaits to get through. This is important, even if your main interest in riding is highly specialized. In her book *Dressage in Lightness*, classical dressage trainer Sylvia Loch says quite bluntly: 'It is a mistake to separate dressage from cross-country work.' And she notes that 'riding out will test the horse's natural skills over undulating terrain, and develop his instincts for sure-footedness, self-preservation and overall awareness.'

For the rider, the advantages are much the same. Fresh air, exercise, a spot of birdwatching or wildflower-gazing, and perhaps the chance to come upon larger items of wildlife like elk or deer at close quarters without disturbing them. And there are the opportunities to test your skills as a rider. But most people who keep horses for hacking do so purely for the pleasure of being out in the open, in the company of an animal they are quietly passionate about, and one that keeps them constantly alert and interactive.

Hacking builds up trust between horse and rider, improves communication, and lets you see the horse reacting in his own way to natural stimuli. As remedial riding instructor Heather Moffet observes, you can 'think about what you are feeling ... when

sports and pastimes

Hacking across country

A gentle uphill canter while out on a hack stretches you and your horse, and adds vital variety to your ride. Before riding in open country, always tell someone where you're going; and once off the road, stick to legal bridleways and trails.

safely out hacking on a loose rein'. For this is an opportunity, as she says, to become more mindful of your steed: 'Become aware of every movement underneath you, because, believe me, the horse is even more aware of every move you make. If a horse can feel a fly land on his back, how much more clearly can he feel you?' That awareness in turn allows you to adjust both your schooling and your riding habits, and the result should be a ride out that's equally enjoyable every time for horse and rider.

The idea of developing a horse's 'instinct for self-preservation and overall awareness' calls for a little examination. It could be said that all horses already have both those qualities in abundance, so much so that they call for control rather than encouragement. At bottom, horses are essentially the same in their responses to the modern world as their wild ancestors were to their world, more than six millennia ago. They are herd animals, inoffensive vegetarians who think there are still lions and bears out there just waiting to attack them. Horses still bunch together for protection, and still regard any strange or unusual object as a potential predator. Their natural reaction to a threat is to run; in the last resort they will defend themselves by rearing and crashing down with their fore feet - aiming to kill with the sharp edges of their hooves.

Some horses can't stand flapping plastic bags, some think all baby carriages contain very small but extremely malevolent dragons, and some have been known to take aversion to cars of a particular colour. Most horses will be startled, at the very least, by the sudden appearance of a noisy motorcycle, or even a game bird breaking cover. They are constantly on the lookout for threats, and their instinct on meeting anything that looks like one is to turn and thunder off. That they don't bolt more often is a tribute to the paradoxical courage of these innately wary

sports and pastimes

creatures, and to the trust they have chosen to put in their rider. Certain things follow from this. One is that the more your horse trusts you, the more courageous he will be. So building trust is crucial to safe and enjoyable hacking, let alone anything more complicated – and the more you hack, the more accustomed the horse will become to the idea of unexpected sights and sounds.

Another, and obvious, point is that the more bombproof your horse is to begin with (see box), the more pleasure you will both have from hacking. Retired racehorses, which are skittish enough anyway, don't make good hacks; indeed most 'hot-blooded' horses, like Thoroughbreds and Akhal-Tekes, generally don't have the placidity to make an ideal hack. Stamina and willingness are qualities to look for so that long, steep hills don't become a matter of dispute, and surefootedness is a must. Endurance is less important unless you are

The bombproof horse

'The bombproof horse' means pretty much what it says – a horse that will turn a blind eye and deaf ear to any kind of intrusion, from a bird flying out of a hedge to a bomb going off. If you're doubtful about your own ability to deal with a tense situation, or have no choice but to spend time on or over busy roads, then look for an animal advertised as bombproof. Alternatively, look for breeds of known placidity and tolerance. With some investment in time and patience they can be trained into the next best thing, although being bombproof is a quality that some horses seem to be born with, regardless of genealogy.

sports and pastimes

thinking of developing into a trek or trail rider. But you will need a horse that, when asked to trot across a main road or out of some other possibly difficult spot, doesn't argue or dawdle. If you are buying a horse, check how much traffic experience he has, and if possible try before you buy; if you can't try him out in traffic, at least make sure he responds quickly and precisely to instructions in the field.

One final point for would-be hackers. The horse's permanent alertness for (his own idea of) danger is one of many reasons why he will get bored standing in a stable for hours on end. But no matter how often you ride out he'll get equally bored – and long before you do – of hacking around the same old circuit time after time, and will let you know about it by 'misbehaving' – refusing to go forward at the yard gate, jumping at every trembling leaf, and so on. If hacking is going to be your kind of riding, then vary your routes, the direction you take around them, the places you rest, the weather you choose to ride out in and, where it's safe and sensible, the speed you ride over different sections.

PONY CLUB AND GYMKHANA

Pony Clubs were born in the UK in the late 1920s, as local organizations run by volunteers for the purpose of 'interesting young people in riding and sport and at the same time offering … light instruction in this direction'. Today, besides the 364 branches in the UK, there are 615 Pony Clubs in the USA, 195 in Canada, 950 in Australia, and 305 in New Zealand, as well as branches in places as diverse as Hong Kong, Malta, Cyprus and Botswana. Continental Europe has its own set of similarly related organizations run through the Euro Pony Club. Membership is limited to riders under 21. All equines are welcome as long as they have a rider.

The heart of the Pony Club is the working rally. These are held throughout the year, and members and their mounts meet to improve their horsemanship, learn about tack and its care, stable management and first aid, and to have fun and games on horseback. Branches also organize an annual camp which, apart from offering the pleasure of spending up to a week with your horse and other like-minded people, involves instruction in most horse sports, lectures and more mounted games. You can also go in for various levels of training and proficiency certificates.

Gymkhana features large at Pony Club meets, and is a fine gateway and foundation for all other riding sports. As a competitive sport, it is perhaps more widely known as mounted games; originally designed for young riders, these are now enjoyed by people of all ages who like some snap in their riding. Gymkhana is fast, almost dangerous, skilful and demanding, huge fun both to ride in and to watch, and very probably character-building as well. Or, as the US Pony Clubs' website puts it: *No guts – no glory!*

At the local Pony Club branch level, what a gymkhana actually involves depends on the inventiveness of those in charge, and games may be run for individuals, pairs or teams. Competitions beyond branch level are usually more formalized team events for five riders, of whom only four may ride at any one time. Among the top prizes in gymkhana for young riders is the Prince Philip Cup. Instituted in the UK in 1957, this competition is now organized at national level by Pony Clubs in several other countries as well, including Australia, Canada, New Zealand and the USA. But the essence of gymkhana remains unchanged: young riders more or less literally jump through hoops on quick, obedient ponies, everyone has a great time, and the fastest horse and rider partnership wins. These games are surreptitious riding classes, in that the skills of equitation are given an enjoyable purpose in an atmosphere of friendly competition; they build the rider's confidence, teach the

sports and pastimes

pony to be both biddable and responsive, and develop trust and cooperation between pony and rider and among team members. Things are virtually designed to go awry, and chaos is part of the fun. When something goes wrong, all the rider has to do is dismount and put it right before continuing. The only time anyone is eliminated from a game is when they are guilty of bad behaviour, cheating, using spurs or a whip, or riding a pony too small for one's weight.

Here is one of the more exacting gymkhana routines, known as the litter race: *aficionados* consider it to be among the most fiendish.

In the litter race, four cardboard containers are put on the ground at the far end of the 'pitch' from the riders; a plastic dumpbin is on the centre line. At the start, the first rider is handed a wooden rod 1m (3ft) long. She must dash to the end of the pitch, pick up a carton on the end of the

Athletics on horseback

For gymkhana, both riders and steeds need to be fit and nimble. Riders may have to dismount and remount at speed, and (as here) be able to throw or drop various objects accurately. Ponies need to be able to stop, start, and turn fast and precisely, as well as tolerate the sudden changes of position their riders make while racing at top speed.

rod while remaining mounted, race to the bin and drop the carton into it, and charge back over the start line to pass the rod to the next rider. This is not as easy as it may seem. Some ponies really don't like the sight or sound of the carton on the stick, flying hooves kick the bin and contents all over the place, and of course the cartons on the ground can be blown or scattered about. Cartons can get trampled – so the rider has to dismount to put them back into shape, but she must be mounted again before she picks one up. Needless to say, the rider is not permitted to clutch the litter to the stick: she must use one hand on the rod only. Pray it's not a windy day.

For this kind of thing you need a pony that can canter from a standing start and turn on the proverbial sixpence (or dime). Given the uproar from spectators and the possibility of mayhem occurring in most mounted games, this is not work for a highly strung animal. It's important to have a pony that is unflappable and will concentrate on the job in hand. It is by no means impossible to inculcate this kind of attitude, but that does take time, patience and skill. And if you're going in for gymkhana, do remember, these are games. It helps to be a good loser, and to be tolerant of others' mistakes too. Your good humour will also keep your horse in good heart.

SHOWJUMPING

Hugely popular as a spectator sport, top-level showjumping offers big prize money and is very demanding on horse and rider – but many people jump their horses just for fun, and not always competitively.

Rules for showjumping are very simple. Depending on the level of competition, the course usually consists of eight to 20 obstacles of various heights, up to about 2.2m (7ft). Jumps may be simple vertical fences and gates (these are actually among the most difficult for the horse); 'walls' that look solid, but with the top row of blocks loose so that they will fall off easily if the horse knocks them with his hooves; 'spreads' with, for example, two or more parallel bars set one

Mounted games: the litter race

Reckoned the most challenging of mounted games, this is run as a relay race for teams (as shown here, with one rider ready at the start line) or as a straight race for individuals. At the centre is a dump bin: riders carry a rod, use it to pick up a carton from the far end, and dash back to dump it in the bin.

sports and pastimes

Showjumping: the water jump

Horses are generally wary of water, and one of the most challenging obstacles in showjumping is over water that's usually hidden behind a hedge-like jump. The horse has to clear the water, which it sees only at the last moment. It's at such moments that the absolute trust that must be built up between steed and rider comes into its own.

behind the other, creating an extended jump with depth as well as height; the 'triple bar' (three bars set at graduated heights); a water jump; and a combination of two or three different jumps a short distance apart. All these have to be jumped in a set sequence, which can be quite labyrinthine. No two courses are the same: designers work with the abilities of the competing horses in mind, and vary colours and textures, types of jump, complexity of the approaches and the level of difficulty accordingly.

The idea is to create a course that only half a dozen or so horses will complete without faults within the given time limit. These are scored as follows: when any part of a fence is knocked down the pair receives four faults. If a horse steps on the edge of, or in, the water jump, the penalty is four faults. A refusal at a fence receives three faults, and

sports and pastimes

six faults for a second refusal. A third refusal sees the pair eliminated from the competition. If either the horse or rider falls, the pair is eliminated. The horse that finishes in the shortest time and with the fewest faults is the winner.

Riders can, and often do, ride more than one horse in competitions; but two riders cannot ride the same horse – the horse would have a clear advantage the second time out. Riders walk the course before mounting, but it will all be new to the horse. At higher levels of competition, the order in which the riders go is settled by a draw, as the further down the starting order one is, the more one can learn from the way preceding riders tackle the jumps.

While there are breeds – the Thoroughbred and Hanoverian, for example – that seem to be born with an aptitude for jumping, individual horses of any kind can turn out to be brilliant jumpers and some just don't want to know. Huaso, whose record for the high jump has stood since 1949 (see box), was talent-spotted after a dismal career in racing, dressage and showjumping, when he spontaneously leapt a 2m (6ft) wall to exit his corral. If you're looking for a showjumper,

How a horse jumps

The hindlegs leave the ground closer to the fence than the forelegs, to give extra upward thrust, while the forelegs act as pendulums to increase momentum. The 'ideal' angle of departure is 45°, but horses actually jump at a much shallower angle – perhaps because they cannot see the fence at take-off, and so start to leap further out to be sure to avoid a crash.

the horse's own attitude to jumping is the first thing to find out, quite apart from checking that he has the necessary strength and courage. You also need a horse who is surefooted and responsive, to negotiate tricky strides between combination jumps, and is sufficiently cool-headed not to be fazed by the unfamiliar.

DRESSAGE

Competition dressage – the discipline of Grand Prix competitions and the Olympic Games – is a sport that has become immensely popular in recent years. This pursuit is distinct from classical dressage, which is more a philosophy of equestrianism than a sport, and different yet again from *Haute Ecole* dressage, which is now a form of demonstration riding involving 'the ultimate communication between horse and rider', performed by professionals.

To quote the US Dressage Federation (USDF): 'Obedience, balance, sensitivity to light aids, and the ability to respond calmly and quickly to its rider's commands: a horse with these qualities will do its job well, whether destined for the ballet movements of the Grand Prix dressage test at the Olympics, or life as a jumper, pleasure horse, or show horse. ... A gradual, logical system of strengthening and suppling exercises, dressage may seem to belong only in the white-fenced arenas at dressage competitions. Yet, the aim of dressage is to develop the ability, suppleness and obedience of the horse – qualities desired in any horse, no matter what its eventual use will be. Except at the highest levels, dressage is not a specialty in itself.'

Quarter Horses, bred for racing and working with farm stock, are not at first sight the most obvious choices for dressage, but the USDF cites the Quarter Horse, Rugged Lark, and his rider/trainer Lynn Salvatori Palm as a prime demonstration of the benefits of dressage training: 'Rugged

High Flyer

The record for the highest jump on horseback is 2.47m (8ft 1¼in), by Capt Alberto Larraguibel Morales, riding the 16-year-old Thoroughbred gelding Huaso ('Cowboy'), at Vina del Mar, Santiago, Chile on 5 February 1949. Larraguibel said at the time: 'In fact Huaso jumped over 2.52m [8ft 3¼in], because the poles were 7m [22ft] long and they curve [down] in the middle. Huaso jumped over the right corner and not in the middle where the 2.47m height was measured.'

Huaso refused on the first attempt and knocked off a fence pole on the second. Recalled Larraguibel: 'As I led the horse for the last jump, I spoke to him, I patted him, I transmitted all my strength and all my faith to him. I said: "Huaso, this is our opportunity. Now or never." Then he sprinted just where I wanted him to and, in a magical show of elasticity, power, decision and harmony, he flew through the air, faultlessly leaping the fence. The most difficult moment was at the highest point of the jump ... I felt as if I'd fall head first. If the horse had felt the slightest hesitation in me, we would've failed. That moment lasted for ever ... it was like sending my heart flying over the other side of the jump and then going to rescue it.' When they cleared the jump, the crowd roared, and the stadium band spontaneously struck up the Chilean national anthem.

Huaso was retired from competition after his amazing leap, and lived to the ripe old age of twenty-nine.

sports and pastimes

The trouble with dressage

Competition dressage has come in for heavy criticism for encouraging the appearance of good riding and ignoring its heart – a natural partnership between horse and rider. Here, using force has put both human and equine out of balance.

Lark has twice earned the prestigious title American Quarter Horse Association "Superhorse" for his winning ways in American Quarter Horse Association working hunter, hunter under saddle, hunter hack, pleasure driving, trail, reining and Western riding divisions. ... Rugged Lark's basic training under Lynn Palm was based on dressage principles. ... [Palm] feels that one of the biggest problems for most riders is not understanding "what is natural and correct for a particular horse".' Dressage training, the USDF says, should take each horse's abilities into account, so that each 'can reach its potential, while remaining happy and a pleasure to ride'.

At the most basic levels of competition, dressage is judged on how the rider (and more particularly the horse) executes its standard gaits, while riding straight, in circles, figures of eight and so on, within an arena 20m by 40m (66ft by 130ft). At the most advanced level, the arena is 20m by 60m (66ft by 197ft) and tests call for flying changes of the lead leg every stride (the effect makes the horse appear to be skipping), pirouettes at the canter, the piaffe (trotting on the spot) and the passage (a slow suspended trot), as well as controlled lengthening and shortening of the stride in all three gaits.

Competition dressage is not without its controversies. The word 'dressage' is French for 'training', with the lurking connotation of bringing something to a finished or ideal state. There are many ways of doing this, and there is an increasingly vocal element among horse trainers, particularly those from the classical school, who have observed that competition dressage has laudable aims but too often achieves them, or an illusion of them, by force. Mental and physical domination of the horse is certainly tolerated, if not encouraged. A handful of top dressage riders are notorious for beating and spur-ring their horses bloody, but everyone, including judges, conveniently looks the other way.

sports and pastimes

Even at the most elementary levels of the discipline, a classic instance of this benighted approach is the insistence on using a tight rein. In the hands of a lazy rider the horse is, in effect, yanked into a position that only appears to be collected – that is, carrying the rider lightly, in balance, with his back up and his haunches flexing freely. But he is actually carrying the weight of the rider on his fore legs – exactly what dressage is supposed to discourage. In a competition, a rider who rode using only a light touch on the rein would be marked down for lack of contact, no matter how well-collected the horse; this is where competition dressage and classical riding part company. The nonsense here is exposed by its irony: dressage grew out of training war horses, who had to be ridden on little or no rein – ridden from the seat – so that their riders could wield their weapons. Prints of François Robichon de la Guérinière (1688-1751), whose teachings founded the modern art of dressage, show him cantering on a loose rein; his book, *Ecole de Cavalerie,* is the Spanish Riding School's bible. In it he remarks: 'It can well be said that sparing use of the aids and chastisements is one of the most desirable traits of the rider.'

Devotees of classical dressage pride themselves on looking at riding from the horse's point of view. By addressing the horse according to its musculoskeletal mechanics and instinctive responses, they aim ultimately for as little distinction as possible between the action of a horse running free and that of a horse with a rider on board, and in perfect physical and mental harmony with it. Both philosophically and practically, it is not surprising that they regard modern competition dressage with a blend of anger and despair for the horses.

Relax like a bullfighter

The bullfighter's life depends on how he rides, and his precise control of his mount. But note how little force he uses: the horse is fully collected, hind legs neatly under his quarters, in a fully natural stance, yet the rider keeps a very loose rein.

sports and pastimes

On the other side of the coin, science writer Stephen Budiansky notes in *The Nature of Horses* that 'when Napoleon created the first modern army, its vast cavalry too large to be filled by aristocrats, the French abandoned the [*Haute Ecole*] and adopted an easily learned method of riding on loose reins. ... the truth of the matter is that these collected gaits are not the ones that a freely moving horse, or a green horse, or a wild horse, will ever select on its own – unless it is highly emotionally aroused. ... the enshrinement of the [*Haute Ecole*] as an ideal continues to do great mischief to our understanding of the natural movements of the horse.'

Since the 1980s Warmbloods have been among the most successful of all dressage mounts. Their built-in athleticism and free movement are certainly essential qualities in a dressage horse: so is 'spirit', although Budiansky's thought-provoking remark – 'How much of a spirited horse's spirit is the consequence of our whipping it into a frenzy remains a valid question' – should not be forgotten in the search for a horse that pleases dressage judges by showing controlled energy throughout its test. Welsh cobs are a breed of horse that make excellent dressage horses because they have a natural sharpness and intelligence that shines out beside the docility and sheer interest with which they do as they're asked; but this is a product of character, not training. There is some truth in the notion that any horse, properly schooled, can do competition dressage to its own natural level. And if, like most people, you want to ride for pleasure rather than from any great ambition, dressage is a fine way to spice improving your riding with a little competitive challenge.

Haute Ecole dressage

Seen here is the levade, as performed by the Spanish Riding School of Vienna. The move is really a skilfully controlled rear, and was originally intended to terrify footsoldiers on the battlefield with the horse's raised, and lethal, fore hooves.

sports and pastimes

The Spanish Riding School

Justly regarded as the epitome of *Haute Ecole* dressage, the Spanish Riding School in Vienna was founded in 1572. Almost from the beginning the school used the white (strictly, light grey) Lipizzaners that are its trademark: the school takes its name from these Spanish-derived animals. Each horse stays with one rider throughout its time at the school, and is trained in three stages – a basic course, followed by training as a cavalry mount then as an equine artist. In the words of an 1898 directive, these stages involve:

1. Riding with as natural a posture of the horse as is possible, not in collection, and on straight lines: the so-called riding forward.

2. Riding the collected horse in all gaits, turns and patterns in perfect balance: Campaign School.

3. Riding the horse in an artistically elevated posture, with increased flexion of the haunches and regularity, manoeuvrability, and dexterity, in all ordinary as well as nature-oriented extraordinary gaits and leaps. Brought methodically to the highest perfection, this type of riding is called *Haute Ecole*.

The most spectacular movements are the 'airs above ground' – the levade, courbette, ballotade and capriole. These are actually derived from military tactics in which the horse became part of the whole cavalry 'weapon system' and joined in the attack. And despite opinions to the contrary, the 1898 directive remarks that such 'extraordinary gaits' 'can easily be observed when horses play and fight with each other in herds at liberty', and goes on to add drily that 'so-called circus tricks are beneath the dignity of the institution and must be strictly avoided in exhibitions as well as at all times.'

TREK, TRAIL AND ENDURANCE

Which of the three pursuits of trekking, trail riding and endurance you go in for depends to some extent on where you live. On small overcrowded islands like the UK, for long-distance pleasure riding you'll be limited to one form or another of trekking – essentially, long-distance hacking – and if the ride takes more than a day you will probably spend the night in a comfortable guest house with the horse at livery.

In the USA, the equivalent to trekking is trail riding, organized among friends, on a club level or commercially, in which you can ride through open country at much the same speed as a cow walks, and will more likely than not spend the night under the stars. For obvious reasons these are not solitary forms of recreation.

Endurance riding can be taken as a form of private challenge, as it was by riders such as Jean-François Ballerau, who to celebrate his marriage took his new wife on an 8000km (5000 mile) trek across South America with four Criollo horses. This was not the first instance of horses being asked to undergo immense journeys through arduous conditions. Usually these were the product of warfare or, as in the long cattle drives of the 'wild' west, from commercial necessity. They have often been undertaken to prove the hardiness and stamina of a breed. All new Russian breeds have been tested in this way, because the extreme climate and immense distances to be covered in that country make vulnerable horses a liability; and most of these breeds were originally developed as cavalry horses. In 1946, a group of Budennys, for instance, went through a 200km (125 mile) test in temperatures reaching 40°C (104°F) that ended in a controlled gallop, and in 1950

sports and pastimes

Budennys underwent a 24-hour endurance test, with the fastest horse, a six-year-old stallion, covering 310km (193 miles) in 19 hours under saddle.

Endurance riding as a sport was recognized relatively recently – in 1950, by the Fédération Equestre Internationale, which creates the rules for Olympic equestrian sports. Endurance is not yet part of the Olympics, although there is an annual World Championship. The sport initially developed in the western USA, inspired by horse trials conducted by European and American cavalries in the early twentieth century. Like the tests for new Russian breeds, these were designed to find the best horses to carry

Riding the trail

Observe how the riders are letting their horses pick their own way across the terrain – riding on loose reins, comfortable in the saddle, saving energy and worry for both their steeds and themselves.

sports and pastimes

weight at speed over long distances, and the trials tested the animals to the limit.

Today the sport is carefully controlled, and the welfare of the animals is carefully monitored: endurance racing leads the field in this concern. Requirements vary from country to country, but all horses have to pass a veterinary check for fitness before the start of a ride or race, and within half an hour of passing the finishing line. The horse is trotted before the vet to show that the animal is sound on his feet; and he must have a maximum rate of pulse (around 64; in Australia it is 55), be breathing easily, and not be suffering from excessive wear and tear. A horse that fails on any of these points is eliminated, even if he has won the race, and may not be ridden any further. For longer rides (the longest cover 160km [100 miles] in a day), checks are made every 40km (25 miles) or so, depending on conditions and local rules. In theory, at the end of the race the horse should be 'fit to continue'; in some European countries there is a further vets' check the next day to ensure that the animal is still fit.

Arabians, Russian horses and 'western' American horses are often top choices for endurance riding, but any horse will do with the right qualities of sound health, strength, stamina, efficient metabolism (a low pulse rate and a large appetite are good signs) and personality. Some horses want to be top in everything, but some are natural followers and will never win endurance races, despite being willing to keep on going regardless: which is fine if you're not competing seriously, or at all. The horse will also need a good sense of balance – very useful in negotiating difficult terrain. Older, fully mature horses are best for long-distance riding, the ideal age is reckoned to be between six and 12 years' old. Medium-sized ones – around 15.2 hands (157cm/62in) and

How big a horse?

The ideal size of horse for long-distance riding is around 15.2 hands (157cm/62in), particularly so for endurance racing which, to maintain the times required, demands trotting over the majority of the course. Although there is very little difference between the amount of energy any individual horse uses whether he is walking or galloping, the trot is probably its most energy-efficient gait. A horse or pony smaller than average will inevitably have to trot faster, and use more energy, to maintain the required speeds; a larger horse will use more energy because, although his strides may be longer, he has more weight to shift over the same distance, and a really hefty horse will inevitably lack agility over tricky ground.

As a general point, you should always try to match your horse's size, strength and energy to your own, regardless of how you choose to enjoy riding. Many young or inexperienced riders' problems stem from being 'overhorsed' – having too large or too energetic an animal underneath them. Don't be persuaded into riding something bigger than you can handle, and remember that no human can ever be as strong as even the teeniest pony. You can't fight that muscle, but you do need to have enough strength in reserve to be able to *direct* your horse's vastly superior power, even in the calmest situation – but absolutely when something goes wrong. Very experienced, skilled and confident riders may be able to ride practically anything. Those less seasoned should ride as many horses as possible to find out what suits them best.

sports and pastimes

under 545kg (1200lb) – are less taxed than smaller or larger horses.

Long-distance riding does not have to be competitive: most endurance organizations offer long-distance pleasure rides, although they will be faster than trekking or trail riding. However, it does require a fit horse with natural stamina, and a rider to match, and that calls for plenty of carefully graduated training well before going on the trail proper for the first time. And be prepared to spend years training yourself if you want to take long-distance riding seriously.

Before any long-distance ride, if you can, ride your horse at least once over the last stretch of the course, so that he has the feeling of 'coming home' at the end of the real thing. This will also perk him up. Most horses get mentally drained after about 120km (75 miles), even though they may be physically fine. (To put this in context, consider the mental and emotional effects on humans of a day spent travelling in a car.) If you want to compete in long-distance riding, make sure you have an animal that won't have to be pushed to the edge psychologically in order to complete the course. Finally, a prime rule on the trail is that you should leave no trace – as far as possible, leave the ground you cover in the same state it was in before you started your ride.

The horse for endurance

Look for these qualities in a horse for long distance riding: good hard hooves, short cannon bones, and well-muscled legs ('a horse is only as good as his legs'), plus deep, sloping, muscular shoulders, a powerful chest and close-coupled back.

POLO AND POLOCROSSE

Polo may well have had its origins in an ancient Syrian game that involved chasing after a (dead) goat's head on horseback; while the word itself comes from the Tibetan, *pulu*, for ball, one form or another of polo has been popular all over Asia for hundreds of years. A seventeenth-century European traveller observed how 'The King of Persia and his nobles take exercise by playing pall-mall on horse back. Their horses were so well trained … that they ran after the ball like cats.' In the 1850s it was taken up by officers of the British Indian Army and their social circles, and they took it back to Europe in the late 1860s, from where it spread to Australasia and the Americas.

sports and pastimes

The vet check

Endurance racing leads the field in concern for equine welfare. Horses are checked at regular intervals to be sure they're fit to continue – even at the end of the race. Rider and back-up crew may help the animal cool down, calm down, and drink in a 30-minute period before the vets look him over, but he must still be trotted to the inspection station.

sports and pastimes

Riding off

One of the more combative ploys permitted in both polo and polocrosse – 'riding off' an opponent who has the ball by charging against his horse's shoulder.

Argentina is now the world's undisputed leader in the game, which has become the country's national sport.

Like most games described in the abstract, polo sounds slightly mad. Two teams of four players on horseback carry long mallets with flexible shafts and charge about on a pitch 274m by 183m (300yd by 200yd) in an attempt to strike an 8cm (3in) ball into the opposing team's goal, ideally without falling off. They do this for seven minutes (a chukka), when a horn is blown and the players take a five-minute break to change ponies. Players continue in this fashion for five or seven more chukkas. When one team scores a goal, the teams change ends. At half-time, the spectators amble onto the field and stamp clumps

sports and pastimes

King of the one-horse sports

The ability to lob and catch the ball with the racquet gives an extra dimension to the play in polocrosse, while the small pitch makes for a fast-moving game. On the field, the penalty area forms the rectangle at each end, where only the attacker and defender may ride; attempts at goal may be made only within the semicircle around the goal.

of turf back into the holes gouged by the ponies' hooves.

One of the game's several curiosities is that a match can start with goals already 'scored' by one team. These are calculated on the basis of the riders' individual handicaps, which can run from −2 to +10. If one team has a combined handicap of 30 and the other has one of 36, the difference is multiplied by the number of chukkas to be played and then divided by six. Thus, in this case, in a six-chukka match, the team with the lower aggregate handicap starts a match with six goals to its credit.

In the US Polo Association's words, polo is 'one of the fastest, roughest, and most dangerous sports played today'. It is also very exciting to play or to watch, as ponies jostle shoulder-to-shoulder or rocket ahead from a standing start, while riders exercise phenomenal hand-to-eye coordination.

But the need to maintain and train a string of polo ponies (one for each chukka in a match) does make it an expensive pursuit. Reflecting this, a recent survey by the US *Polo* magazine found that American polo players have an average annual income of $966,000. About a quarter are women, and another quarter are between their mid-forties and mid-sixties in age, so neither sex or age is a limitation. Skill and courage are paramount, however.

Originally, only ponies up to 14 hands (142cm/56in) were allowed to play polo, and then the Australian Waler, the South African Basuto pony and the Indian Manipur

sports and pastimes

Polocrosse

In 1938–39, a trio of Australians – Mr and Mrs Edward Hirst and polo player Alf Pitty – took an exercise that was being used at England's National School of Equitation and turned it into a fast, exciting game for people who either couldn't, or didn't want to, invest in more than one horse for their sport. Polocrosse really became popular in Australia and Africa after World War II, and it is now played all over the world.

The sport is something like the game of lacrosse, played on horseback. Players (six to a team) carry a flexible 'racquet', which can be of any length, that has a loose net at the head. They use this to pick up, pass, catch and bounce a soft 10cm (4in) ball. Knocking the ball from an opponent's racquet with an upward swipe is permitted, as is 'riding off' – charging an opponent at an oblique angle from behind to drive her away from the ball.

The pitch is 146m by 55m (160yd by 60yd) wide, and divided into three main zones (see diagram below). Each team is divided into two sections of three: an attacker, who is the only one allowed within the opposing penalty area and the only one allowed to score; a 'swing' or centre, who rides the midfield; and a defender, who is the only player on her side permitted within her side's penalty area to prevent goals being scored. The game is played in four to eight chukkas, each of between six and eight minutes' duration. One section of each team plays a chukka while the other rests its horses; and mounts are not permitted to play more than 54 minutes in a day. This is how it is possible to make polocrosse a one-horse game.

Polocrosse was designed to be played on any horse by any rider of any age. Retired polo ponies obviously make good polocrosse mounts, but at the amateur level a rider's good humour is probably more important than a flash steed. As one Australian devotee remarks, 'Polocrosse is much more of an activity than just a game played at tournaments. From just messing around by yourself with a stick and ball, playing a little impromptu one on one, or perhaps two on two with some friends to full scale tournament play. It's all polocrosse, and it's all fun.' As for the horses, he remarks in the same Crocodile-Dundeeish vein: 'Any horse will do. Horses pick up the game quickly and seem to enjoy it as much, if not more, than their riders. Any size, age, or breed. Lame or otherwise unsound horses are not permitted to play, neither are stallions. Blind horses are not allowed to play, neither are blind people, even though many players would swear that there are plenty of blind umpires.'

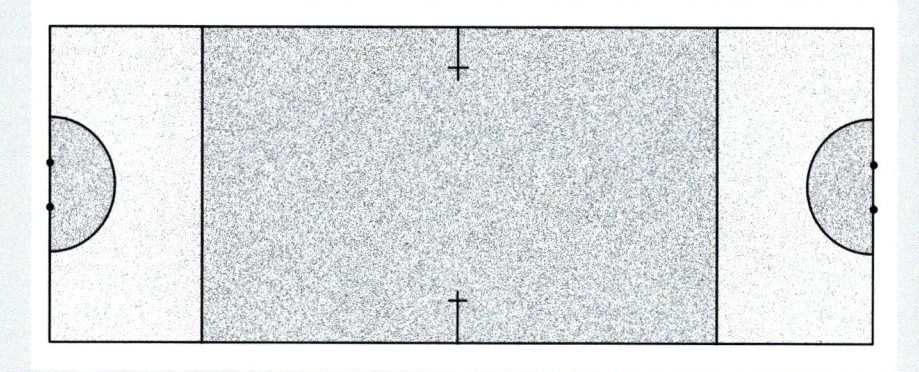

sports and pastimes

Riding to hounds

The hunting partnership between humans, horses and hounds is one that has been in play since the 1700s. Today, there are 20,000 working hounds in the UK alone. These dogs, mostly foxhounds, with smaller numbers of harriers, beagles and bassets, live in kennels in packs of up to 60 and from an early age are trained to work alongside horses.

were the mounts of choice. Since the height limit was abolished, Argentinian Criollos (often bred specially for the game) and Thoroughbreds of around 15 hands (152cm/60in) have been preferred. The polo 'pony' is now a very fast small horse, and mares seem to take to the game better than geldings or stallions. The game clearly does not suit timid animals, or riders, and both have to be very fit to play.

HUNTING AND POINT-TO-POINT

Foxhunting is more or less a British invention, going back at least five centuries, and it certainly helped to shape much of the British countryside with its combes, spinneys and hedges, which were (and are) planted and managed to provide cover for foxes and jumps for hunters. Ireland, France, Australia, New Zealand and the USA are other major hunting nations: in the USA, red and grey foxes, coyotes and bobcats are hunted, but only until they run to earth, not for the kill.

Some hunts are highly formal affairs with strict dress codes, membership by invitation only, and a certain one-upmanship regarding the horses. Others are more relaxed and come-as-you-are, and the variety of horseflesh rather wider and untidier. The essential rules on the field remain the same, however, for reasons of practicality.

Hunting takes place between last harvest and first sowing. The hunt initially meets at a prearranged point, and consists of two groups: the huntsman, hounds (usually 12–20 'couple' or pairs) and whippers-in, and 'the field' – the mounted followers – who are under the direction of the field master. The huntsman, hounds and whippers-in then proceed to 'draw' a chosen field or wood where foxes are believed to be. This means that the hounds sniff out the scent of a fox and follow it in the hope of forcing the quarry from cover. Hounds are controlled partly by the huntsman's horn, to whose specific calls they are trained to respond, and partly by the whippers-in, who round up strays or redirect the pack if it splits in pursuit of more than one fox. Once the fox has left cover, the field master and field will follow at speed. Most hunts will divide the field into jumpers and non-jumpers, so that the inexperienced or faint-hearted are not obliged to take hedges or broad ditches at a gallop. The fox will often run from one set of cover to another: in that case, the field waits at a decent distance while the huntsman and his team draw the fox again. Both foxes and coyotes have been known to go from cover to cover in relays.

Hunting calls for a fast horse that jumps well and surely. In no circumstances should you hunt on a tearaway or a disobedient animal, or one that gives you a hard ride by refusing to gallop long and low. Thoroughbreds are often the mount of choice where the hunting country is mostly grass, because of their speed and boldness; but in areas where land is ploughed in winter, or on mountain and moorland, surefootedness, balance and common sense are much more important, and Thoroughbred/local breed crosses often make excellent hunters in these circumstances, although it is not at all unusual to see pure-bred local ponies or cobs in these areas. The Irish hunter (a type not a breed) is always worth considering. Traditionally a cross between a Thoroughbred stallion and an Irish Draught mare, it appears to have a natural ability for hunting, usually keeping its feet in even the most exacting conditions. Following years of campaigning, The Hunting Act 2004 is an Act of the Parliament of the United Kingdom which bans the hunting of wild mammals (notably foxes, deer, hares and mink) with dogs in England and Wales.

Point-to-point racing is directly connected to the hunts in Britain and the USA. The hunts organize the race meetings, design the courses and benefit financially from the gate. To run in a point-to-point, a horse must have been 'regularly and fairly' hunted during the previous season (at least three times, in practice). Point-to-point races started as an informal way of testing hunters against each other, and even as late as the 1960s some were still being run across open country. In the nineteenth century, steeplechasing split off from these amateur, local contests to become formalized and professional, and took to permanent racecourses, although it has never forgotten its roots in hunting. At a point-to-point today, there have to be at least 18 jumps and eight fences on a course, which can be any shape, of 5km (3 miles) or so in length. Men and women may ride in the same race subject to carrying a minimum weight. Professional riders are not permitted, but many jockeys ride point-to-point full time as a prelude to a career in steeplechasing.

WESTERN EVENTS

The American cowboy's stock-handling techniques of cutting, roping and reining – which take years of practice for both rider and horse – now form part of a challenging competition held at shows and fairgrounds in many parts of the world. Such skills still have their practical application out on the range today as, in the words of the International Museum of the Horse in Lexington, Kentucky, 'although jeeps, trucks and even airplanes provide much of

sports and pastimes

Point-to-point

Small purses (low prize money) help ensure point-to-point racing is still an amateur affair, with races run at full tilt and plenty of rough and tumble over fairly makeshift fences.

Drag hunting

For a day out hunting guaranteed not to involve a fox, growing numbers of people are turning to the sport of drag hunting. This involves the field of riders following a pack of foxhounds trained to hunt a runner or rider dragging an artificial scent. Some hunts use bloodhounds, which follow the natural scent of a runner (called 'hunting the clean boot'), rather than an artificial trail.

Like foxhunting, drag hunting takes place in autumn through to early spring and, as far as possible, the hunt is organized over natural countryside – so there is plenty of jumping over ditches, streams, hedges and walls. If natural obstacles are few and far between, the hunt builds its own fences or brings in portable jumps. The ride is usually very fast, since the artificial scent laid by the runner or rider is strong and encourages the hounds to travel swiftly across country. (Hunts using bloodhounds are much slower, since the natural scent they follow is quite weak.) A typical day may mean following between three and six 'lines', each 1.5–8km (1–5 miles) long. Each line usually presents a different level of difficulty– some will suit novices, others will challenge more confident riders.

the transportation for modern ranchers, no machine can displace the versatile and savvy cow pony.' A case in point is the 'cutting' horse, specially trained to separate a cow or calf out from the herd in order for it to be rebranded or treated for an injury, or to allow bullocks to be separated from heifers.

Much of this task was, and is, actually done by the horse. In a modern contest, the competitor has two and a half minutes to cut (separate) as many cows as she can from a herd. Horse and rider move slowly into the herd, and select a cow to cut from the others. Having herded the cow out from the crowd, the rider loosens the reins and holds onto the saddle horn. It is then up to the horse to keep the bovine from rejoining the herd by various blocking manoeuvres. The rider may not make noises, use the reins, prod the cow with her boot, or otherwise interfere at this stage, and there are penalties if the horse paws or bites the cow. Once the cow loses interest in returning to the herd, the rider lifts her reins and re-enters the herd to select another cow – points are lost if she selects an animal on the fringes for cutting. A good partnership will extract three cows within the time limit.

Roping is a team activity whether on the range or in the rodeo ring. Two riders are required, the first called the 'header', the second the 'heeler'. In competition, a steer is released into the arena and given a 3-4.5m (10-15ft) head start. The header rides up on the running steer's left, throws her rope around its neck or horns and secures it around the saddle horn, and then rides to the left, forcing the steer to follow. This move also exposes the steer's hind legs to the heeler, who now rides up and loops her rope around the steer's hind feet. As she wraps her rope around the

The sliding stop

Generating clouds of dust, the sliding stop involves getting the horse to sit down on his hind legs while continuing to lope forward with his forelegs before coming to a complete halt. Up to 9m (30ft) can be covered in this spectacular fashion.

saddle horn she brings her horse to a spectacular sliding halt to bring the steer down and anchor it. At the same time the header turns her horse towards the steer. The 'run' is over, and has taken perhaps 15 seconds – a time real experts can shave to under five seconds. In US championships, teams rope four steers in a row, and the fastest aggregate time wins. Prizes can go into tens of thousands of dollars.

One of the great appeals of roping (apart from the skill displayed) is that it is open to virtually anyone prepared to invest the time and energy in practice and training. Children do it, and so do septuagenarians. Roping was the fastest-growing equine sport in the USA in 1990s.

Reining is the nearest Western riding comes to dressage, except that its origins lie in the acrobatic abilities cowboys looked for in a horse, rather than in the demands of the battlefield. And it is rather more flamboyant than dressage. In competition, the US National Reining Horse Association (NRHA) calls for horse and rider to perform one or more of a set of 10 'patterns'.

All patterns include moves such as backing up, flying lead changes, and the spin, sliding stop and rollback, all of which should be executed with imperceptible cues or aids to the horse. The NRHA describes the spin and sliding stop, which are peculiar to Western riding, as follows:

- Spins are a thrilling manoeuvre both to watch and ride. The horse is asked to turn his front end around in a series of 360-degree turns, executed while his inside back foot remains in one spot. Correctly done, the horse will cross the outside front leg over the inside front leg, effortlessly moving his front end around in a smooth, flowing manner.
- In a Sliding Stop, the rider, while loping, cues the horse to stop. The horse brings his back legs up underneath in a locked

sports and pastimes

Reining patterns

Pattern 10 of the official US NRHA series calls for the rider to enter the arena (start at bottom of diagram), come to a sliding stop, back up (dotted line) and perform four spins to right and left (small circles); next, three circles are ridden to the right, and then to the left, at different paces. Horse and rider then run down the right side of the arena, perform a rollback to turn, ride around to the left side and rollback to turn, and finally return to the ride side to end the pattern in a sliding stop. The rider then dismounts and drops the bridle.

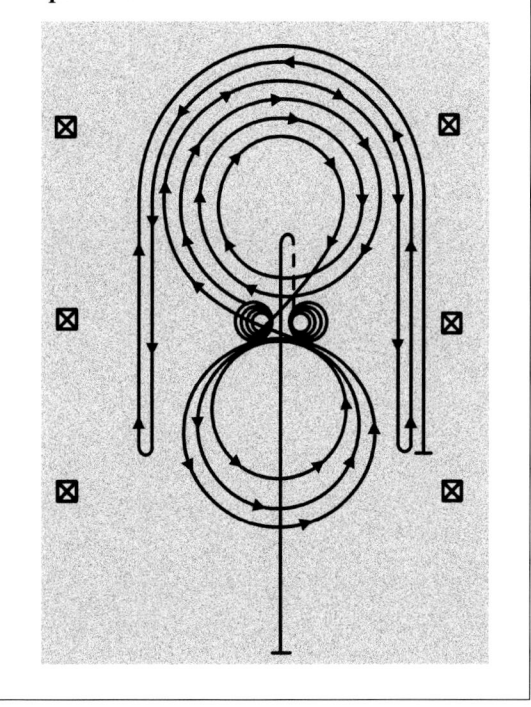

position that will cause it to begin sliding on his back feet. The horse continues to maintain forward movement by continurunning forward with the front feet and using his head and neck for balance. Throughout the stop, the horse continues in a straight line while his back

sports and pastimes

Campdraft riders

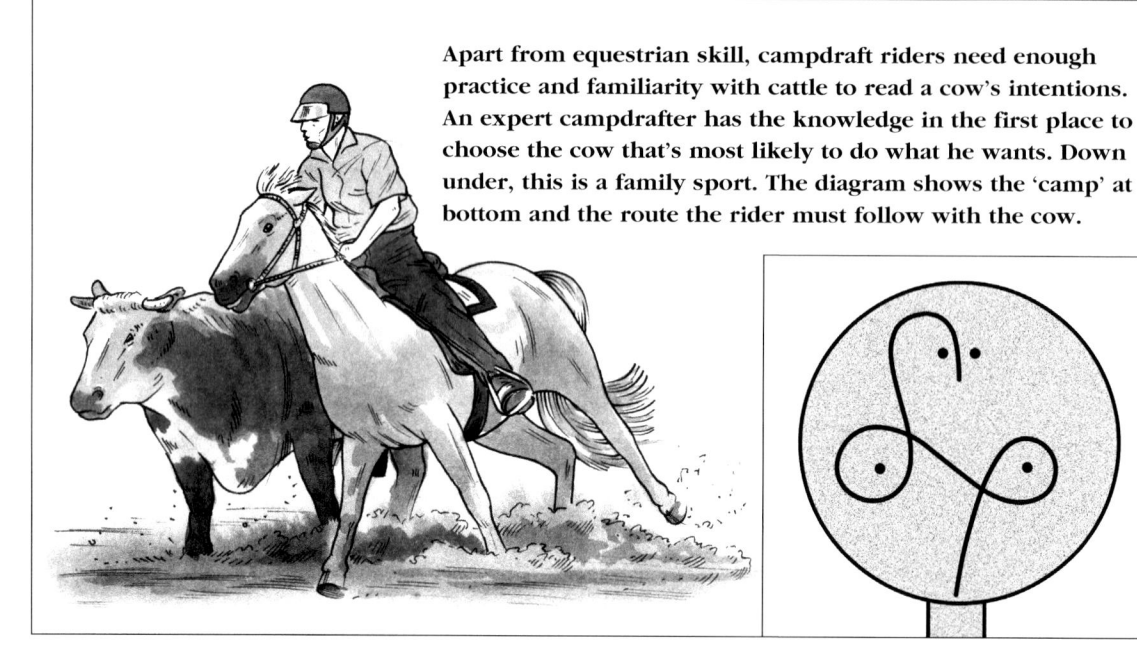

Apart from equestrian skill, campdraft riders need enough practice and familiarity with cattle to read a cow's intentions. An expert campdrafter has the knowledge in the first place to choose the cow that's most likely to do what he wants. Down under, this is a family sport. The diagram shows the 'camp' at bottom and the route the rider must follow with the cow.

Campdrafting

Campdrafting is the uniquely Australian version of handling stock on horseback, and bears a resemblance to Western cutting. The sport evolved from precisely similar requirements on the vast cattle pastures of Queensland, where stockmen in their few idle hours turned working skills into a challenging game. Between 1880 and 1890 it became a sport.

The campdrafting layout consists of a 'camp' (a pen) holding a 'mob' of at least six and perhaps a dozen cows or calves. Horse and rider enter the camp, cut a beast out from the mob, and herd it towards the gate into the arena. Next they block and turn the animal across the gate, keeping it from returning to its fellows, until the rider considers she has demon-strated complete control of the cow. She then calls for the gate to be opened: once in the arena, she has 40 seconds to herd the beast in a circle around first one peg (usually in fact a small tree) and then another, then up the arena and behind and back through two more pegs (the 'gate'). The diagram shows a right-hand course: the judge may call for a left-hand one, which means taking the cow around the left-hand peg first. A good campdrafter can complete the full course in 25 seconds or under, but will win or lose on points – the judge can award up to 26 for camp work, 4 for the arena course, and 70 for horse work.

Australians swear by the Australian Stock Horse for campdrafting; at the very least, they say, the mount should be 'a horse with cattle sense, athletic ability in the camp, and the ability to gallop fast, do small circles on the course and yet remain responsive to the rider's control.'

feet slide over the ground. When done properly, this has the effect of causing the horse to slide anywhere from 10 to 30 feet [3-9m]. (Used in roping, the sliding stop also buffers the effect of the lariat around the steer's hind feet, bringing it down relatively gently, and avoids breaking any bones.)

In the rollback, the horse slides to a stop from a fast lope (canter), then while still collected from the stop rolls 180 degrees over his hocks, bringing his fore feet down in his own tracks, and launches himself back into the lope again.

In April 2000, reining was recognized by the Fédération Equestre Internationale, which gives the sport a toe on the ladder to eventual Olympic status.

The physical qualities of a horse with good reining potential include low head carriage, good pasterns for soundness and way of moving, excellent overall balance, sloping shoulders and strong hindquarters. Athleticism, agility and the ability to stay calm while learning and performing these tricky manoeuvres are also crucial – in the rider no less than in the horse.

For cutting and roping, as might be expected, the favoured mounts are Western horses such as the Quarter Horse; the Criollo is also a real contender, as is the Icelandic horse. Native ponies like the Welsh have been used by hill farmers for equivalent work with sheep, so they too might take well to Western riding.

EVENTING

Eventing, also called horse trials or combined training, brackets several equestrian disciplines into a single gruelling series of tests. This is probably the toughest of all horse sports, for the rider and the mount: both need to be immensely fit and determined – physically and mentally – as well as skilful. As eventer Michael Hillman comments, 'Two minds and bodies have to work as one, and a true partnership between horse and rider is necessary to win.'

Eventing developed from training exercises for military horses, and the structure of the competition was based on the mission of a cavalry officer charged with delivering a message through enemy lines and returning to base. The sport first appeared at the Olympic Games in 1912 at Stockholm under the title 'The Militaire'; then, only military men were allowed to take part, but the competition was opened to civilians in 1920. The attributes sought in the horses are 'precision, elegance and obedience; stamina, versatility and courage; jumping ability and endurance; and finally, the horses' fitness to remain in service'. These qualities do not come amiss in riders, either.

Both informal and formal eventing competitions are often held over one or two days; these may be qualifiers for competing at national and international level, in the three-day event. On the first day there is a dressage test; on day two, speed and endurance tests; and finally a showjumping test. By themselves these are not as complicated or demanding as their single-sport equivalents, but together they constitute a shrewd and daunting trial. The sequence of the tests is not arbitrary. Ideally, in a dressage test, the horse should appear to be performing on his own, as if only incidentally carrying a rider. In eventing, apart from the intrinsic display of accomplishment, the dressage test is designed to show the equine's fitness (there should be a sense of huge but controlled energy), suppleness and obedience, and his harmony with the rider – all qualities vital to tackling the following day's work successfully. Training for dressage also conditions the horse's muscles to become strong and elastic, able to cope easily with extended galloping.

The second day of a three-day event has traditionally consisted of four different tests,

sports and pastimes

all performed in the open against the clock: first, 'roads and tracks', a brisk walk and trot over about 5.7km (3½ miles) to warm up; next, a steeplechase galloped over 3.4km (2⅛ miles) and eight brush fences; a second roads and tracks phase over about 11km (7 miles), to cool down, regain wind, and relax – during this, some riders dismount and run alongside their horses; and finally a 5–6.5km (3–4 mile) 'cross-country' gallop at more than 30km/h (20mph) over a course of some 24–36 artificial obstacles up to 1.2m (4ft) high. Riders walk the course beforehand, but the horses see it for the first time when they are at full tilt: this is a real test of courage, stamina and equine trust in the rider. Starting with the 2004 Olympics, the second day of the eventing competition has been limited to a cross-country test of 45 jumps over 5.7km (3½ miles). Experienced eventers regard this as bad news for the equines, who without the prior warm-up risk starting overconfidently and becoming exhausted part-way through.

Before the cross-country phase there is always a compulsory 10-minute rest, and the horses' temperature, pulse, breathing and general soundness are checked by vets. There is a similar test immediately afterwards as well. Any unfit or unsound horse is eliminated at this stage for his own good. At lower levels and in one- or two-day eventing, not all these endurance stages are included, and are of course somewhat less strenuous than those expected of Olympic contenders. For example, for novices the endurance phase consists of the cross-country only, and is run at a steady canter for approximately 2.5km (1½ miles), over about 15 obstacles that are no higher than 90cm (3ft).

The third day of show-jumping consists of a demonstration designed to show, in the words of the Fédération Equestre Inter-nationale, 'that, on the day after a severe test of endurance, the horses have retained the suppleness, energy and obedience necessary for them to continue in service'. There

Dressage in eventing

This first stage of an eventing competition is designed to show that both horse and rider are fit, supple and in harmony – all vital ingredients for the tests of skill and stamina that are to come in the later stages of the competition.

sports and pastimes

The cross-country stage

In showjumping, the horse has to clear the water in the water jump, but in cross-country he has to jump into it. This is a much greater test of the steed's trust in the rider. The horse will not have run the course before, and has no idea how deep the water is. Cross-country jumping skills must be highly developed, for obstacles are fixed, and do not forgive errors.

is a formal vets' check immediately before this final stage. In Olympic eventing, showjumping involves 12–15 jumps; including a water jump, a combination jump and two 'spreads'. As with the other tests in eventing, Olympic showjumping standards are not expected: what is important is that the horse still has the precision, agility and desire to clear the jumps accurately.

The cynics' view of eventing is that horses and riders are jacks of all trades and masters of none: which is perhaps unjust to the sheer determination and stamina that both require for this discipline. Assuming you are confident that you have these qualities yourself, for eventing you need a mount that is bombproof both physically and mentally (without being insensible to the rider's aids), is capable of extreme precision, and has a clean and careful jump, especially

sports and pastimes

in the cross-country stage. Some Russian horses, including the Akhal-Teke, match this description; professional eventers' favourites are probably the German Warmbloods and the Selle Français, as well as the Thoroughbred. Those with more interest in eventing as a recreation should consider horses such as the Conne-mara, the Irish Draught and Shire crosses, which have affability and willingness in equal measure to their stamina, as do certain lines of Morgan and Quarter Horse.

GETTING STARTED

How do you find out what it is like to go round a show-jumping course or to ride in an endurance race? Whether you have a horse or not, there are plenty of ways to get first-hand experience, or the next best thing, of most equestrian pursuits.

The showjumping stage

This is a final demonstration after the rigours of the cross-country and 'roads and tracks' stages of eventing that the horse is still in top condition, and willing and able to perform with agility and precision – 'fit to continue' in the jargon.

Local riding clubs make a good start. These regularly hold classes on virtually all aspects of riding, and newcomers are always welcome whether as spectators or as participants. Riding clubs are usually informal, welcoming and friendly affairs, and members range from the knowledgeable to complete beginners. Most people there will be doing this for fun, and no one in the horse world claims to know everything. They will also be able to put you in touch with more specialized local groups, as well as instructors, dedicated to particular sports and disciplines. If you don't have a horse, these local organizations are always looking for people to help run their events, so by volunteering you can do something useful, pick up a lot of tips and information, enjoy the sport that interests you, and meet some interesting people and horses, all at the same time.

Riding schools, too, often have open days on which you can try out different equestrian activities; they also hold demonstrations at which you can watch (and ask questions of) other, more or less accomplished riders following their particular pursuits. Schools may vary from those run by a sole instructor to highly organized commercial concerns – try out a few of those available near you, and see which one you like the best. Sometimes the smaller schools can be the most helpful, because their approach is often more personal.

sports and pastimes

The risk is real

It would be mealy-mouthed not to mention the risks inherent in eventing. In 1999, five world-class riders died in four months; seven were killed in 1998, and two fine Australian riders died early in 2000. Horses, too, number among the casualties in eventing. So it was that the 2000 Olympics in Sydney were regarded by many as a test of whether the sport would continue to feature at the Games. There were no fatalities (although there were some broken human bones), but nonetheless there has been a persistent rumble since, that perhaps eventing should be banned as too dangerous.

When eventing accidents as a whole were analysed, the irony and the true tragedy of that cluster of deaths became apparent. In sailing and mountaineering (for example) fatal accidents tend to occur most frequently among the inexpert and the inexperienced. But in eventing, the worst accidents happened during the cross-country stage, to the most accomplished riders. The reason: horses were catching a hoof on the obstacles (which are solid and immovable, unlike showjumps); the horse would twist or somersault, fall and land on the rider. This tends not to happen in steeplechasing, where the high stirrups help tip the jockey off if the horse falls. The eventers were such good riders that they stuck on when lesser eques-trians would have been saved, however ignominiously, by falling off and away from the horse.

This is a good moment to point out a fundamental of being around horses. If you ride at all, you are implicitly rejecting the contemporary delusion that life can be purged of risk and responsibility. A horse can be dangerous even when it doesn't mean to be, and sitting on one only boosts the potential hazards. Horsey people regard horses with respect and deep caution, just as sailors rationally fear the sea, and climbers their mountains. And so fatalities are statisti-cally rare in all these pursuits.

Local Pony Club branches provide a great practical introduction to riding if you have your own horse or pony; even if you don't, you can learn a vast amount just by watching a Pony Club class – just as you can at your local riding club.

All kinds of horses turn up at local Pony Club meetings, and very few riders are unwilling to talk about their horse or pony. Everyone has a horse story to tell. They will happily introduce you to theirs, tell you why they have a passion for a particular breed or a particular sport, and so on. Remember that they all started out in the same position as you, and all know they never stop learning about horses. This is also a great way to compare lots of horses, both in action and face to face. This will help you sort out in the flesh the characteristics and temperaments of different breeds, and show you how different one horse can be from another, even those of the same breed.

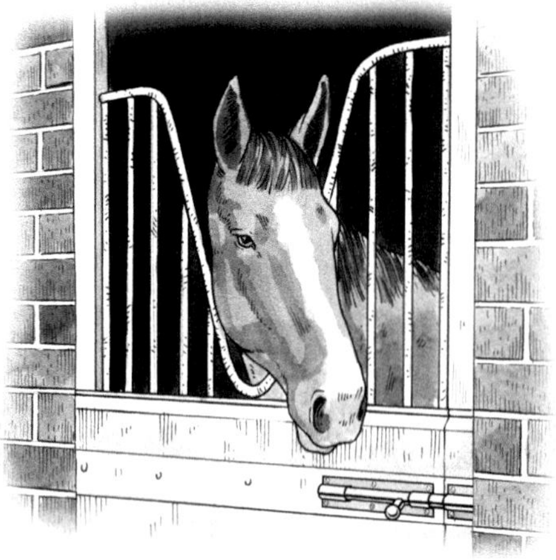

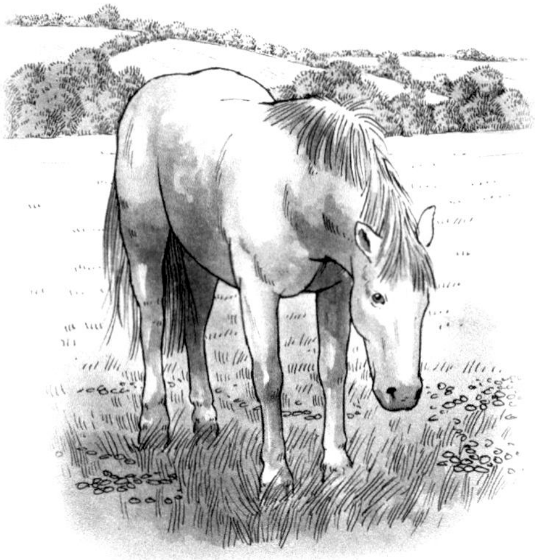

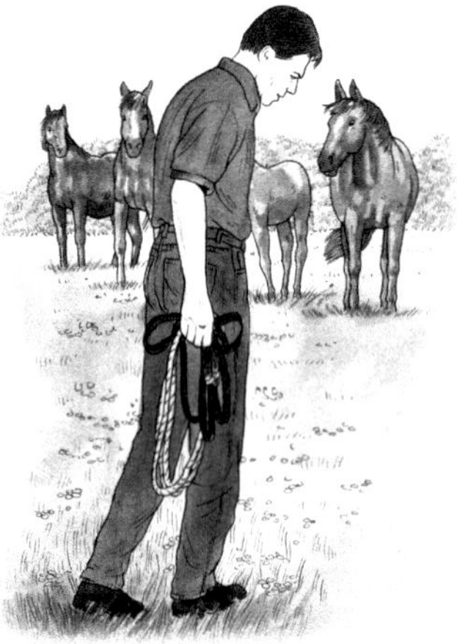

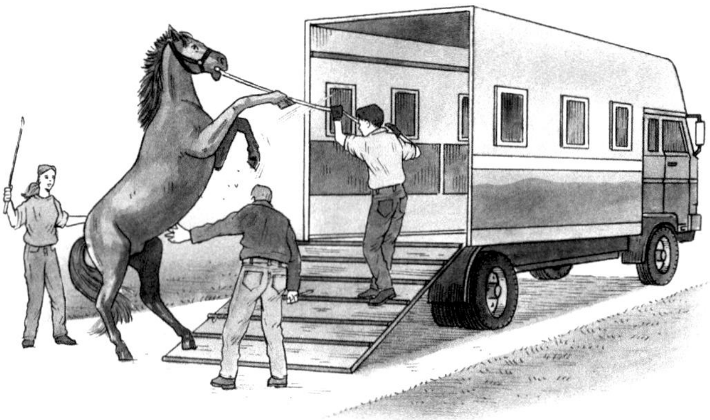

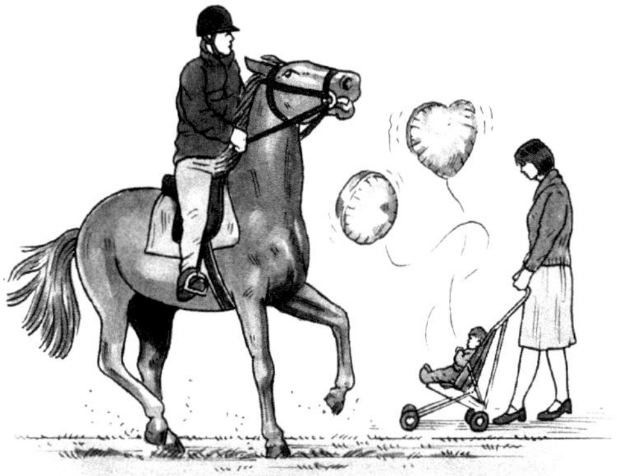

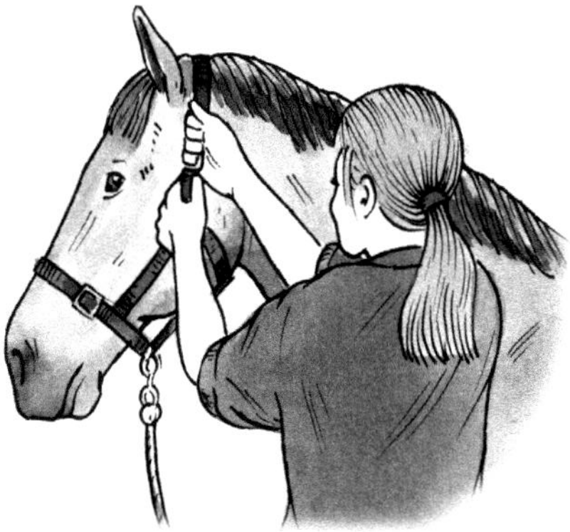

CHAPTER TWO

The Nature of the Horse

Horses are highly intelligent creatures with senses of smell, sight, hearing and sociability very different from ours. Appreciating how a horse thinks and feels is vital to managing his welfare, and to being a good rider.

People have been handling horses for millennia. But what, exactly, is a horse? A one-toed ungulate, the biologists will solemnly tell you - meaning a large, hoofed mammal - but this doesn't begin to describe the complexity of this fascinating animal. Most of your dealings with equines will revolve around three things: his physical strength; his mechanical structure - which you have to be able to manage and direct in order to ride; and his intriguing view of the world - which you have to understand at all times, and sometimes outwit, if you are going to have a real partnership with him.

THE WORLD ACCORDING TO THE HORSE

Horses are essentially no different today from the creatures that first came into close contact with people as they roamed the Asian steppes around 6000 years ago. They are at the mercy of the same instincts, fears, and hungers, and in need of the same satisfactions and gratifications today as they were then. All of these traits evolved and developed because they were the very attributes that allowed horses to survive in the wild. Thwarting them throws horses mentally and physically out of balance. To put it in human terms, it makes them unhappy, because their overriding instinct to survive is frustrated. Consequently the essence of good horsekeeping is to try to provide a domesticated equine with as few instinctual obstructions as is practically possible.

This does not mean that the only happy horses are wild horses, or that it is unkind

the nature of the horse

to ride horses, and so on, although some animal rights extremists take this view. The only issue is whether what people demand of their horses does any physical, mental or emotional harm to the animals. Racing, for example, doesn't of itself call for equines to do anything that horses don't enjoy. The horse is built to run – and does so spontaneously, sometimes alone and sometimes in gangs: watch the stam-pede when a new mare is introduced to a herd in a field, or a couple of foals as they go charging about together. Even a solitary foal will break into a gallop of his own accord, from a standing start, and not just to rejoin his mother.

There are different reasons for all these things, but no one could sensibly claim the horses are deliberately giving themselves a hard time – what animal does? If there are problems with horse racing, they arise from the age at which animals are put on the track (when they are far from fully grown) and the conditions in which racehorses are traditionally kept and trained (which are not remotely 'natural').

Stephen Budiansky's remark in his book *The Nature of Horses* bears repeating here: 'Those who claim it is "unethical" to ask a horse to do anything it would not do of its own inclination are being naive and foolish; but equally naive and foolish are those who expect to teach a horse to do their bidding without taking into account its natural inclinations.' And in thinking about how to look after a horse we should bear in mind his further observation: 'Horsemen have always been susceptible to one great foible, and that is the belief that the categories and terms and concepts they apply to their art are ones their horses hold too. The art of riding is just that – an art – and it has evolved its own language and techniques that contain a whole suitcase of assumptions.'

A HORSE NOT A HUMAN

We need to be careful not to project our ideas of what is good and bad, natural and unnatural, onto the horse. For example, his ideas about what is good for him may be very different from what he may meet in even the most reputable yards. But what is natural, for a horse? Most obviously, this is a herd animal: wild horses, and those kept under the 'tabun' system in Russia (see Chapter 3), live in groups, and the herd has a specific social structure. The horse is also a prey animal – meat for wolves, bears and big cats; it is itself a herbivore, grazing on grasses and browsing on leaves. Virtually everything else about horses flows from these salient facts, and from horses' status as highly evolved, sentient beings with emotional and even intellectual lives of their own.

All animals that humans have domesticated have certain things in common. The innate curiosity of sheep, dogs, goats, cats, cattle and so on is apparent to anyone who's so much as passed one on the street or in a field, and along with their need for food this inquisitiveness almost certainly contributed to their initial association with human beings. In the wild, these animals are also migratory and adaptable. Horses

Horse names

A quick guide to the terms commonly used to describe horses of various ages:
- A baby horse is a foal. If female, it's a filly foal, and if male, it's a colt foal.
- A foal's mother is its dam; a foal's father is its sire.
- A year old foal is called a yearling
- At three years old, horses are reckoned to be sexually mature, and fillies are then called mares. Colts are either called stallions (or, more rarely, entires) or, if they've been castrated, are called geldings.

the nature of the horse

Horse solitude

Being in the company of other horses is fundamental to a horse's emotional well-being: solitude is misery. Among wild horses, being exiled from the herd is a major punishment.

The senior mare will drive away a member of the herd – usually a youngster – who misbehaves, and not allow the offender back into the herd until he shows remorse.

share all these traits. The archaeological record shows that after 55 million years of evolution, horses as we know them today appeared about two million years ago. The modern horse, *Equus caballus*, became extinct in the Americas 10,000 years ago at latest, and survived increasingly tenuously on the Asian steppes as once plentiful grazing lands disappeared under encroaching forest. By the fourth millennium BC, the Asian herds had dwindled to perhaps only a few hundred animals. There are 60 million equines in the world today because around 6000 years ago a tribe of hunters and pastoralists living near Dereivka, in the area that is now the Ukraine, domesticated these creatures for use as a source of meat, and then, eventually, learned to ride them. Two thousand years later, horses had once again spread all over Europe and Asia; but this time they were always in the company of humans.

Horses have been horses about four times longer than *Homo sapiens* has been a distinctive species of mammal. Besides that, they have been domesticated for only three-thousandths of their time on earth. So it should hardly be surprising if horses still behave as though they were roaming the steppes fending for themselves.

Animals that graze tend to live in nomadic herds, ambling from one feeding ground to another. As a result they have a less urgent sense of their own habitat than animals that live solitary lives and have to defend their food supplies. Horses do mark the general area they inhabit by leaving strategic piles of droppings, but these are designed more to warn roving-eyed stallions away from the mares than as markers of territory as such.

the nature of the horse

The innocent victim

Many domesticated horses are kept on their own. While they may have fine grazing and otherwise caring owners, they will become depressed and hard to handle from lack of equine company. Never keep a horse in solitude if you can avoid it.

FAMILY LIFE

One might get the impression, initially, from seeing a group of wild or feral horses that they consisted of a harem (usually of between two and ten mares), with offspring at various stages of development, under the leadership of a stallion. But close observation shows that the major decisions are made by a senior mare - usually, but not always, the oldest. She will resolve when to move on to new grazing, will keep order among any unruly young (handing out punishment when necessary), take precedence at the water hole, and so on. Apart from providing the mares with foals, the stallion functions as a guard and protector against predators and also against competition from other stallions wishing to take over his harem. Feral herds are taken over by a new stallion as often as every two years, but otherwise the herd's essential structure - a group of mothers and their daughters and their foals - remains stable. Colts and defeated stallions will join 'bachelor groups' of unattached male horses, and will then try either to be accepted by a group of mares without a stallion (they don't always succeed) or to take over a herd from a resident stallion.

Since horses are not naturally limited by loyalty to any particular territory, they create cohesion within the herd through bonding between members. Although there is a hierarchy within the herd, the most frequent forms of equine social behaviour have less to do with arguing over social status than with forming and maintaining friendships. Thus there is a paradox: while horses are herd creatures, they have a powerful sense of one another's individuality. They recognize one another by sight, sound and smell, which they remember like elephants (so to speak). Domestic horses will greet each other with whinnies of joy (and none of the squealing that occurs initially between strangers) after years of separation. Wild stallions are able to identify and reclaim an errant mare who has drifted

the nature of the horse

From the horse's mouth

Horses make a fairly small range of vocal sounds. In order of increasing excitement, their basic calls are the nicker (also called a wicker), blow, whinny (or neigh) and squeal. With the possible exception of the first, they make these noises to express their state of mind, to alert other horses that something is up, or to scare off a predator. Equine noises are valuable to the animal because they cause something to happen, rather than because they mean anything strictly translatable into human terms.

NICKERING

This is a deep, gentle, nasal sound, made with the mouth closed. Mares and foals use it to call to each other; horses in general use it as a friendly greeting, to people as much as to other equines. It is similar to a cat's purr, which essentially means 'I am a very nice cat and mean no one any harm.' (Cats purr like small furry tractors when pleased, but also when in pain. The intention is to placate anything hostile.) Animal communications expert, Eugene Morton, suggests that the nicker was originally meant to be felt rather than heard, a vibration made by a foal snuggling up to his mother. Young animals are not threatening, so the sound continues to be used to signal friendly intentions when the foal grows up.

BLOWING

This tends to happen at times when a person would sigh – when the horse is fed up with waiting around, or being led off to do something he doesn't really feel like doing. The blow is also used as a warning of, and to, a possible threat – a startled horse will blow, wait, and then cautiously investigate whatever disturbed him.

SNORTING

A rarely heard variation on the blow is the snort, a harsh noise that sounds very like a human doing a bad impression of a pig. Horses snort to show disapproval or dislike, with a strong hint of aggression – 'Keep away, or else.' Unruly foals, people with alarming tools such as chainsaws – and indeed pigs – may find themselves snorted at.

WHINNYING

A whinny can be very loud, even from a very small horse. It is used to announce a horse's presence, and designed to carry over long distances. Sometimes it's a complaint ('I'm alone/lonely', or even 'Wait for me!'), sometimes just a loud hello. There are horses who, when travelling, whinny at any other horse they see out of the horsebox window. Horses can recognize the whinny of another horse they know; wild horses use it to keep in touch with others in their band who are out of sight. This is what the whinnying horse, left alone in the yard while the others are out hacking, is trying to do.

SQUEALING

The squeal sounds a lot worse than it is. Two stallions will squeal on meeting; so will a mare and a stallion, and so will an older horse after exchanging perfectly amiable greetings with a politely submissive juvenile. It's an assertion of seniority or dominance, made with angry-seeming flat ears but with a measure of uncertainty: the head stays up, without the low-down, tooth-baring 'snake face' that signals real aggression. Wild stallions will go in for quite long squealing contests to decide who is top horse. The one who squeals longest shows that he has the bigger lungs and stronger chest muscles, and would most likely win a fight. Contrary to their reputation, stallions will avoid violence if they can: this is one instance of how they do so.

the nature of the horse

into another herd. The general stampede that often occurs when a new horse joins an established group of domestic grazers may be designed to let the horses work up a quick sweat and exchange their personal odours. The neutral umbrella of a high-spirited group romp saves not only time but much energy that would be taken up with individual meetings. In this speedy set of introductions, horses seem able to identify, perhaps from their smell or perhaps from subtle visual signals, one another's ages, or at least their capacity for dominance or submission. Certainly hierarchies have been seen to change immediately within a herd after such communal dashes, with the new horse slotting into place (including top place) with no further discussion or objection from other members of the group.

Living in the herd involves more than observing its hierarchy, however. Horses have particular 'best friends' whom they allow into their 'personal space', which extends to about 1.5m (5ft) around them, to graze and with whom they enjoy mutual grooming sessions. In these, the two horses

Actions speak louder

Horses' very acute vision and their original existence, with the herd spread out over a large area, have made it both possible and necessary to develop visual signals – a body language – that is subtler and more informative than their vocal 'language'.

In his book, *The Nature of Horses*, Stephen Budiansky suggests that in some cases we may be able to read a horse's mind better than another horse can. Humans read one another's faces all the time, and can accurately interpret a horse's. Equines can look everything from smug to mischievous, patient, vacant or focused. A puckered upper eyelid shows mild worry or pain – or self-pity, in a histrionic nag; ears flopping sideways demonstrate contentment; a wrinkled nose, irritation; a drooping lower lip, relaxation, on the verge of sleep; and so on. No one knows to what extent horses notice one another's facial expressions, or even if they're actually intended to communicate how they're feeling. Some horses will pull lugubrious faces with every muscle available, almost crossing their eyes, and twisting their heads every which way over the stable door, to get attention; they won't do this at another horse, only at humans.

HORSE GESTURES

Horse-to-horse communi-cations consist of signs of annoyance, submission and friendship. Of the latter, the most obvious is mutual grooming. Annoyance (which can be very mild) may be shown by lashing the tail, or flattening the ears backwards and swinging the head at an intruder, in an obvious prelude to a bite. Or one horse may swing his hindquarters at another, perhaps raising a hind leg at the same time. Actual contact in the form of kicking or biting is rare, and is prolonged only long enough to make the point. Usually, long before things get this far, the other horse will read the signs, drop his head and tuck in his tail in the classic posture of submission, and move off.

Foals and young horses will ritually make a champing motion with their mouths open and heads lowered when greeting an older horse. This is a bit like a flag of truce, but can be a sign of submission too, for foals will 'mouth' when they've been told off by their mothers, as well, and even by another foal who's higher in rank.

the nature of the horse

Fear of the unknown

Horses generally hate strange objects that wave, jiggle, flap or bob about, or that make a lot of noise and can't keep still – such as small children. Their instinctive reaction is to shy away, or even to bolt. Some never get over their alarm at 'ordinary' things like plastic bags or balloons, but with patience and gentleness most can be trained not to worry when meeting something unusual.

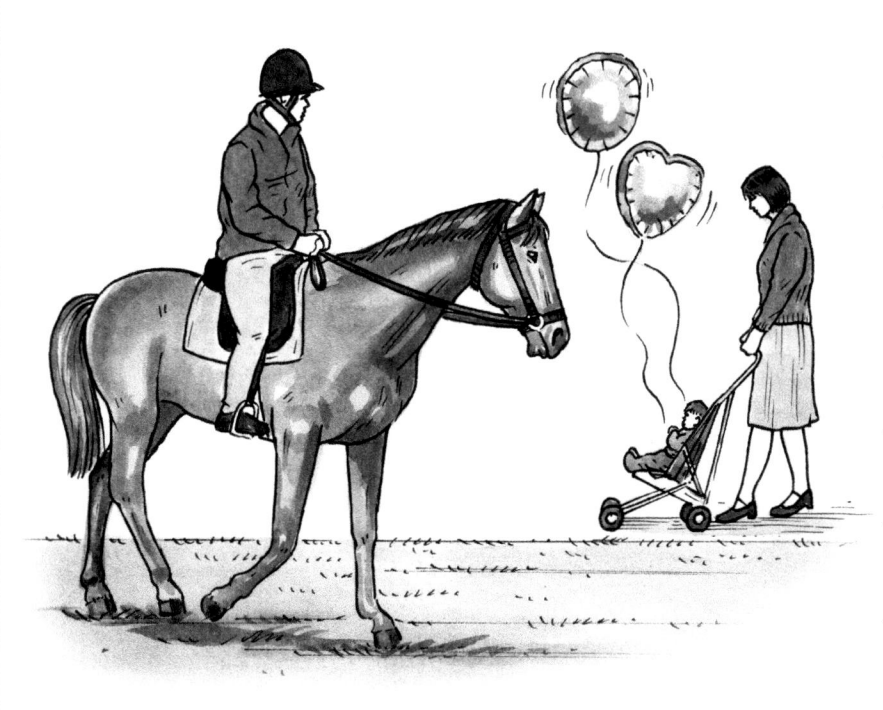

A horse who trusts his rider will be more likely to let himself be pushed through a frightening encounter than one who doesn't. But never use a whip – just ride him firmly past the obstacle. He will eventually realize there is nothing to fear, whatever he meets.

the nature of the horse

Real aggression: the 'snake head'

A horse who's really angry puts on a display that makes him look remarkably like a prey animal – with flat ears, neck and head in line, flaring nostrils, and wild eyes with the whites showing. All this signals a serious intention to attack.

FACTORS FOR SURVIVAL

Horses long ago evolved to thrive on the least digestible grasses – the food that other grazers rejected, and would starve on. This is one reason why horses are so reactive to the diets that humans feed them in buckets – for their guts are phenomenally efficient. It is also the reason why horses eat continually – they have to consume large quantities of grass if they are to extract the energy they need from it. This accounts for horses' large size when compared with other land mammals. The bigger the animal, the smaller the surface area (skin) it has in relation to its mass, and therefore the less energy it loses in the form of heat for a given quantity of food.

stand head to tail, and with bared teeth scratch each other down the neck and withers, and less often along the loins, on the croup and around the shoulders.

Interestingly, the favourite areas for grooming coincide with a major network of nerves, and stimulating them lowers the pulse rate. Grooming is calming. Such close friendships may form between horses of distant, or the same, social ranking, and one horse may have more than one such close friend. The resulting criss-cross of relationships binds the whole herd together, not just pairs of horses. This kind of social living, along with the reduction of most aggressive behaviour to symbolic gestures (see 'Actions Speak Louder'), leads many observers to conclude that the horse's life in the wild is essentially cooperative rather than competitive or contentious.

Nosing around for food keeps the horse's mind occupied, and his feet as well: a horse will cover about 40km (25 miles) in a day, even in a field, as he goes from one patch of grass to another. At the same time, his long nose gives him the ability to graze while his eyes remain high enough from the ground to spot predators. An inborn curiosity about the world about them, and excellent long-distance vision, became powerful factors for survival.

Life as a prey animal meant that horses survived to breed if they were able not just to see but to outrun the animals that wanted to eat them. Horses survived too who were wary of unfamiliar-shaped objects, and ones given to sudden movements, and if they avoided shadowy spaces, holes in the ground and other dark places where something lithe, clawed and lethal might be hiding; those who were not so careful were eaten.

the nature of the horse

Horse senses

Like all mammals, horses rely on sight, hearing, touch, taste and smell to take in information about their environment.

TOUCH

When stroking a horse you should reach out slowly and give a good hard scratch along the top of the neck where horses groom one another. Tender little strokes feel too much like flies' feet landing, especially around the face, and will annoy the horse. Apart from the networks of nerves on his skin, a horse's major touch organ is his vibrissae, the whiskers around his nose and mouth. These are as important to a horse as whiskers are to a cat: they are used to judge distance in an area where horses can't see, and to test textures, particularly of food. The vibrissae are often clipped off by people who either don't know this or, worse, don't care, for the sake of 'neatness'.

SMELL

Horses have a very highly developed sense of smell. It has been estimated that their smell-sensitive cells cover an area equal to their entire skin. Humans can distinguish at least 10,000 individual scents; but this is a fraction of what a horse can detect. In the wild, sniffing at a pile of dung made by various passing horses will tell any horse which stallions have added to it, how long ago, what their relative ranks are, and whether any contributing mares are alone, in a harem, and in heat or not. Like other animals, humans secrete different chemicals in their sweat depending on whether they're feeling calm, happy, wary or frightened. We can't pick up these subtle aromas, but a horse can – and reacts accordingly.

TASTE

Horses' tongues, like humans' tongues, have sensors that can detect sweet, sour, salt and bitter flavours. This extremely acute sense is used to sort nourishing food from poisonous plants.

SIGHT

Horses have a virtually 360-degree field of vision. They have two small blind spots: an arc of about 3 degrees directly behind the head, and a small area immediately in front of the nose. Directly ahead, horses have binocular vision. Here, they see three-dimensionally, in depth. When relaxed, equine eyes are naturally focused on the distance, but horses can see very sharp details only within a fairly narrow, horizontal band of their field of view.

Ironically, horses don't know that grass is green, whichever side of the fence it is. Equines have only limited colour vision, although it is still enough to help them to see through camouflage used by predators. Equally important in this respect is their highly efficient night vision. This doesn't work too well in twilight, however, and neither does their day vision. Horses get understandably twitchy and skittish at dusk, because this is when predators are most frequently on the prowl, so it is easier for all concerned to bring them in or put them out to pasture while there's still full daylight. Even moving horses after dark is easier than doing it in twilight.

SOUND

Horses' ears can turn through 180 degrees, and research suggests that they can pay equal, simultaneous attention to a sounds reaching one ear from behind them and the other ear from in front. Their ability to hear weak sounds made more than 4km (2 ½ miles) away is a crucial aid in detecting a predator's movements. They can also hear very high-pitched sounds (up to 33.5kHz, compared with our limit of 20kHz), giving them yet more sensitivity to stealthy activity at a distance.

the nature of the horse

A major part of a horse's intellectual stimulation comes from being on the alert for potential threats. This might appear to us, seeing horses in a world in which we generally feel entirely safe, to be timidity, even cowardice. Actually, it is the result of equine curiosity and caution, acting together in the interests of self-preservation. And if in doubt, the horse will do his best to bolt.

A SENSE OF TRUST

The horse's unmatched reputation for courage may seem curious, even inexplicable, in light of the above. How, for instance, did such a chary creature become a weapon of war? A war horse in battle array must indeed have been a terrifying thing to behold. But something had to induce him to go into battle in the first place – to be not only fearsome, but fear*less*. In the same way today, something will persuade an eventing horse to fly in the face of his own instincts and jump into a darkened barn and take yet another jump into water to get out of it.

We can only start to understand this by remembering that it is in a horse's nature to bond with other horses. As more than one horse enthusiast has wistfully remarked, they

Keep your distance

Horses avoid fighting as much as possible: they prefer to cooperate with one another. Consequently, one horse has only to indicate irritation – just lifting a leg to signal the start of a kick – for another to get the message and back off.

the nature of the horse

bond well with people, but only for want of something better – namely, another horse or, preferably, a whole bunch of them. It is often said, but it's not quite true, that to a horse a human being is the herd leader, and that is why horses do as we want. In fact, we do very few of the things that horses do together, and we certainly don't *look* equine. Perhaps because horses stabled in the traditional European way probably get more human than equine company, and interact more with people than they do with other horses, humans become trustworthy in their eyes. (At least if they're treated kindly; and humans are also an important source of food.) Yet this happens too with horses kept out with other horses much of the year. When someone they know walks into their field, they will sooner or later stroll over to see what is what and exchange greetings. They'll allow themselves to be approached and caught, even when they've jumped out of their own field and are lunching on the hay field or the lawn; some even come when they're called. Why should they?

Herd life, as we've seen, is essentially a cooperative affair, and if they're not violently abused it would appear that horses, in their own heads at least, make a kind of deal with humans. We don't frighten them, we do feed and shelter them, and we groom them, satisfying some of their tactile needs at least. In return, they go along with us when we do something as strange as to sit on their backs, and even before that fit them with all kinds of odd equipment. They need convincing that this is okay, and most won't be convinced in a hurry; but they do it. And not because we are their 'leader-who-must-be-obeyed', but because all the other things we've done with them have turned out to be

Saving energy

Horses have a 'passive stay' mechanism in the hind legs: the patella (kneecap) slips into a groove in the femur, locking the legbones together in a rigid parallelogram. The horse can then stand comfortably for hours, as it is using no muscular energy.

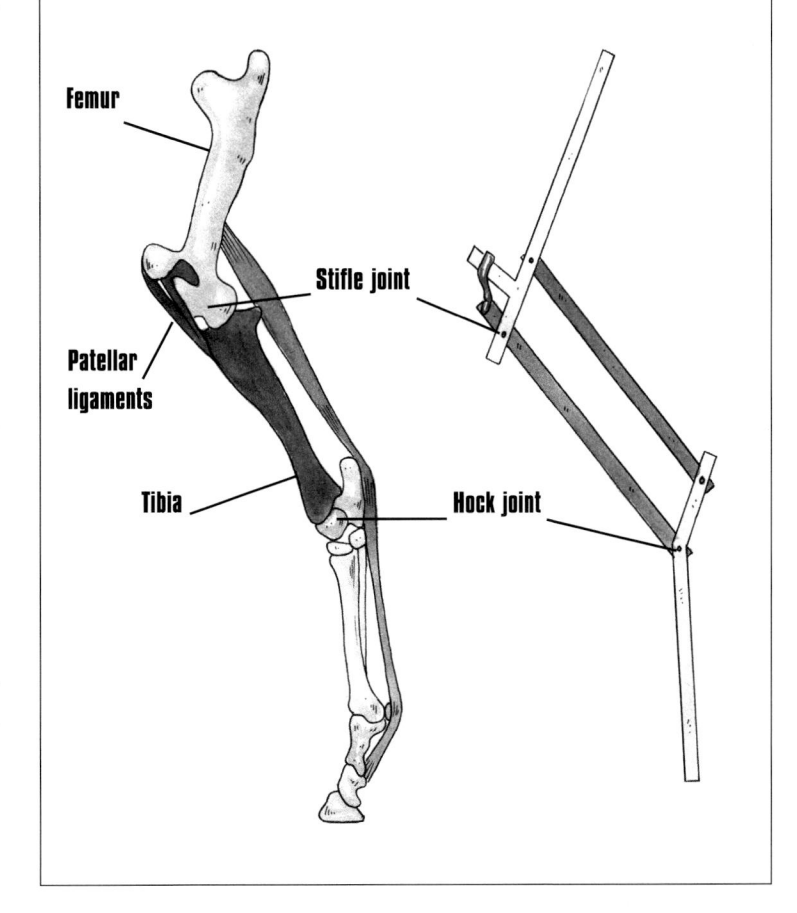

- Femur
- Stifle joint
- Patellar ligaments
- Tibia
- Hock joint

the nature of the horse

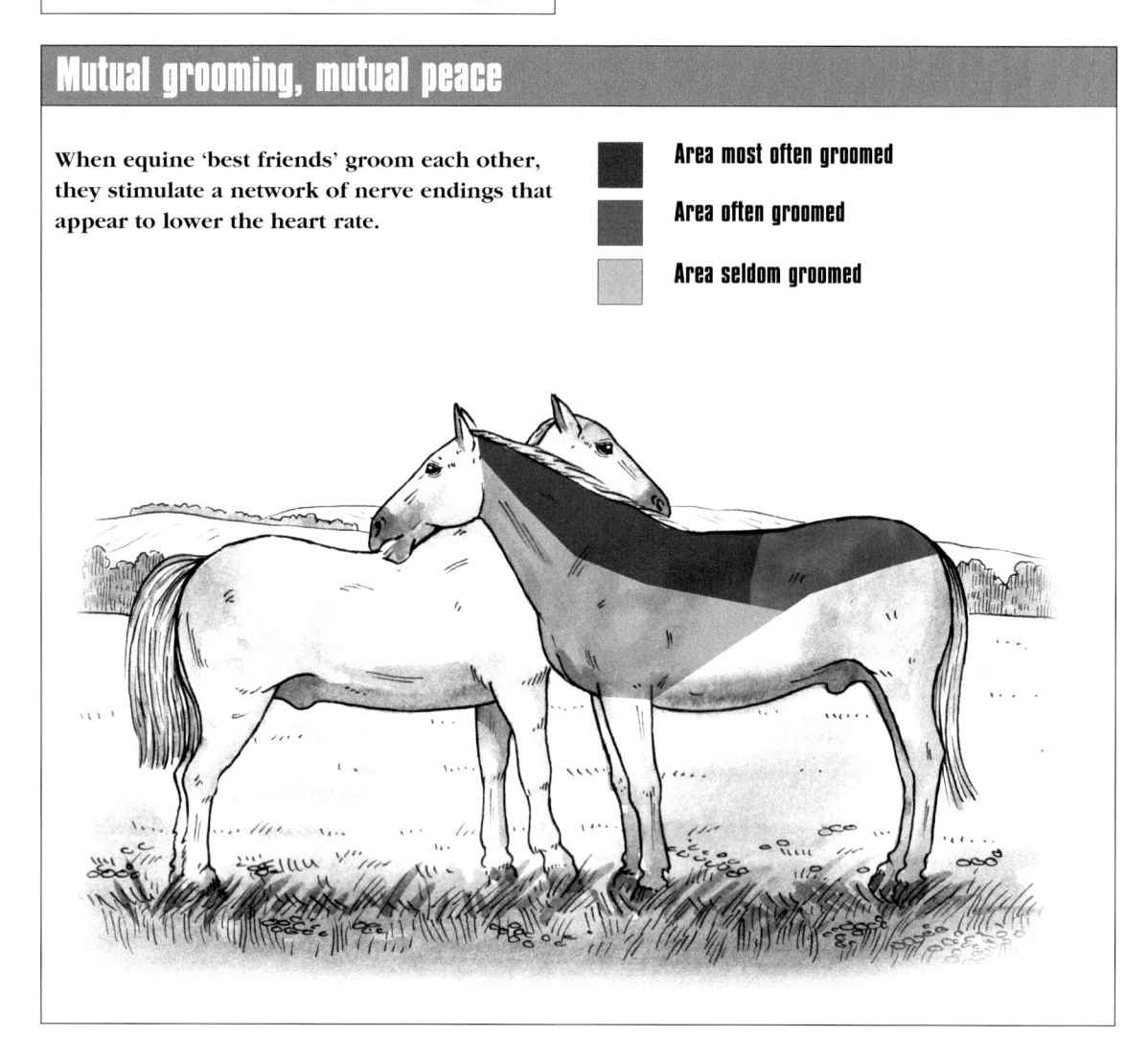

Mutual grooming, mutual peace

When equine 'best friends' groom each other, they stimulate a network of nerve endings that appear to lower the heart rate.

- Area most often groomed
- Area often groomed
- Area seldom groomed

safe, non-threatening and even enjoyable. So they trust us not to ask them to do anything impossible or dangerous. If we ask a horse to jump into a dark place, they trust us, in effect, to have cleared tigers out of it first.

WORK IS PLAY

It is not necessarily obvious that a horse's courage is a product of trust, but once we realize that, it immediately becomes clear that beating a horse in the hope of making him do what we want is exactly the wrong approach, as it destroys trust. In nearly all our dealings with horses we need to rethink and re-imagine things in their terms.

This means not only learning to act in a way a horse understands and accepts from within his own view of the world, but keeping him in a manner that accords with his nature. For example, the more time he can spend in the company of other horses, preferably out on grass when he's not being worked, the better. He will be happier, and consequently will be more interested in cooperating with you and learning new skills when it comes to riding. Horses may be idle, lazy, grass-munching good-for-nothings on one level but they are naturally curious creatures and most of them enjoy learning things and overcoming a challenge.

All highly intelligent creatures (although not all domesticated animals) seem to have a latent desire to add to their store of knowledge and even accomplishments. Dogs enjoy learning new tricks, and invent some for themselves, as well as goofing around; think how many routes a cat will take to go from one side of a room to the other. This kind of behaviour seems to be a persistence of juvenile play into adulthood – grown cats will still chase their tails, for instance. In wild animals, childhood games are a serious practice of survival skills, and the real business of hunting or foraging, fighting or fleeing takes their place in adulthood. In many adult domesticated animals (sheep are a notable exception), these games seem to continue to be played for their own sake. Perhaps because their survival needs are largely met through human care, domestic animals 'fill in' the resulting blank in their mental lives through play.

Where does the horse fit into all this? Veterinarian Andrew Fraser suggests that adult horses find an outlet for their desire to play through their association with people – through learning new activities (as in the schooling arena, or jumping, or out on a hack), and through equestrian sports like hunting and racing, which involve being in a group of horses, and which all occur in different environments. The mental energy that a horse would have used in searching for food, water, predators and mates in the wild is redirected to learning and exercising new skills. There is a human counterpart to this: arts and especially sciences have developed only in societies that have been able to support an affluent class with the leisure to think beyond the immediate questions of survival. This channelling of otherwise frustrated mental energy would explain why horses take so enthusiastically to work, and will often (for instance) learn how to play mounted games better than their riders.

AGAINST NATURE

'Live free or die' runs the motto of the American state of New Hampshire. Would that it stood in giant lime-green letters above every domestic horse for all to read.

We have seen how the essentials of equine nature are tactile sociability, constant movement and more or less constant eating. Horses that are permanently stabled clearly can't be said to be living a normal life, since they have little room to walk, rarely have continual access to hay, and are usually cut off from actual contact with other horses by floor-to-ceiling walls in their stables. In some yards, they are shut behind doors so that they cannot even see other horses. Comprehensively deprived of natural stimulation, many stabled horses consequently develop 'stereotypies' – that is, they take up obsessively repetitive activities to help endure their stupefying boredom and frustration. These are traditionally called 'vices'. They include weaving, crib biting, box walking, and door and wall kicking; and they are never seen in horses living wild. There are other habits that are conventionally called vices, but that are entirely harmless, and one or two that almost any horse will indulge in when out in a field, given certain circumstances. We'll come to these in due course: let's first deal with the most common problems of stabled horses.

Weaving

The horse sways from side to side on his fore legs and weaves his head (the nose follows a figure-of-eight) from side to side along the width of the stable door. This is distressing to see, although like other repetitive activities it is highly likely that it gives the horse a fair degree of pleasure. What seems to happen is this. Deprived of

the nature of the horse

anywhere to walk, the caged horse produces an exaggerated form of marking time – walking on the spot. This activity releases opium-like substances, called endorphins and enkephalins, into the brain. These are natural, powerful anaesthetics, and they are produced, by any mammal, as a counter to severe stress (such as a fright or a wound). This is why people who are badly injured in sporting or automobile accidents or in the midst of battle may fail to notice what has happened to them or, if they do, can retain their wits long enough to seek help before the pain kicks in.

A weaving horse is under stress, but by persisting in his exaggerated behaviour he continues to stimulate the release of endorphins, which relieves the *sense* of stress. A weaver is, in other words, addicted to his own drugs. He will also lose condition, because he cannot (or will not) rest and often loses his appetite, and can eventually make himself lame. This is why people install anti-weaving bars on stable doors, or hang bricks and tyres and other deterrents at the sides of a weaver's door. This protects the horse from the consequences of his addiction but doesn't remove the cause, so one can expect his stress to find some other outlet. Many horses simply step back and weave inside the stable.

The best way to deal with weaving is not to let it start in the first place – by enabling the horse to spend as much time as is practicable at grass, in the company of other horses, and by breaking up periods of exercise so that the animal doesn't have enough time to become stressed by being in a stable. If you find you have a weaver on your hands, these measures should cure the condition too. When in, the horse should be loose in the stable, not tied up in a stall (why anyone ever thought this was a clever way to leave a horse for hours on end is incomprehensible). Plenty of water and bulk food (hay or straw) should be available, too – put the food in a net with small holes, so that he has to work quite hard to get it and so it will take longer to eat. Some people advise isolating weavers and crib biters, to stop other horses copying them. Since isolation and frustration are the main causes of this obsessive behaviour, this advice is neither astute nor kind. What the horse needs most is company and space to move naturally. If for some over-riding reason he can't be let out, even illusory company seems to work vastly better than none (see 'Reflections on Weaving').

Cribbing and wind sucking

The horse bites onto any projecting object (such as the end of a fence rail, or the top of a stable door: some will gnaw on their own limbs) and sucks in air – actually swallowing it, so that the air gets into the gut and interferes with the digestion. Horses may also simply suck wind without fixing their teeth onto anything, arching their necks as they do so. The activity appears to be a pathological form of grooming, indicating that the cause is loneliness. Cribbers add to their problems because persistently gnawing at hard material can wear their incisor (front) teeth so badly that they cannot graze. This may account for some extreme cribbers' failure to lose the habit when put out to graze with other horses – where they should have been more often in the first place – and given a varied and challenging course of work. The more likely reasons are that either the specific underlying cause of stress is still present, or that the horse has simply become too powerfully addicted to his own endorphins to let go of them.

While prevention and cure for cribbing and wind sucking are generally the same as for weaving, a 'cure' commonly recommended for relentless exponents is the anti-crib collar. Essentially this causes discomfort when the horse contracts his neck muscles to suck air. While its advantage is that the horse punishes himself, it doesn't deal with

the nature of the horse

A good sniff

On meeting a smell that is new, horses will curl back the upper lip, stick their noses in the air, open their mouths, raw the scent in and trap it around a smell-sensitive region called the Organ of Jacobsen in the roof of the mouth. This singular action is called 'flehmen', and it looks as if the horse is literally turning his nose up at a vile odour – which can be particularly embarrassing if he's just had a good sniff at you. In fact, he's fixing the scent in his memory and, scientists believe, analysing its chemical make-up. Among other things, horses can tell if another animal is calm or fearful from its smell, or whether it is sexually receptive.

Reflections on weaving

It is estimated that between three and 10 per cent of stabled horses weave. Research by veterinary scientists at the University of Lincoln, England, indicates that the underlying cause is isolation. Dr Daniel Mills, who led the research, says: 'Abnormal behaviours, such as weaving, are only seen in animals in confinement. … The horse has a lack of control over his situation and is faced with a problem he cannot resolve. With weaving, the scenario would be: "There's another horse but I can't actually get closer to him. I can see him but I can't interact, I can't groom with him." On traditional yards all the stables face one another so the horses look into the centre. That's like us being able to see our favourite food but not being able to eat it.'

Dr Mills and his team found that their test horses stopped weaving entirely, and almost at once, when they were allowed nose-to-nose contact with one another. Recognizing that rebuilding stables to allow direct contact between horses is usually not an option in most yards, the scientists tried installing hoofproof, highly polished stainless steel mirrors in standard stables to give the horses at least the illusion of company. They found that the horses regarded their own reflection in a full-length mirror as a threat, but a mirror 1m (3ft) square (which was more like a window into another stable) worked a treat.

Thoroughbreds that had weaved for as long as seven years reduced their weaving by an average of 86 per cent when able to have nose-to-nose social contact. The same horses showed a 77 per cent reduction in weaving when housed in a stable fitted with a mirror – and did so within 24 hours of it being installed. Mirrors have also been found to reduce loading and travelling problems when fitted in horseboxes and trailers.

the cause. More expensive, but perhaps more effective in the long term if making the animal's life more interesting doesn't work, is to discuss with your vet the possibility of giving a course of narcotics-blocking drugs. Apart from the cost, however, the treatment may cause side-effects not unlike low-level colic, and it is not a cure. The dose (a slow-release pellet placed under the skin) has to be maintained, or the horse will revert to his previous habits.

Box walking

The horse constantly walks at a great rate around his stable, often apparently oblivious of anything or anyone else – they may well get barged out of the way if they venture in. Given that grazing horses, even domestic ones, will cover about 40km (25 miles) a day as a matter of course, this is clearly a statement of frustration at being restricted. But it may be expressing more, or some other frustration than that.

For once, albeit probably fortuitously, the traditional remedy for box walking has some horse sense in it. This is to place tyres randomly around the floor of the stable and/or hang empty feed bags from the ceiling – the idea being that this will make the manic animal's bad habit harder to execute, and deter him from continuing with it. Success under that plan is counted as the horse eventually standing still, although that is not what horses naturally do most of the time. What a series of 'obstacles' might more construc-tively do is make the stable more interesting to chug around – in which case the obstructions should be as varied as possible. Success won't be measured in horses standing stock still (and bored stiff), rather in their slowing down and taking note of their surroundings, and even playing games with all these new toys.

As with weaving and cribbing, you should do a thorough analysis of everything that's going on in the horse's life – as well as giving him the freedom to wander around at will in a grassy expanse with other horses, and plenty of bulk food and water in the stable if and when he has to be in. It's possible, for instance, that a box walker is only voting with his feet – trying to escape some pain in his body. If so, this will almost certainly be more apparent from the way he behaves in the field. If things don't look right, get experienced or veterinary advice as soon as possible.

When is a vice a vice?

It is really a misnomer to call disturbed behaviour in a horse a 'vice'.

The word suggests that such disorders are the fault of the horse, when it is humans' treatment of the horse that ultimately causes them. None-theless, the term 'vice', as a kind of shorthand, carries a certain weight in law that one has to abide by.

In some countries, one is legally obliged to declare certain 'vices' when selling a horse. These are usually the habits of weaving, crib biting and wind sucking, since a horse suffering them cannot be guaranteed sound. If one untruthfully advertises a horse as having 'no vices', one lays oneself open to civil or even criminal proceedings. Caution suggests that even when you believe you have cured a horse of a 'vice', it's wisest to declare his history when you sell him. If the animal is put under stress in his new home, the old habit can reassert itself. Even though this is not your fault (or the horse's), you'll be landed with the responsibility if you haven't declared the problem to the new owner.

the nature of the horse

Door and wall kicking

This habit is largely self-explanatory, but not to be confused with outbreaks of enthusiasm and impatience at or approaching feed time. This latter is roughly equivalent to small children banging their spoons on the table while waiting for the ice-cream to appear. You can reduce this carry-on to a minimum by feeding the horses strictly according to their rank in the herd, or by changing the order they get their buckets every feed time. They soon get the idea, and reduce their

Panoramic vision

Horses can see almost all around them, although only a little over one sixth of their field of vision, directly in front, is binocular, allowing them to judge distance. They have a narrow blind spot directly behind, and another that extends about 30cm (12in) in front of their noses. Their vision is sharpest when looking directly at an object.

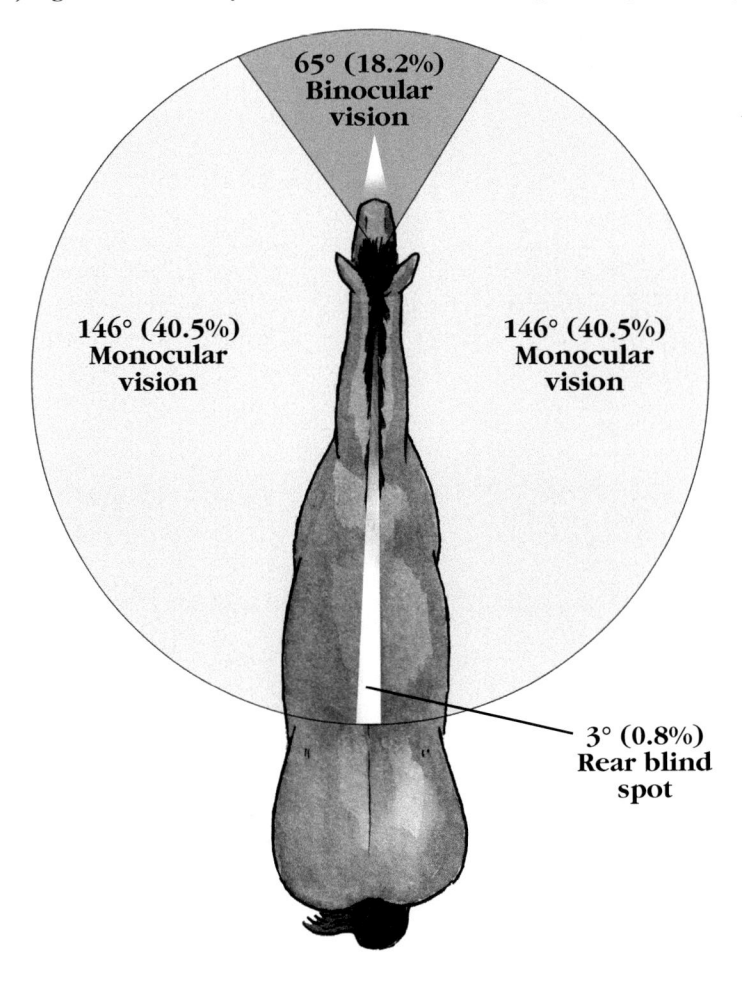

65° (18.2%) Binocular vision

146° (40.5%) Monocular vision

146° (40.5%) Monocular vision

3° (0.8%) Rear blind spot

the nature of the horse

Looking for company

A horse left alone too long in a field may develop the habit of fence-walking – trotting along, leaving a bare, muddy track behind it, with its head over the fence. It's not at fault – just lonely, and desperately seeking companionship.

signs of eagerness to a few seductively appreciative nickers.

Serious (pathological) door and wall kickers are consistent, rhythmic and persistent, and put themselves at risk of damaging cartilage and tendons from the constant percussion. They are presenting at least two messages. One: I am bored and idle, and making this racket at least livens the place up a bit. Two: I'd like to get out of here. There may be simple material reasons for wanting to get out: there may be mice or rats in the stable, or not enough to eat. Or the horse may be trying to tell you he's irritated by mites around his feet, or by some other parasite. Check that these non-psychological causes aren't at work, especially if the horse normally gets a decent amount of company and time outside: they can often be dealt with swiftly.

There are, as ever, various recommended 'cures' that stop the symptoms but not the cause, such as hanging a bale of straw behind the horse's hindquarters (quite how is an interesting question), hobbling the horse and putting on kicking chains - a length of iron chain attached to a strap buckled around the foot, so that the chain lashes the horse when he kicks. Ideas and kit like these are well suited to a medieval torture chamber and should stay there. In the equine mind, anything that restricts his ability to gallop out of danger is tantamount to a death sentence. If there isn't a physical problem with your kicker, make sure his daily life is varied and interesting, with a good portion of time spent out with other horses, multifarious schooling, hacking and so on.

At the same time, remember that no two horses are the same. Some are claustrophobic (it is surprising that more are not), whereas

the nature of the horse

Punishing the victim

Bars like these set on stable doors are intended to stop horses 'weaving' – but this treats the symptoms, not the cause, of the horse's problem. Confirmed weavers will simply step back and continue their distressing habit away from the door. The problem arises in horses who are constantly stabled, and is really an illness, not a defect – they are trying to compensate for not being able to walk around all the time, as horses naturally do. The best cure is to let the horse out to grass with other horses in the first place, not boxed up, unable to exercise, and out of contact with other animals.

a few feel happier and more secure in a stable than out. Some have idiosyncratic friendships: the renowned Hungarian racehorse Kincsem actually refused to travel unless accompanied by her favourite feline. Some horses make a commotion or start developing a 'vice' because they've been s tabled next to a horse they don't like or who bullies them, or because they're too far from a best friend. Keep an eye out for subtle factors like these. And never forget that whatever situation a horse is in, he doesn't know that it may be only temporary. Now and forever are the same words to him.

HARMLESS HABITS

There are a few things that conventional wisdom holds to be objectionable in horses but that are entirely harmless. One is eating straw bedding. A horse in the wild spends about 60 per cent of his time eating. When the bucket and the hay net (or heap) run out, the stabled horse's natural instinct is to look for the next nourishing thing to chew on. If he eats his bed, who should be surprised, and so what? Describing this, as one authority on horse management does, as a 'sign of a depraved appetite' is grotesque. Straw is unlikely to make him fat, keeps him occupied and content, and it's usually cheaper than hay. If he also eats his droppings, on the other hand, you may have a problem. He could have worms (has he missed a worming date?) or he may be trying to increase his intake of mineral salts lacking in his diet (leaving a salt lick in the stable should help).

It is normal for a very young foal to eat small amounts of his mother's droppings.

the nature of the horse

Mind your head!

To get attention (or a treat) foals nudge their mothers with their heads and, unless they're trained out of it, some will carry on doing the same to you when they're grown up. Head-butting is often a demand for a titbit, so avoid giving food treats from the start. Give treats for only specific, preferably lengthy, achievements, so the horse knows he will get them only after a long bout of work. Some horses butt because they've had their vibrissae (whiskers) cut off, and simply don't realize that you are in range. Sometimes head-butting is a sign of being in pain: he may have a headache from over-tensed muscles, and this may be his way of asking for a massage. As with other 'bad' habits, you need to ask why the horse is butting, and address the underlying cause. At the same time, you must wean him off this particular way of expressing himself. Being bashed around the head or face by a large and bony equine nose is not pleasant, and can break bones.

If you have a head-butter, don't respond by hitting the horse in the face: you could very easily make him fearful of anything touching his head or ears. Instead, rapid but very gentle tapping with the knuckles on the cheek just under the eye usually gets the message across. Make a specific signal at the same time (such as raising your weaker hand, palm open at the horse, to shoulder height) and use this combination *only* for head-butting. The horse will soon associate your weaker hand's signal with punishment for his misdeed. You can then use the signal by itself, as a warning of the consequences if he does it again, until he's entirely given up the habit – while leaving your stronger hand free to do something useful, and pleasant, like scratching his neck.

Gnawed and ignored

Cribbing – incessant chewing at fences, doors and so on – can be seen as a neurotic reaction to being fed only occasionally: horses naturally eat almost constantly.

Several reasons have been proposed for this, and all may be in play at once. The foal may be getting a mineral supplement, or taking in his mother's gut bacteria so that he can digest grass properly, or he may be learning to recognize what she eats so that he avoids poisonous or non-nutritious plants when he begins grazing in earnest himself.

SIGNS OF DISCONTENT

A couple of other signs of boredom or loneliness are worth looking out for. One is fence walking – patrolling the edge of a field and carving a track of mud or bare earth alongside the fence. Not to be confused with horses' irrepressible conviction that the grass in the next field is tastier than the stuff at their feet, this is usually a cry of loneliness from a solitary horse. Or it may be that the animal is being bullied by another in the group he's grazing with. Changing the

the nature of the horse

social arrangements should effect a cure in both cases. Look out too for your horse biting and tearing at his rug. If this happens, first check that the rug fits properly – if it doesn't, there will be rub marks on the horse's coat. Next, check for skin diseases, such as ringworm, or insect bites that the rug may be irritating, and treat accordingly. And, as with all other 'vices', see that the horse isn't simply doing this to get your attention or giving himself something vaguely interesting to do, because he's idle, bored or lonely.

Finally: remember, there are two stages to the worst 'stable vices'. If the horse is over five years old, they're probably ineradicable, because their addiction has become second nature to the horse, who will continue with them even when the original cause has long since disappeared. But if the 'vices' have developed before the horse is about five years of age, you should be able to get rid of them with imagination and patience. This may include simply turning the horse out to grass for six months, giving him time to recover from being cooped

A magical, imaginary friend

Putting a metre-square steel mirror in a stable dramatically reduces weaving. Horse mirrors are commercially available, and come with a full fitting pack and advice. Do not attempt to fit a house mirror in a stable as the glass is too fragile.

the nature of the horse

Time budgets

The accompanying charts show how horses kept under different conditions spend their time. What is clear immediately is that a stabled horse whose social life is limited to no more than looking at other horses (chart B) spends a vast amount of time just standing about. He's not eating because most of the time there's nothing to eat, which for a horse in this situation means there is nothing positive to think about either. His 'lifestyle' is almost exactly the opposite of a horse living in the wild (chart A). The degree of boredom, and the potential for developing psychopathic 'vices', can easily be imagined.

Two simple changes to the stabled horse's regime can dramatically improve his quality of life. Allow him to touch as well as see his yard companions; and let him have access all the time to bulk food (chart C). If you're concerned about him getting fat, put straw in a hay net: the nutrient value is low but the psychological value enormous, and the net will slow down the rate of consumption as well as giving the animal a bit of a mental challenge.

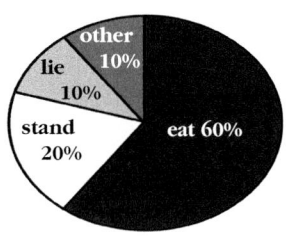

A The average time budgets for Camargue horses throughout the year. (After Duncan 1980).
other 10%, lie 10%, stand 20%, eat 60%

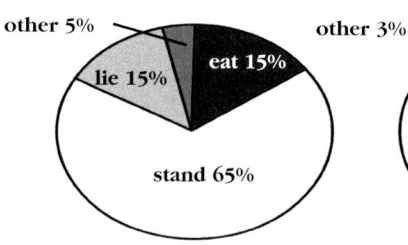

B The time budgets for horses in stables where they can see, but not touch each other, and only have limited food.
other 5%, lie 15%, eat 15%, stand 65%

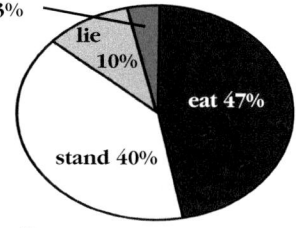

C The time budgets for three horses kept in individual stables with unlimited access to bulk food and able to touch and see each other.
other 3%, lie 10%, eat 47%, stand 40%

up, and then reintroducing him gradually to being stabled, but only as part of a varied programme of work and play.

Some flinty-hearted characters might ask why anyone would take on a horse with such a problem in the first place – why not look for another that's just as nice? The question seems reasonable enough, but drastically underestimates how a particular horse can appeal to a particular person, or what other actual or potential qualities one can see in him. Most of all it overlooks a natural human desire to rescue an animal from unnecessary misery. Much space has been given to this aspect of stabled horses so that you know from the start how to avoid creating the conditions that cause this kind of dispirited behaviour.

BASIC HORSE HANDLING

Whatever our previous experience of equines, we are always looking for sound advice on keeping them – but the best kind is counsel that comes, as far as possible, from the horse's mouth. This doesn't mean giving the horse everything he wants all the time. That would either spoil him, or mean that he would never be ridden, since he would obviously rather be living in a free herd with his other large warm friends than messing

the nature of the horse

about with us. The trick is to balance the horse's needs with ours, and in such a way that the equine wants to do what we want – because it's non-threatening, interesting and enjoyable – and has a contented life when left to his own devices.

This philosophy inevitably means managing your horses in ways that collide head-on with many long-standing practices in horse yards, which have long been run for human, not equine, convenience. Nonetheless, people do have lives to live, and not all horsekeeping traditions are pointless or misguided all of the time. Horses are a combination of powerful instincts and very strong opinions based on their own particular experiences, which is why they are highly individual creatures. What works with one, or a hundred, won't necessarily work with another. Horses never let you stop learning, thinking or feeling, but all your efforts will be in vain if you don't try to work out what the horse's point of view is when you run into a problem.

So, even something as simple as leading a horse on a head collar or halter may have to be done slightly differently in each case, depending on the particular horse. It's also something you'll be doing a lot of – going in and out between field and stable, when mucking out, before putting on his tack, when loading for travel, and so on.

How to frighten the horses

Raising your arms, with fingers stuck out like a predator's claws, staring straight at a horse and walking directly at it (or worse, up from behind) will all be taken as signs that you mean trouble – and the horse will do his best to avoid contact.

CATCHING THE HORSE

When you're fetching a horse in from a field, you shouldn't have any difficulty approaching him if you do it steadily and unaggressively, without any jerky movements (too bad if you trip over a tuffet). But some horses just don't like being caught, and most will occasionally think they've got better things to do just then than to

the nature of the horse

come along with you. And all horses have a profoundly personal space extending roughly 1.5m (5ft) around them, plus a less intense one that starts about 6m (20ft) away. A horse that is feeling awkward will definitely take umbrage if you storm into this space, intent on making your presence felt, without giving a thought to the offence it might cause him.

Softly, softly

When you approach a horse that's out on grass, go indirectly, keep any headcollar out of sight, adopt a submissive posture, and avoid eye contact with the animal. He will read these signs as a message that you mean no harm, and want to cooperate.

But speak a language the horse understands and you shouldn't have a problem. Slump your shoulders as you slowly but steadily approach. Lower your head. Keep your hands by your sides or behind your back. Avoid eye contact and turn your head and shoulders slightly away from the horse. Talk soothingly, meanwhile. The rest of you, though, is speaking the body language of a submissive, cautious horse asking for acceptance. You should be allowed to come close enough to exchange greetings (hold out a free hand for the horse to sniff, chat and give him some strokes in return) and then put the head collar on. Once you've done this, always show your appreciation, physically and verbally.

If this doesn't work, and the horse scoots away (probably not more than a few metres), retreat quietly until you're at least 6m (20ft) away, still retaining your submissive posture. Wait for a few minutes, then advance again. Continue this advance and retreat, if need be, until the horse decides you aren't, after all, a threat or a nuisance and lets you right up to him.

For really determinedly uncatchable horses, equestrian journalist Lesley Bayley suggests 'walking down'. You will need to set aside plenty of time for this. Just follow the horse around in his field, maintaining your non-aggressive stance, but staying close enough to keep him on the move. He

the nature of the horse

Putting on a head collar

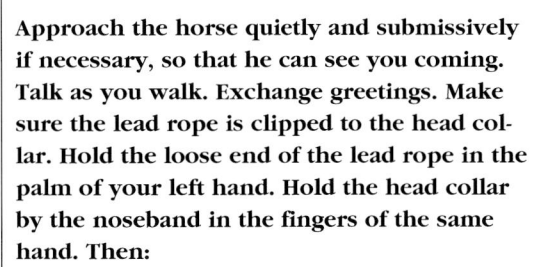

Approach the horse quietly and submissively if necessary, so that he can see you coming. Talk as you walk. Exchange greetings. Make sure the lead rope is clipped to the head collar. Hold the loose end of the lead rope in the palm of your left hand. Hold the head collar by the noseband in the fingers of the same hand. Then:

1. Stand at the horse's left shoulder, facing in the same direction as he is. Some people put the lead rope over the horse's neck at this point, but it can distract the horse, or slip out of reach, down the side away from you. So this is by no means a golden rule. Just do what works best for you and the particular horse, but don't let the rope dangle on the ground.

2. Pass your right hand under your horses' chin and put it palm down on the bridge of his nose, not so quickly that you make him start, but firmly enough so that you have his head under gentle control. Slide the head collar up over his nose so that the noseband is in place. Hold it there with the your left hand.

3. As you slide the head collar on, use your right hand to catch and bring the headband round behind his ears. Make all these movements smoothly so you don't startle the horse, and talk to him all the time.

4. Do up the buckle (not too tight), take the lead rope in both hands, give a scratch or pat as thanks for the cooperation.

the nature of the horse

Positive reinforcement

Always end a lesson or schooling session on a high note, immediately after the horse has performed well. A good scratch and some sweet nothings in his ear is always better than a pat.

The pressure halter

The pressure halter, made of soft knotted rope, can be a very effective device in teaching a horse to be led and to load. When the horse resists or pulls away from the direction you want him to go, the system of loops in the halter tightens like a slip knot, and applies pressure on the horse's nose and poll. This causes no pain, but presses on a network of nerves so that the horse gets a powerful ticklish feeling. Naturally, the horse wants this to stop. The lead rope should be held so that as soon as he moves in the right direction, the rope slackens and the pressure is instantly released. Don't speak to the horse when he puts pressure on himself, so that he doesn't associate you with the peculiar sensation. But do praise him as soon as he takes the pressure off himself by going in the right direction.

---

has no option but to focus on you, and will eventually decide you mean no harm and will be curious to find out what you want. He may stand still and let you stroll up, or he may walk up to you. Put on the head collar, give him lots of praise, then take it off again and walk calmly out of the field. Lesley Bayley did this, and found that after a half-hour break, her uncatchable mare – whom she'd had to follow for several hours the first time – took only 10 minutes to give in the second time. More often than not, she reports, this mare will now let her walk straight up to her, and never resists being caught for more than five minutes. The method worked because the horse decided for herself what to do, and then was rewarded for it.

LEADING THE HORSE

Leading a horse should be straightforward enough provided, as ever, that you do it in a calm, unaggressive manner. To begin with, put the head collar on while standing at the horse's shoulder, and stay in that position once you start to walk on. If you lead the horse from in front and something spooks him, you could be bowled over or, worse, find yourself on the receiving end of his lethal front feet.

Talk reassuringly to the horse all the time. Don't use high-pitched, whiny or mocking tones: they'll only agitate him. Keep a good firm grip on the end of the lead rope in the hand that's furthest from the horse, but don't loop it around your hand. If you do and the horse shies, rears or tries to bolt, that loop will pull tight, and you could be left with crushed or broken fingers. The 'leading' hand, the one nearest the horse, can be up on the rope just below the clip, or about 30cm (1ft) away from it, or by your side (hold your forearms parallel to the ground, elbows in by your sides – not unlike your basic riding position). In all cases, the rope should be

the nature of the horse

hanging slack between your hands, and in the latter two it should be slack between head collar and leading hand (which should hold the rope very lightly) except when you need to put on brief pressure to start the horse off, turn him or stop. As soon as he responds correctly, release the pressure.

The third style is perhaps to be preferred, because the horse is free to look about as he walks along, and he's walking with you, not needlessly dominated by you. If he decides to stop to gaze at a cat on a fence or gets distracted by a bird rising from the next pasture, a quick pressure on the rope to remind him what he's supposed to be doing is more noticeable from a slack rope than from one you've already got under pressure. And if something goes awry, you're in the best position to keep him under control. However, some horses will have been led 'under pressure' or with the leading hand up under the chin for so long that they will only walk on if that's the way the rope is held. If so, lead him the way he prefers, but keep the pressure to the effective minimum.

The worst that can happen if the horse spooks is that he'll rear. Let go of the rope in the leading hand and let it play out while keeping a firm grip

Two ways to use a lead rope

Leading the horse with your hand high up the rope gives you good control as long as the horse is 100% calm. Horses like to look around as they walk, and keeping plenty of slack on the lead rope is comfortable for them and less strain on you.

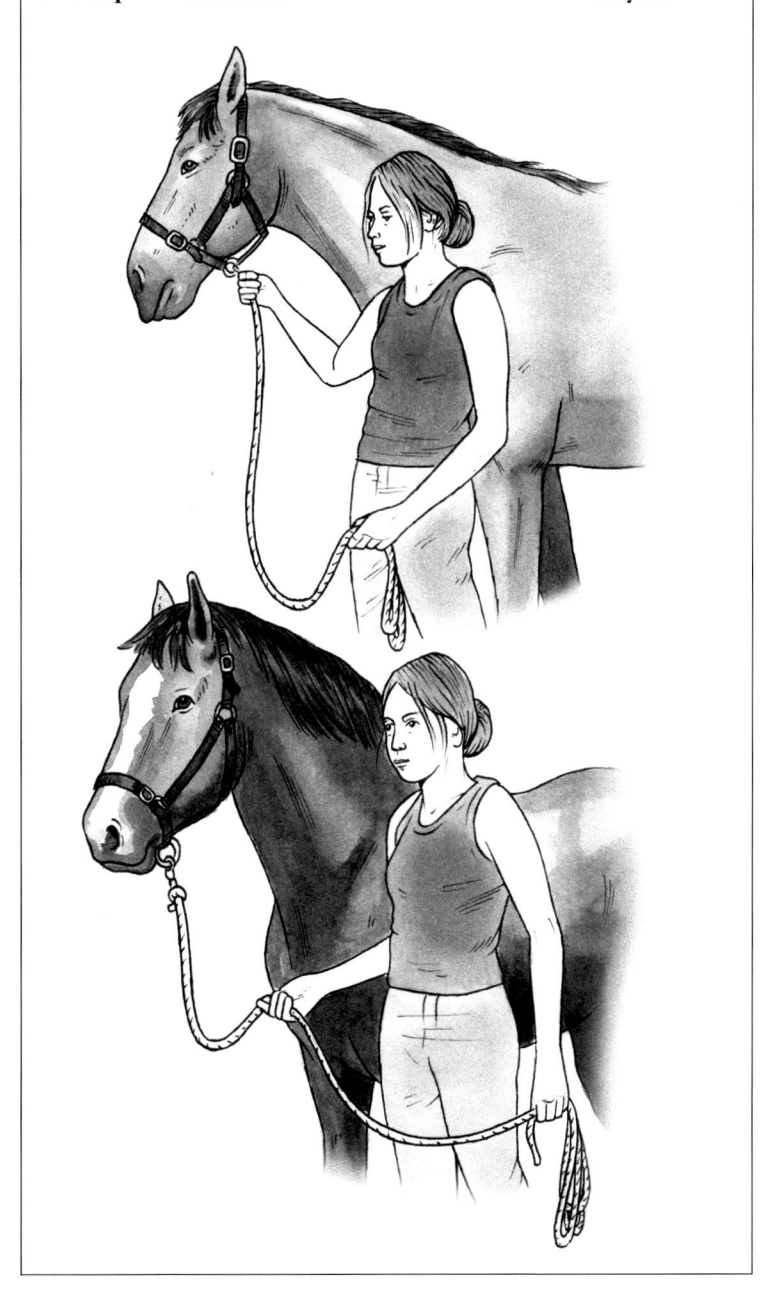

the nature of the horse

How not to load

A horse who's slow or stubborn to load, or just afraid, won't be cured of his problem if you try to force him on with whips, shouts, and crowding. He may even react violently (as here), and do himself or you serious harm. Even previously good loaders can turn into bad ones with this kind of treatment. Take it gently – you'll be glad you did.

on the end with the other hand. Make sure you don't lose it. Absolutely do not pull down on the rope. The horse is infinitely stronger than you, and he'll go on going up in reaction - and you're at his side, and can tip him off balance and over on his back, which can have disastrous results. Instead, shove your shoulder in hard against his shoulder as he begins to go up, and keep pushing. This will put him off balance, but soon enough for him to land squarely back on all four feet, and will almost always be enough of a surprise to take his mind off the original problem. Soothe him with strokes and quiet talk, staying at his side. As soon as he's calm, carry on walking as before.

Once a horse has reared on you a couple of times you'll be able to 'read' when he's about to go up. As soon as you get that first hint, simply lead him firmly in a tight circle. With his body bent, he won't have the balance to rear, and a couple of revolutions is usually enough to make him forget why he wanted to.

These tricks won't cure rebellious rearing in a horse. Trainer Richard Maxwell suggests whacking the horse on the belly with a length of rope, when he rears. The idea is that he will soon associate rearing with being attacked in a place he can't see – which a horse naturally hates – and he'll stop rearing to avoid being attacked. There

the nature of the horse

One step at a time

Horses need to learn for themselves that a horsebox isn't a scary place to be. Leading them up the ramp, a pace or two a day, with a bucket of feed gets them used to the box and gives them the chance to explore it on their own. Once they've satisfied their curiosity, and feel safe around the box, you should be able to lead them on and off without trouble.

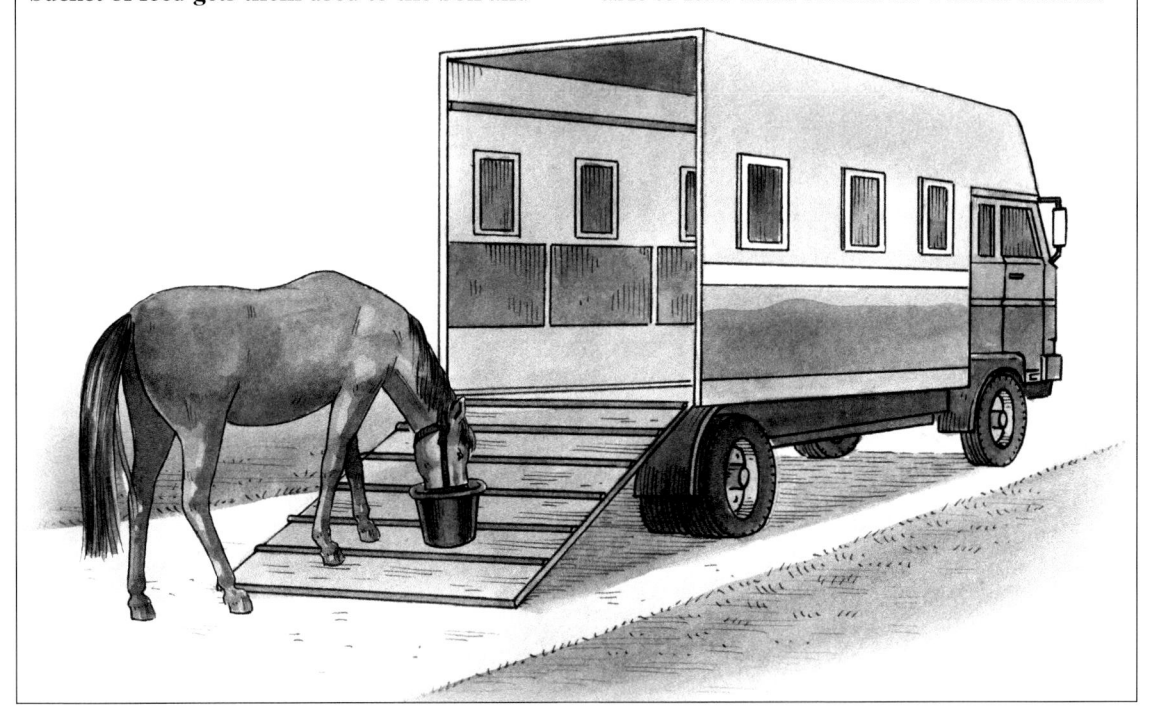

is a drastic but effective ruse to cure a foal of habitual rearing against the halter. Take him onto the soft surface of a schooling arena, let him rear, and then tug him off balance so that he falls over. He will give himself a nasty fright, and won't rear again. However, you should only do this in an arena, or on very soft ground, and it's not a method to use with a full-grown horse, whose vastly heavier weight and less flexible body will put him at risk of injury.

LOADING AND UNLOADING

Getting into a horsebox or trailer goes against the equine grain. They are usually dark, are even more restricted than a stable, and feature a ramp that often doesn't feel at all solid to a human, let alone a four-footer weighing half a tonne and more.

Horses who refuse to load either have not travelled before, or have had a nasty experience on the road. The latter could be anything from a tyre blowing out with a terrifying bang, or undergoing an emergency stop, to being driven too fast for comfort or being beaten into loading. (Beating is self-defeating, because all it does is link the box and a good whacking in the horse's mind.) So, they have to be convinced, in their own time and way, that the box is not a bad place to be. The following method of accustoming a horse to a vehicle works even better for foals, who

the nature of the horse

haven't anything but their innate caution to overcome. You need to allow plenty of time for this in a day, and the whole process may take several days.

On Day 1, open up the box, let down the ramp, and shift the partition so that there is as much room as possible inside. Put a bucket of feed just far enough up the ramp that the horse has to put his front feet on the ramp in order to eat. Lead him to the bucket. Don't tie him up. Just let him eat, and give him enough time afterwards to go further up the ramp if he wants to. A problem loader probably won't at first, but a foal, out of sheer curiosity, might decide to explore the box, or at least the feel of the ramp under his feet. If he does, let him nose around for a few minutes before leading him down (with lots of praise). Better still, build his confidence by letting him find his own way down. On Day 2, put the bucket another pace up the ramp. Continue creeping the bucket up the ramp day by day until it's at the front of the box. Rare is the horse that won't succumb to its magnetism.

Once the horse is used to going into the box or trailer like this, move the partition back to its usual place for travelling. Put the bucket at the front, and lead him on board for his meal. Tie him up for this. When he has finished eating, let him stand for a while before you lead him out. This interval is important. If you simply lead the horse on board and then out again immediately, he'll get it into his head that this is what he is always meant to do.

Once the horse is comfortable going into the box and staying there for a while, you can start teaching him how to back out, if you don't have a side-loader (or a front ramp on a trailer). Horses really don't like going backwards more than a step or two, and some will turn round on the ramp so that they can go down it head first. If

The herringbone position

Left to themselves in a horsebox, horses will take up a stance at 45° to the direction of travel, as here. If you can, load yours in this 'herringbone' position for a comfortable ride.

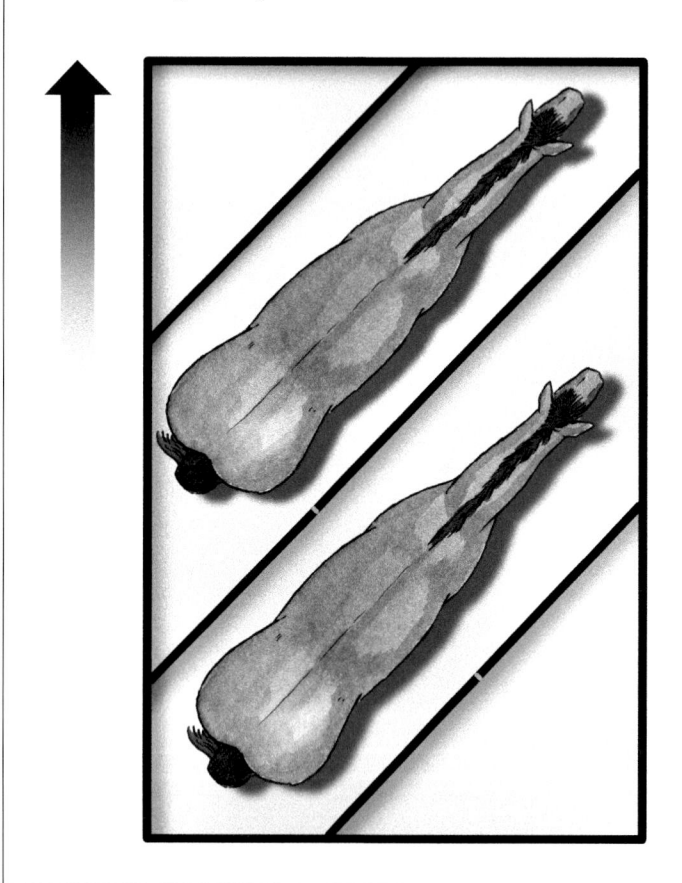

the nature of the horse

this happens, always load him in future on the side of the box he came from when he decided to turn on the ramp. Because he'll always turn in the same direction. Load him on the wrong side, and he'll step backwards off the ramp into thin air when he turns – which could be disastrous. Once he's learned how to go down the ramp, backwards or forwards, you can begin loading him between meals, leading him on, tying him up for a bit, and then bringing him out again. The bucket will still be a great motivator, so always have one – just a few nuts in it will do – at the front of the box, for the horse to aim for whenever you load.

A couple of other points about horseboxes – Research has found that, given enough room and left to themselves, horses will angle themselves at 45 degrees to the direction of travel. If you're buying a horsebox, try to get one big enough to carry your horses this way.

Make sure too that the box has strong internal lights that shine from the back, forward into the box, so that when there's little or no daylight the horse can see he is going into a bright, visibly safe space. (It's not a bad idea to turn these on in daylight, as well, to add reassurance.) Turn off the vehicle's own exterior lighting immediately before loading, as well, so the horse isn't dazzled, and can see where he is going. And before unloading in the dark, make sure your yard lights are on for the same reason.

Finally: drive carefully, smoothly, and not too fast!

NEW WAVES FOR OLD

In all these activities with the horse, we have been trying to speak to him in his own terms – which amount to a kind of sign language. If, at these very basic levels of handling, it's important to do this to create and maintain a partnership between you and the horse, it is surely vital to continue to treat the horse as if he were a horse, and not a motorbike or a parrot, in every other aspect of our dealings with him. As early as 1973, writers such as Candida Geddes and Neil Dougall were publishing articles pointing out that herd animals like horses should not be kept on their own, and that locking a stallion in solitary confinement in a dark stable was a cruel recipe for disaster. Monty Roberts, who has done as much as anyone to promote the treatment of horses on their own terms, came to international attention in the late 1980s, when he demonstrated his technique of 'join-up' – a non-violent, horse-centred and simple way to 'break' a horse – to members of the British royal family. Since his work became widely known, other 'horse whisperers' – some trained by Roberts and some who had developed their own approaches to 'natural' horse management – have made names for themselves.

How to tie up with a lead rope

Never attach a lead rope directly to a hitching ring or rail. If the horse rears, it could damage itself. Tie the rope with a quick-release knot to a loop of string. If there's trouble, the string will break.

the nature of the horse

Rough play is normal play

Young horses tussle together all the time, and even grown adults will go in for mock fights and galloping races now and then. Horse games look rough to tender humans, but very rarely result in real damage. Better, then, to let equines run free and have fun – and maybe risk the odd nick in the skin – than be locked up in isolation all hours of the day.

At the heart of this approach is the principle that the wild horse and the domesticated one are essentially the same, speak the same language and have the same emotional and physical needs. Therefore everything from persuading a horse to let someone sit on his back ('starting' the horse, rather than 'breaking' it), through stable design and management, to riding techniques, would be more successful if we tapped into and redirected the horse's instinctive nature than if we followed the traditional route of dominating the animal through force. Horses are cooperative creatures among themselves: why not build on that in their relationships with people, to mutual advantage? Such techniques have been shown time and again to be faster and more effective as well as kinder than those based on dominance. Cooperative trainer Lucy Rees, for instance, and a top Western trainer using conventional methods caught two wild mustangs at the same time. After six weeks, Lucy Rees was able to ride her test horse calmly in only a head collar, while the Western cowboy still hadn't managed even to mount his. Yet he complained that he 'did not have time to spend letting the horse get used to him and doing things quietly'!

A whole movement to change traditional attitudes to horses is now under way and there is a great deal of scientific research to back up this 'new wave' approach. Much of the 'new' thinking looks like no more than applied common sense, once one understands where a horse is coming from. Yet despite this pressure for change, people continue unrelentingly to force their own standards onto horses and ponies, rather than adapting their attitudes and their standards to equine needs (see 'The trouble with showing').

However. Unless you're extraordinarily fortunate and can spend all your time on your horse, there'll always be a tension between what is practicable and possible from your human point of view and what is ideal for a domestic horse. Practices recommended here as 'best' are often ideals, which will almost certainly be constrained by the time, money, energy, or even climate and geography, of your particular circumstances. They may not always even suit your particular horse. But one really should always do the best one can, with the horse's interests constantly in mind. It's all too easy to slip into the belief that what's convenient for you, or for the owner of your livery yard, is also good for your horse. How best to balance human and equine needs in terms of housing, feeding and general care is addressed in the next chapter.

The trouble with showing

The world of competitive showing would probably win most prizes for putting human interests above those of the horses. In her book, *Equine Welfare*, Marthe Kiley-Worthington reports that, in Europe, judges of showring Arabian horses look for 'a very straight back with a high set of the tail. This can result [in mares] in a curious angle of the vulva which [because it cannot drain naturally secreted fluids] causes infection and sometimes lack of breeding ability. Dartmoor and Exmoor ponies have been selected according to various set standards which were developed in order to try and produce the aesthetic "ideal" of those who are interested in them. The result is that they are less able to live on the moors where they evolved.'

One of the problems for show horses, notes Dr Kiley-Worthington, is that they are over protected, 'to ensure that their bodies are not damaged in any way which will be penalised in the show ring. ... If contact with others might cause one to bite or kick another then no contact is allowed; one rubbing another's tail thus ruffling it, is prohibited. So these most sociable of animals are never allowed to run outside or form normal bonds with other horses.'

Another practice inflicted on show horses is trimming off their whiskers, depriving them of their major touch organ. Injury may be added to insult. 'Before showing the animals may be kept in the dark so that when they come out their pupils are enlarged – and so on.' And there are persistent rumours that some Arabians 'are made cocaine addicts to ensure they correctly follow the stick around with their heads and thus pose in the particularly curious position required by in-hand arabs... .'

Of course there is nothing wrong in showing horses at their best: but one has to ask why showing demands so much that is clearly not in the horse's own interests.

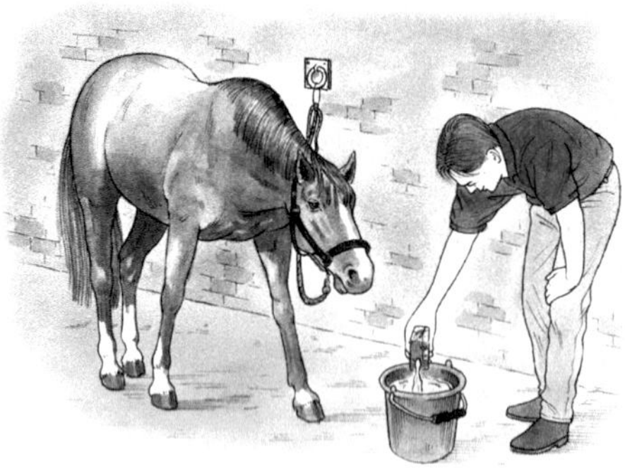

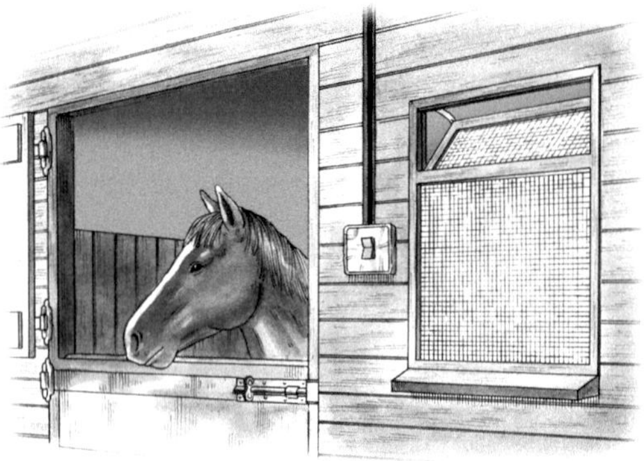

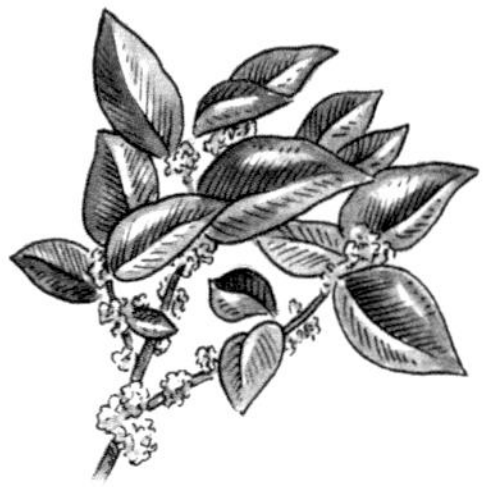

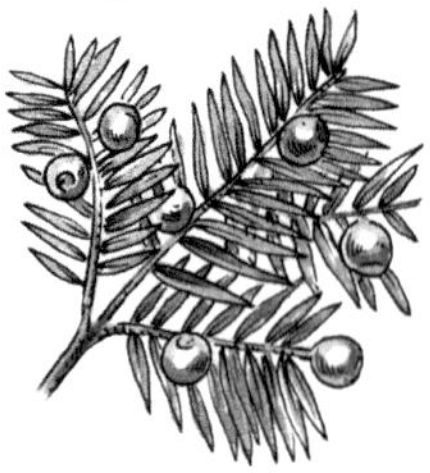

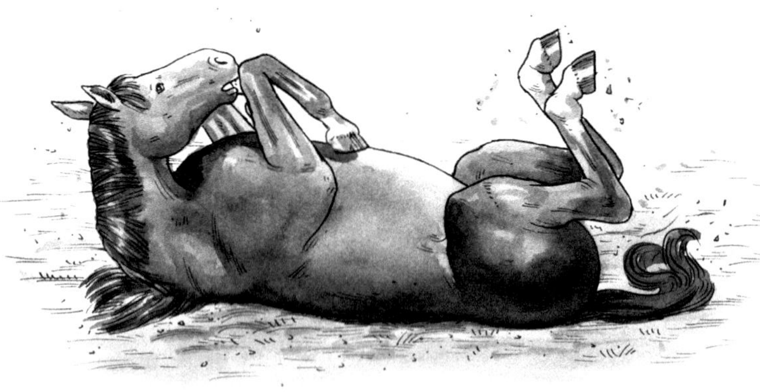

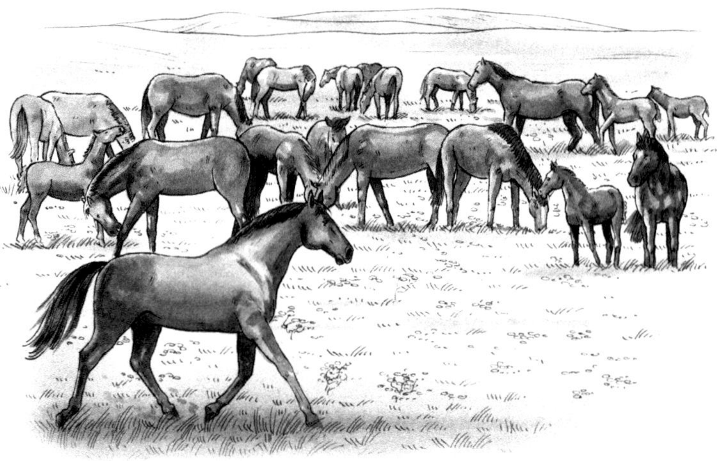

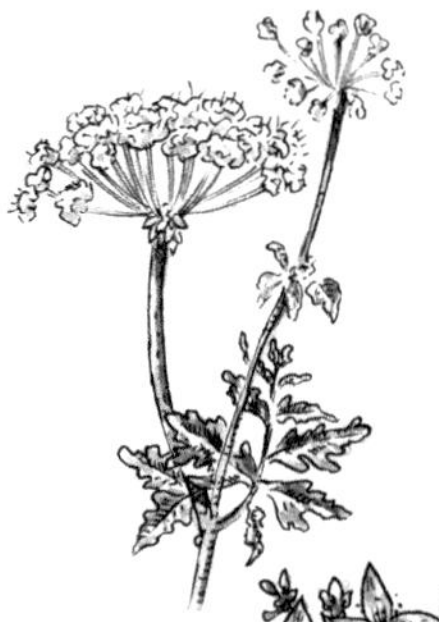

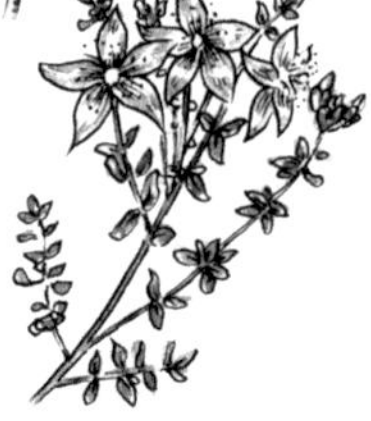

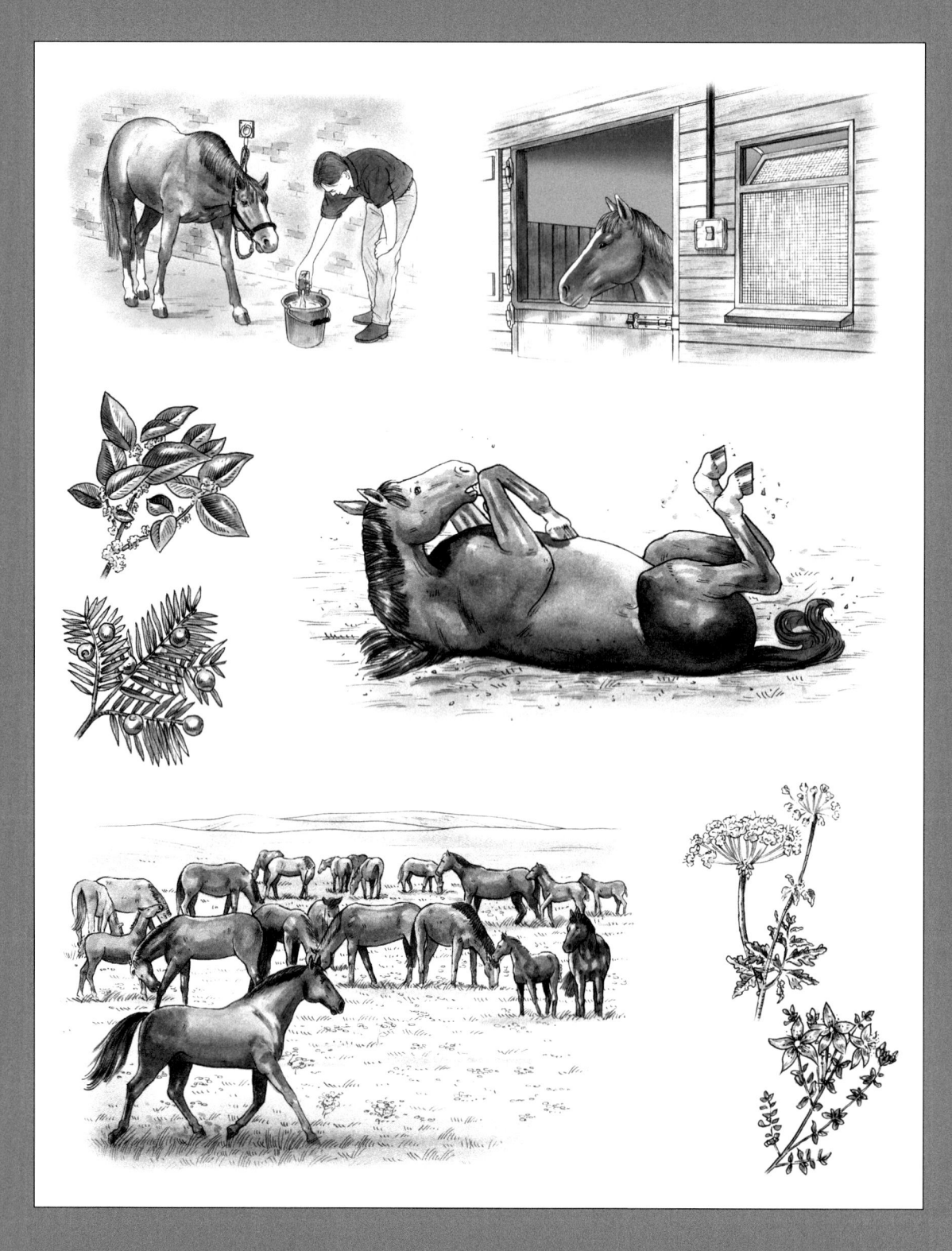

CHAPTER THREE

Stables, Fields and Food

Nature made horses to live in the great outdoors, and that's still the best place to keep them. For all kinds of reasons, that may not be practicable for you – so here is a guide to caring for both indoor and outdoor equines.

There is a good case to be made for keeping horses out on grass all year, and hardly bothering with stables at all. That is what horses evolved to do: living out in the company of other equines gives them a fulfilling social life and forestalls the development of so-called vices, while a properly managed pasture will give most horses all the nourishment they need. However, it isn't practical for all horses all the time, and for a variety of reasons it does not always work for the people looking after them, either. On the other hand, anyone who decides to keep horses stabled, even part time, has to realize that this involves a serious, major commitment. Every day, without fail, a portion of your time and energy has to be devoted to looking after them. If you go away, you have to find a reliable, knowledgeable horse-sitter. And even part-stabled horses need regular exercise and social contact in a way that those living out with other animals do not.

Any horsekeeping system has to take account of the particular nature of the horses involved, the amount of land available and its location, and other individual circumstances. But whatever precise scheme is used, it's vital to know the best way to handle all its various aspects.

KEEPING IN VERSUS KEEPING OUT

Besides wild or feral horses like those of the Carmargue in France or the North American Mustang, there are domestic breeds, such as Connemara and Welsh ponies, and many

stables, fields and food

Russian and Asian breeds, that still normally live out all year. Britain, Europe, Australia and the Americas all boast native, domesticated breeds that do just this. Troika, the Internet's most authoritative resource on Russian horses, notes: 'Many inherently Russian horses have been bred in herds under semi-wild conditions, in the open, exposed to the elements, most often extremely rigorous elements. This especially pertains to steppe, forest, mountain, and desert horses of Russia. Some of them may be called extreme breeds, produced under extreme conditions: extreme temperatures, extreme aridity, extreme altitudes, extreme feeding regimes, and so forth. These breeds were kept out all year, getting food from under snow. ... At the other end of the spectrum, you find Akhal-Tekes, [desert horses that] are bred on a rich-protein diet literally from the hand.'

Some Russian steppe horses (such as the Don) live year-round in the open, enduring frost, snow and drought and temperatures as low as -40°C/F in winter or up to 40°C (104°F) in summer. Explains Troika 'The steppe horses' system is used to seasonal variation in the level of feeding, with days of lush growth followed by long spells of drought or frost. Therefore, in

The Russian Tabun

The enormous numbers of horses bred in Russia – for riding, driving, farm work, food and the military – has made it impossible for them all to be stabled. Instead, horses have largely been kept in tabuns, in which the horses are maintained in conditions very like equine life in the wild. The Russian word tabun (pronounced 'ta-boon') translates roughly as 'a group of horses kept on a common grazing ground'.

This cheap and simple way of raising horses is still very common in many parts of the former Soviet Union. Only in the most dire weather conditions will additional food be given; in some cases lean-to shelters are provided to protect the horses from the elements. Life in the tabun contributes to good health and weeds out horses who cannot survive the sometimes stressful conditions of outdoor life.

The traditional tabun system allows very little control over breeding, and is not used with valuable breeds or those humans want to improve. The most sophisticated tabun method, used with breeds like the Don and the Budenny, combines the outdoor life with regular supplements of food. In winter, Budennys are kept on grazing near thick hedges to shelter them from wind and cold. In exceptionally foul weather they are stabled and given hay; yearlings get some oats. In high summer, the horses are brought to water three times a day, journeying more than 25km (15 miles) a day in the process. To protect them from insects, the herds are grazed 'against the wind' and on high ground.

The composition of this form of tabun is tightly controlled. A herd of 100–150 is considered best. Horses are divided by sex and age, especially when they are young, or when mares are in foal or have recently given birth. At the start of the breeding season in May, stallions are distributed to a kosiak (a small group of 15–25 mares). In August, at the end of the breeding season, the mares are returned to the tabun. Depending on their value, the stallions are either collected into a stallion tabun or kept in individual stables until the next breeding season.

stables, fields and food

good seasons the horses quickly accumulate reserves of fat, which also protects their organs from heat losses, and lasts them through harder spells.

As noted in the previous chapter, the ancestors of all modern horses were adapted to life on the steppe. They did not evolve to live in stables. Most horses can tolerate exposure to far greater extremes of weather than their owners allow, or perhaps even realize. There are, of course limits to this principle. But, even if it plainly doesn't suit a desert horse like the Akhel-Teke to languish in the misty climes of the Newfoundland seaboard, horses in their own habitat can safely live out all year. Even the generally rather conservative British Pony Club's *Manual of Horsemanship* says that, '... in addition to savings in time and money, the grass-kept horse exercises himself enough to keep healthy, and ... is less likely to be over-fresh when ridden'; he is also less likely to suffer respiratory problems and limb

The wild herd

A herd of horses living in the wild is guarded by its single stallion, who keeps a constant lookout for predators and for rival stallions. But he is not in charge: that is the senior mare's job. The herd may include a sub-group of 'bachelor' stallions who are not yet ready either to challenge the current sire or to leave the herd to found their own harem.

stables, fields and food

Solitary confinement

A horse that's unable even to look out of its stable to see its yard companions, and has floor-to-ceiling walls keeping it from contact with its neighbours, will get depressed and will possibly develop 'vices'. This one doesn't even get fresh air (note the closed window). Yet an astonishing number of horses are still kept in conditions like this.

injuries than a stabled horse, and can 'indulge in a hearty roll ... whenever he feels like it'.

Besides encouraging the development of so-called vices, one of the drawbacks of keeping a horse constantly stabled is that his legs are prone to 'fill up'. A horse's circulatory system depends on internal pressures generated when his hooves strike the ground to keep blood and lymph in motion and to pump them back up his legs. A stabled horse can't move around very much, obviously, and so blood and lymph collect in his legs, and they swell up. Apart from being painful, this impedes the waste management operated by the bloodstream, and in the long term will impair the immune system.

So the question naturally arises: why, then, are so many horses stabled, most or part of the time? A very short answer is: because people ride them. It is from this that a profusion of interventions in the equine's life arises – rugs, clipping, complex diets and, of course, the stable itself. One shouldn't be too hard on the stable. For most of the horse's history since being domesticated it has been a weapon system, the major motive power for farming and transport, and a symbol of wealth. The vast majority of horses had to be immediately

stables, fields and food

available or at least near at hand (for soldiers, coachmen, ploughmen, carters), and many horses lived in cities, where there was no grazing. Their social life as herd animals may not have been that great, but they were not bored: they were too busy. Very few led lives of stabled idleness.

Even so, the needs of the past have bequeathed us a whole clutch of horsekeeping traditions that continue to be recommended for, and practised in, modern stables. The Pony Club *Manual*, for instance, suggests a daily routine that, leaving aside any time on horseback, would consume about four hours a day per horse. This kind of drudgery may have been appropriate for keeping soldiers occupied in peacetime, or for the mews of a city mansion where there were servants to tend the horses day and night. But the key point is that the traditional way of keeping horses was designed not for the good of the horses, but to satisfy humans. Today, our dealings with horses are rooted more in pleasure and fascination than necessity, and we look after them ourselves in what time we can fit between work and family. We now know enough about the essential needs of the horse to be able to rethink our approach to stabling, and yard routines, from square one. Curiously enough, the more we take the horse's needs into account, the more we can save ourselves time and effort.

Stepping outside the box of traditional thinking about horsekeeping is not always easy to do. Monty Roberts, has succeeded in doing just this though. He is famous for cracking the codes of equine communication, and for promoting non-violent techniques for breaking horses – which he rightly prefers to call starting or gentling them. Roberts has spent countless hours observing equine social life in the wild and has brought a rare understanding to it. He seems absolutely to understand the psychology of the individual horse as a flight (prey) animal. Yet when it comes to day-to-day horsekeeping he appears not to have cottoned on to the full implications of their needs as herd animals. Reading between the lines of his books one has the impression that the horses on Roberts's Flag Is Up Farm spend more time in stables than they do pranking about together. Mares and stallions at Flag Is Up do not run together to breed, but are called upon to perform to order in a breeding barn. Mucking out is a large enough operation to make it worthwhile to contract the task out to a small, efficient company. Do horses at Flag Is Up have a restricted social life, despite the many other advantages they enjoy? If so, there could hardly be a better illustration of how deep the fangs of tradition can bite, for in other respects Roberts is an admirable and original

Choosing a livery

If you have no choice but to keep a horse at livery, bear in mind that there is more than one kind. Some livery operations don't have turnout fields, while others do; some will simply provide stabling, and leave the customers to feed, muck out, turn out and bring in their horses; others will do everything for you, including exercising horses, and yet others will do some things but not everything.

Prices vary with the type of service provided.

Choose your livery carefully. Don't be afraid to ask the owners pointed questions, and don't put up with evasive answers. If you are left in any doubt about the quality of the care your horse will receive, look elsewhere. Above all, ensure that the horses get turned out in good company for as long as is practicable every day.

stables, fields and food

thinker whose concern for equine welfare is unquestionable.

The relationship between horses, humans and stabling needs to be recast along the following pragmatic lines. First, horses evolved to live in the open, among their peers, feeding on coarse grass. Second, therefore, the more time they can spend outside in the company of their own kind, on the right kind of pasture, the happier and healthier they will be. Third, the more time horses spend out with other horses, the less time people need to spend on a system of caring for them that is in neither their own nor the horses' best interests.

WHEN TO STAY IN

In winter, chill winds and cold rain plague horses; in summer, flies and hornets take their place. Rain and snow in winter can so lash a horse's coat that he suffers from weatherbeat, also known as rainscald. His skin gets chapped and covered in scabs. Persistent storms can saturate even the best-drained pasture, and the good earth will turn into a swamp. Horses paddling about in the mire may get mud fever (also known as scratches). Waterlogged skin on the horse's legs and belly is invaded by bacteria from the ground, and the resulting scabs seal the intruders in. In summer, midge bites can cause sweet itch, flies of all kinds can infuriate as well as bite the horse, ground previously grazed by other livestock may turn out to harbour ticks, and various stinging insects abound. No matter how well one manages the pasture, freak weather conditions – which have been more common in recent years – can turn fields into a quagmire or provoke a supera-bundance of bugs. And some horses are more susceptible to some or all of these afflictions than others.

Prevention being better than cure, one can sidestep many of these tribulations by operating a system of part-time stabling. For some reason, fewer flies venture into stables than infest fields. In summer, in places where horses are especially bothered by insects, they can be brought in during the day to rest and sleep. In winter, when the weather is particularly bitter, they can be brought in at night for protection from (yet) lower nocturnal temperatures.

A HOUSE CAN BE A HOME

Stables, whether used very much or not, need to be well lit, properly ventilated and insulated, and properly floored. There are dozens of ways to achieve these apparently simple aims. No great detail will be given here, but it is useful to know the basic principles, particularly if you're converting barns or outbuildings into stables, as so many people do.

If you're sufficiently well founded to create a yard from scratch, then the whole layout of the place can be designed to be both practical (from your point of view) and calculated to give the horses a social life and a stimulating environment. One such layout is illustrated on page 87; you'll notice straight away that it's set in an ideal world. All the grazing fans out from the yard, so that turning horses out into a field involves only a short walk from the stable, and a minimum number of gates to negotiate. There's enough hard standing to drive your trailer or horsebox in and unload with the minimum of reversing. Insulation is improved by building the hay barn into the end of the complex to protect the inner yard from the weather, and by putting the feed and tack rooms at the weather end of each row of stables.

The horses can look out at one another, as well as see one another from side to side, and can also watch work going on in the arena. The interiors of these stables should have walls separating them that are low enough for next-door neighbours to have physical contact. There is a barn for keeping in

stables, fields and food

An ideal stable yard

Note how all the buildings face away, or are sheltered, from the prevailing winds (blowing in the direction of the arrow). Hay and straw are within easy reach of the stables, which are further protected by the tack and feed rooms adjoining the haybarn. The large building backing onto the stables is an open barn housing several horses together.

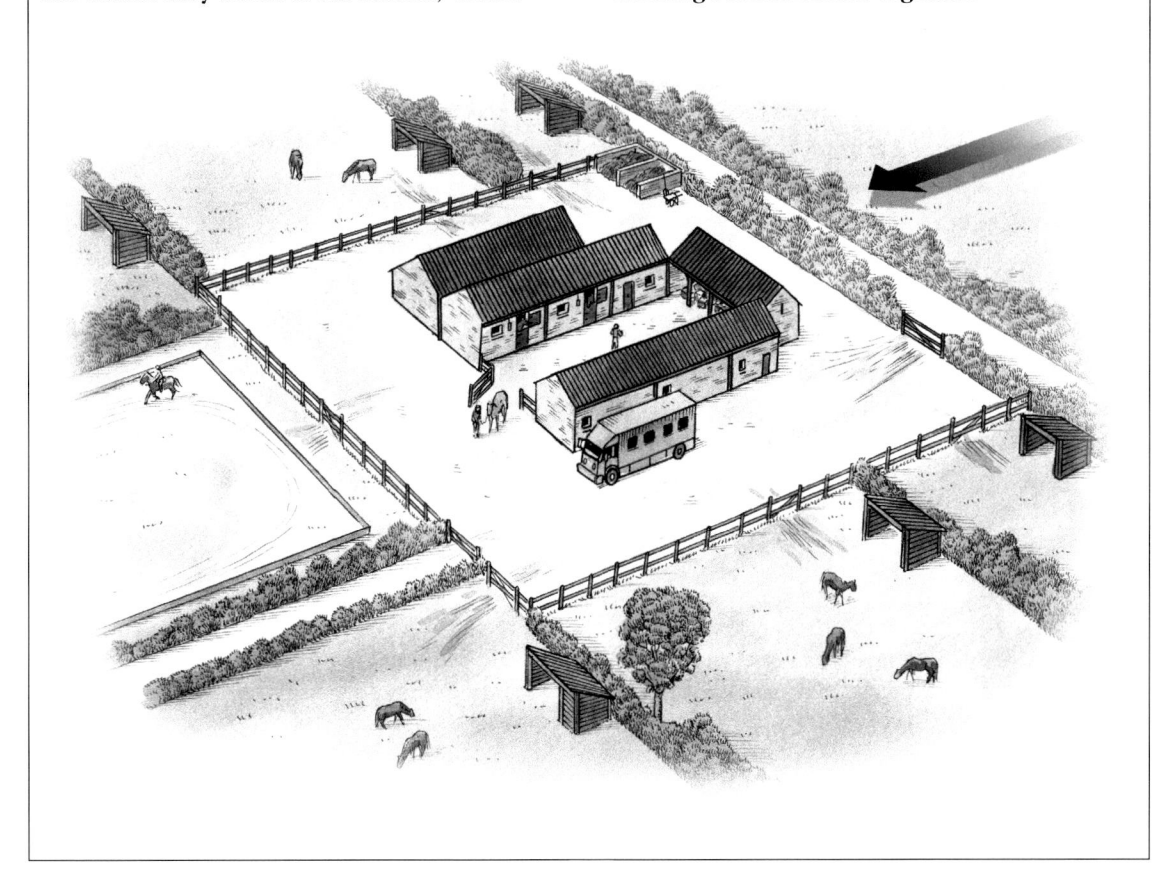

more than one horse (such as mares with foals, or newly weaned foals) with easy access to two fields. You could, where appropriate, gate off this barn so that horses can shelter in it but have free access to the pasture opposite. The rear wall of the barn could also have openings that allow physical contact from adjoining stables (but see 'Ventilation' below). The exterior of the yard should have powerful artificial lighting, both for your sake and so that the space is patently free of threats in the horses' eyes.

General stable design

Two basic systems of stabling are common. In the barn system, horses have individual stables arranged under a single roof. The walls of the stables don't reach to the ceiling, and in larger barns the stables are set back to back and side to side, with a broad walkway between facing rows; so

stables, fields and food

The cast horse

Horses 'cast' themselves when they lie down facing a wall, fence, or hedge, and so close to it that they can't get their legs down to the ground when they want to stand up again. This can cause the animal to panic, and can take several burly humans to put right. Double-banking straw at the base of stable walls is said to stop horses getting close enough to the walls to get cast.

opportunities for equine socializing are much greater, and the horses can see all the others in the barn. There's usually also an area for tacking up under cover, and perhaps one or two larger pens for mares and foals or youngsters to be in together. These spaces are also handy for vets' visits. More usual in Europe are outdoor yards, with stables set along the sides. These are somewhat less sociable from the horses' point of view, particularly when side walls are built at full height.

Individual stables should be as large as possible, but at least 4m (13ft) square. The roof should ideally be pitched, and high enough to prevent a startled horse going up from hitting his head, as well as to provide a good volume of fresh air: allow at least 40 cubic metres (1500 cubic ft) per horse.

Doors should be of traditional split design, so that the horse can put his head out and see what's going on outside. The top door need be closed only in the worst of weather. Don't put grilles up. Door frames should be at least 1.2m (4ft) wide and 2.4m (8ft) high, which should accommodate the largest horses. They should also open outwards, unless you really want to have a debate with the equine every time you go into the stable. Latches are easier to operate than bolts (especially at floor level), although some waggish nags take great pleasure in learning how to undo latches. As remarked, walls between stables should be low enough to let neighbouring horses have physical contact; they should also be high enough to discourage bed-swapping games.

There should be no sharp edges on any fittings, and nothing projecting from the walls on which a horse could cut or tear himself. A couple of rings for tying the horse up and attaching a hay net, a hay manger, and perhaps a fixed water trough are all the fittings you need. Mangers should be about 1m (3ft) from the ground. Don't put them above the horse's head height, or he'll be forced to feed in an unnatural position, and will risk getting dust and seeds in his eyes. If you use buckets for hard food and water, though, the stable is easier to clean.

Lighting

Install powerful lights so that you can see what you're doing on dark winter days, and to give the horse a bright, safe space to enter. Switches (and the light fittings, and as much wiring as possible) should be outside the stable and/or out of horse-reach, or the horse will, sooner or later, try to gnaw on them, even if just out of curiosity. Switches must be weatherproof, and insulated so that if a horse ever gets the opportunity to play with them he can't electrocute himself. It's useful if they have a pilot light that glows when they're turned off, so that you can find them easily in the dark.

Ventilation

To prevent draughts, windows (with glass protected by bars or wire) should be on the same side of the stable as the door, and placed so as not to be darkened by the open top of the door. They should open inwards at the top: this lets air enter over the horse's head and prevents draughts. There should be a ceiling vent that doesn't admit rain or offer a nesting place for birds, through which stale air can escape. In back-to-back stables (see illustration on p87) you can have an opening in the rear wall to allow contact between horses in adjoining stables. But you must beware of creating draughts, so you need to be able to close this opening on cold or windy days. A hatch that folds up or slides, so that the horse can't catch himself on it when it's open, is best.

Horses can tolerate much greater extremes of temperature than we can and, as long as they're not in a draught, those in what are to us cool or even cold stables are better fitted for hard work, and more resistant to disease, than coddled ones. A hot, tired horse standing in a draught risks catching a chill; the same horse standing in still cold air doesn't. In really cold weather it's better to put a rug on the horse than to keep him warm by depriving him of fresh air.

Insulation

Stables should be damp-proof, and walls and roof should be constructed to prevent draughts (see above) and to maintain a cool environment in hot weather and a warm one when it's cold. There are many ways of achieving this, and it's best to take expert advice, whether you're converting an existing building or starting from scratch.

Flooring

Arguments continue to resound over the best material for a stable floor. All floors should be non-slip, long-lasting and dry (waterproof). You may need to install land drains to ensure a dry floor. An earth floor is warm and comfortable if it's well drained; its drawback is that it's not easy to disinfect. Clay floors are warm and natural too, but need re-laying annually to stop holes forming in them. Concrete floors are cheap and easy to construct, but not ideal. The surface must be roughened to prevent slipping, and can get very cold: you have to use lots of extra bedding in winter to avoid chilling the horse. Vitrified, non-slip stable bricks have a good reputation – they are both warm and easy to keep clean and dry. Rubber matting

stables, fields and food

'Not bad for a stable'

With an open door, low wall between it and the next stable (so that the horse can have nose-to-nose contact with his neighbour) and a draught-proof window, this stable is designed to give its occupant an indoor life with minimum stress. Note the covered, water- and horse-proof light switch, and how the open top door does not block the window.

is soft underfoot and warms up the surface of a brick or concrete floor, but for both comfort and hygiene should always be usedin conjunction with bedding. Mats are not necessary if you are using deep litter.

Stable floors should drop slightly from front to back, with outlets in the back wall to a gully leading to a drain. If the base of the stable walls is of wood, the outlets need to be sheathed in metal to prevent rot. A drop of 1:48 (a 2 per cent gradient) is reckoned to be best. Since horses like to look out of their stable doors, it's not a good idea to have them standing with their feet in a wet gulley – which is what happens with front drainage unless the gulley is covered with a strong grille of some kind, which reduces its efficiency. With rear drainage, the mangers and water supplies can be sited away from the drain and on the door side of the stable, which also happens to make access easier for the horsekeepers.

stables, fields and food

BEDS AND BEDDING

Traditionally, in temperate climates, straw has been the bedding of choice for the owners of equines. It has been cheap, plentiful and locally available. Wheat straw is usually preferred, partly because it is light and long-lasting, but often for no better reason than that horses find barley straw and oat straw rather tasty. A better reason for not using barley straw is that it doesn't last as long as wheat straw, and remnants of the sheath holding the grain ('beards' or 'awns') can irritate equine skin. Straw is a useful bedding in that it's easy to handle, comfortable for the horses (as long as it's dust-free) and once rotted down it can be recycled as a natural fertilizer. It's also available in treated form – chopped fine to deter bed-eaters, with dust extracted. Some processed straw beddings have deodorizing herbs added.

One of the great advantages of straw is that it can be used for deep litter bedding. With this system, you start with a good deep bed of straw. Then, instead of mucking out the whole stable daily, you simply skip out, that is lift the day's droppings from the top layer of straw, then scatter fresh straw on the bed. This makes for short daily work, and is very economical in the use of straw, but calls for a major clean-out every six months or so. Without mechanical assistance, this can take a day per stable. An alternative is a system of semi-deep litter, which involves skipping out and adding fresh straw daily and mucking out thoroughly once a week. As long as the stable is properly drained and a decent top layer of fresh straw used each day, deep litter need not (as some horsekeeping manuals allege) cause problems for the horses' feet, and the thick bed is both warm and soft.

Muck heap administration

To make the most of them, muck heaps need to be organized into at least three sections. Reserve one for freshly removed bedding, one for partly rotted manure, and the third for manure that is completely rotted down. In practice this means juggling with more than three actual heaps, and shifting some of the muck around from time to time. As long as it is really well rotted, the muck can be used to fertilize resting fields in winter. Or you can earn the thanks of gardeners all over the neighbourhood by selling it or giving it away as garden compost.

However, straw may not be cheap or easily available in your area, or what you can get is so dusty that it makes your horse cough. You may need to keep a sick horse off straw temporarily, or permanently, if he has a chronic respiratory problem. If any of these circumstances apply, there are literally dozens of alternative beddings you can use. Among the most common are sawdust and wood shavings. These call for daily mucking out (so you can't use deep litter) and may block stable drains. Proprietary variations on these basic wood products include demoisturized pine fibres, which are highly absorbent and deodorizing, virtually dust-free, and long-lasting. Once rotted down, they can also be used as garden compost. A popular alternative to wood products is recycled, dust-extracted cardboard and newsprint. Some shredded newsprint can leave a mirror image of bygone news stories on a pale horse's coat, which might give you something to read while grooming but may not please judges in the show ring. These paper-based products biodegrade, but don't always make good fertilizer; once damp, they can also be quite heavy to lift on a fork.

One of the more interesting commercial beddings is made from the core of organically grown hemp plants. This spongy product drains in such a way that liquid is absorbed (and its odours contained) by the lowest layer, which needs to be removed only every 7-10 days. Droppings can be skipped out from the top layer, which remains warm and dry. Mixed with droppings, the hemp rots down to a useful compost.

If you're not using deep litter, when the horse is in during the day you should remove droppings as often as you can, which makes the daily mucking out a lighter task. When mucking out, always take the horse out of the stable first, so that when you put down fresh straw he doesn't get dust or stalks in his eyes or up his nose. Take out any feed and water buckets too. Remove droppings and the wettest straw from the bed, and make an even layer of the remains, putting the driest bedding on top. Then add fresh straw, shaking it out with a fork - about half a bale is usually enough, depending on the productivity of the individual equine. If the horse won't be coming back in for some time, throw the remaining used bedding up against the wall on one side to let the floor air (heap it against the opposite wall the following day). Then, before restabling the horse, relay the bed and add fresh straw.

A traditional way to make a stable bed is to cover only the rear three quarters of the floor with bedding - making it deep enough to cushion the floor thoroughly - and then bank it up, double height, against the walls. The reasoning behind this is that you gain a clear floor space on which to stand feed and water buckets - and these are less likely to get infested with fragments of bedding. You also save a little money on straw bills.

There's also an advantage for the horse. Besides adding some extra draught-proofing, the banking at the sides is supposed to stop a horse 'casting' - that is, lying down with his legs so close to a wall, or up against it, that he can't wriggle himself upright again. In theory the horse won't walk on the banking, so he never lies down close enough to the wall to get cast. But even if all this works as planned, banks are still no help if the horse casts at the front, where there's no bedding at all.

In practice, boxes that start with neat three-quarter beds often end up with bedding over the entire floor, as any horse is quite bright enough to scuff the straw into a pile wherever he wants it, whether to make a thicker section of bed to lie down on, or wants warm forefeet while he's peering out of his stable door. So you may as well save the horse the trouble and cover the whole floor with a thick, even layer of bedding to start with. Bank it against the walls by all means if you want.

RUGGING AND CLIPPING - OR NOT

Many breeds of horse grow very thick coats to stay warm in winter - in Siberia, where the people know as much as anyone about bucking the cold, they actually make hats and gloves from the winter coats of deceased equines. Competition and pleasure horses, however, are often wholly or partly clipped all year round, and some breeds such as Thoroughbreds and Arabians don't grow a particularly substantial winter coat. Even in temperate climates, winter weather can be exceptionally harsh on occasion, and horses living out may need extra protection then; stabled horses can't move about much to keep themselves warm. This is where rugs come in. They can also be useful in summer. Some horses are more vulnerable than others to biting insects (just as some people are), and those living out can benefit from a light summer sheet that stops bugs bothering them.

As with all matters equine there is some disagreement about whether rugging horses in winter is strictly necessary, or even sensible, since a rug inevitably restricts the animal's movement to some extent. Obviously a closely related question is whether it's necessary to clip them in the first place.

stables, fields and food

Yard and stable kit

Minimum equipment for keeping the yard and stables clean and tidy consists of:
- Barrow
- Rubber dung skip
- Shovel
- Yard broom
- Hosepipe
- Stable broom
- Mild disinfectant
- Hay/straw fork
- Buckets
- Shavings fork
- Rubber gloves

It can be argued that clipping and rugging horses is a self-sustaining cycle. Critics call it a vicious circle. In favour of clipping, it is true that it's easier to keep a clipped horse clean, whatever the season. Some horses are just very hairy all year round, and become uncomfortably sweaty and visibly unhappy when worked, even on cool summer days and even when fit. But as anyone who has seen horses at dressage competitions, on a racecourse, or being shown in-hand knows, people regard a clipped horse as an elegant, gleaming, tidy creature. Many, if not most, horses are clipped because that is the way people like to see them.

One reason often given to justify clipping is that working a horse in a long winter coat causes him to sweat his weight off, and he cannot maintain condition to sustain competitive speeds because he's sweating out nutrients. There are no reliable scientific studies to back up this assertion. Indeed,

stables, fields and food

Rugs and rollers

Choose an outdoor rug with shoulder pleats so that the horse doesn't strain against the fabric when he bends down to eat – which he'll be doing most of the time he's out – and doesn't get sores where the rug has rubbed.

The roller-and-surcingle system (left) of keeping a rug on is fiddly, and usually has to be fastened too tight for real comfort. A cooler (below) whips sweat and rainwater from the horse's coat and dumps it outside – leaving him warm and dry beneath.

stables, fields and food

endurance horses in the USA, who undergo training schedules as arduous as any, are routinely raced unclipped in temperatures down to -30°C (-22°F), and after 80km (50 miles) at an average of 16km/h (10mph) have had their pulse rate down to 48 beats per minute within half an hour of finishing the race. This is markedly lower than the maximum pulse rate the sport allows (see Chapter 1), and does not suggest these unclipped horses are even remotely unfit.

Another reason given for clipping and rugging is that a horse with a thick coat will come in from work wet with sweat, and the coat takes so long to dry that the horse risks getting a chill. The answer to that problem is indeed a rug – a cooler, made of fabric woven in such a way that it extracts moisture from a wet coat while remaining dry on the surface that rests against the horse. If the equine is rubbed down in a draught-free environment before the cooler rug is put on, and is left in the rug, out of draughts, until he is thoroughly dry, there is no reason why he should catch cold. Once again, unclipped American endurance horses are treated like this and survive night-time temperatures of -50°C (-58°F) after a race, with no ill effects.

Rugs aren't, however, entirely risk-free. First, horses can get tangled up in the straps: for a flight animal, not being able to run at will is a death sentence, and a terrified horse can go into a frenzy and injure itself, possibly fatally, long before anyone sees what has happened. Second, no matter how well fitted, all rugs restrict the horse's movement to some extent, especially around the shoulders. In her book *Equine Welfare*, Marthe Kiley-Worthington gives a poignant example of the possible consequences: 'One of our young horses with a particularly good movement was kept clipped and rugged from the age of three for two years every winter by his new owner. His free flowing movement was reduced to a short-strided "pit-a-patter" even without the rug thereafter.' The moral is that while rugs are sometimes necessary, they would ideally

Putting on a rug

Fold the rug in half, from back to front, so that the inner surface is outermost and the straps are dangling freely. Fold it again so that the quarter containing the straps is on top. Stand at the horse's nearside (left) flank and put the quartered rug flat over his near hindquarters. Gently tip the other quarter over so that it's hanging down on his offside. Make sure all the offside straps are over and not caught up under the rug, and that the rug (still folded in half) is centred on his back. Now unfold the front half, taking it over the withers, and pull the rug forwards a little up his neck to make fastening the front straps easier. Duck under the horse's head to do up the front straps. Next, fasten the surcingles (belly straps), so that they cross under the belly. Now pull the rug back to smooth it down, check that it's still centred, and make it snug to the hindquarters. Then do up the nearest leg strap. If you can trust the horse, step around behind him and thread the offside leg strap through the one already done up, and fasten it. If in any doubt about the horse's tendency to kick out, walk around his head and fix the second leg strap by leaning under from the flank.

Reverse the procedure to take the rug off. As you undo each leg strap, be sure to fasten it back in place on the rug, or you risk the clip banging against the horse's legs.

stables, fields and food

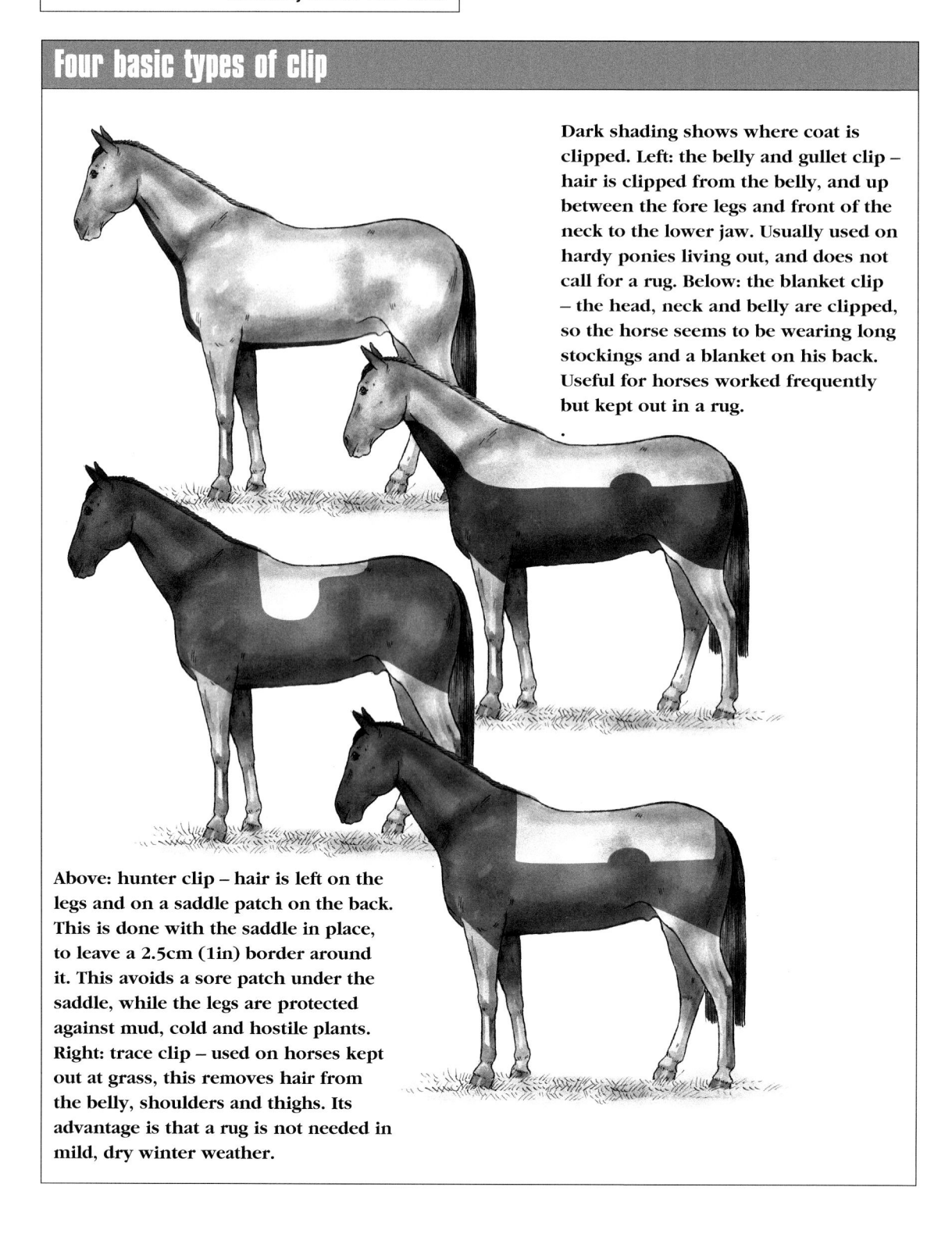

Four basic types of clip

Dark shading shows where coat is clipped. Left: the belly and gullet clip – hair is clipped from the belly, and up between the fore legs and front of the neck to the lower jaw. Usually used on hardy ponies living out, and does not call for a rug. Below: the blanket clip – the head, neck and belly are clipped, so the horse seems to be wearing long stockings and a blanket on his back. Useful for horses worked frequently but kept out in a rug.

Above: hunter clip – hair is left on the legs and on a saddle patch on the back. This is done with the saddle in place, to leave a 2.5cm (1in) border around it. This avoids a sore patch under the saddle, while the legs are protected against mud, cold and hostile plants. Right: trace clip – used on horses kept out at grass, this removes hair from the belly, shoulders and thighs. Its advantage is that a rug is not needed in mild, dry winter weather.

be used as sparingly as possible, and horses living out in rugs should be checked as often as practicable.

THE RUG FOR THE JOB

As already mentioned, the summer sheet serves a valuable purpose in protecting the horse against insects. The cooler rug, which draws moisture from the coat onto its outer surface, is ideal for helping the horse cool down and dry out after hard work, for drying him out when brought in wet from the rain, and to let a horse who sweats while travelling finish his journey warm, dry and protected from chills when he leaves the trailer or horsebox.

Stable rugs are used to keep the horse warm when he has to be kept in; they're not waterproof. They are traditionally made of jute lined with wool; but these can shrink when washed, and they're heavy. Ones made of synthetic material are much lighter, don't shrink, and are machine-washable. Stable rugs tend to get soiled when the horse lies down, so keeping a spare is a good idea. They also lose their bulk (and therefore their warming properties) over time.

Standard, wind- and waterproof outdoor wear for horses is the turnout rug. As with stable rugs, the traditional canvas-and-wool-lined type (known as a New Zealand) is heavy and restrictive. Those made from synthetics are much lighter and often more effective as windcheaters. Turnout rugs have to withstand the horse rolling in them, scratching himself against trees and posts, and the rough-and-tumble of horseplay. They can get torn or become heavy with mud, and in very foul weather they can get soaked through. Keeping a spare is essential.

Both indoor and outdoor rugs are now available with pleats at each shoulder. Known as freedom or action gussets, these give the horse much greater liberty of movement than standard rugs, and are highly recommended.

stables, fields and food

Rugs should be fitted with as much care as a saddle. They should not be tight, and their shape around the neck and hindquarters should follow the shape of the horse. Take special care that the fit around the neck and chest is deep enough to allow the horse to reach down to feed without strain on either animal or fabric, and that the rug will not rub around the withers and points of the shoulder. However, the rug should be snug enough to stay in put without having the fastenings done up tight. Leg straps must be long enough to let the horse gallop without rubbing or pulling; they also need to be placed so that his legs don't catch in them when he rolls or lies down. Fastenings need to stay done up under this treatment – spring clips are better than the hook-and-eye type of buckle. Keep them oiled and rust-free so that they don't stiffen up. Outdoor rugs should be deep enough to protect the belly from rain and wind. Rugs held in place with a roller and pads (a leather or webbing strap, running over pads placed either side of the spine) generally need to be kept too tight for comfort if they're to stay in place. These are best avoided.

Horses don't instinctively wear clothes, and need to become accustomed to rugs – in particular outdoor ones, with their straps around the hind legs. They perhaps need even more to get used to the business of getting them on in the first place (see 'Putting on a Rug'). Practice a few times with the horse tied up in the stable, and leave the rug on for 10 minutes or so with the horse untied. He'll probably explore it with his mouth and wriggle about a bit. Once he's used to the feel of it, you can put him out in the field with it on, but do keep checking throughout the day to make sure the rug and its straps are still securely in place.

CLIPPING

Clipping is usually first done in late October in northern latitudes as the winter coat

stables, fields and food

begins to show through, and then repeated as necessary, usually every month or so. The summer coat starts to grow about three months later, and can be spoiled if clipped. When clipping the head, never remove a horse's vibrissae (nose and chin whiskers – see Chapter 2), the long hairs around his eyes, or the hair growing on the inside of his ears. The four basic types of clip are shown in the illustration on page 96. Not shown is the full clip, in which the horse has the whole of his coat shaved off. Clipping demands skill and experience, and a calm temperament on the part of both horse and human. It's an art that can only be learned first hand, and under the guidance of an expert, not from a book. You will also have plenty of time then to decide whether you believe it is really necessary.

THOUGHTS ON FOOD

Forage foods like grass and the herbs growing with it are the most suitable food for horses; these are what they have evolved to eat. When the horse is stabled or if grass is in short supply, the next best option is a bulky food such as hay or straw. There is also an enormous range of hard (concentrated) feeds available – from simple grains like oats and barley to costly and specialized commercial mixes. Hard food used to be considered the most important part of an equine's diet, but has now become a somewhat contentious issue (see 'How much hard food?').

Generally speaking, a horse worked once a day needs to eat 1.5-2.5 per cent of his body weight every day. Besides water, he needs fibre, proteins and fats in his diet. There are basic requirements of each of these for the horse simply to stay alive in reasonable health; but the proportions vary between horses and ponies and from individual to individual, according to intrinsic needs, their metabolic efficiency, the work they are doing (which includes the weight

How much hard food?

Some advocates of natural horsekeeping maintain that hard (concentrated) feeds are unnecessary, even for horses competing regularly, if horses spend enough time eating good grass and bulky food. Specialist hard feeds are, they will even say, simply a way for feed companies to make money. It may be true that not all horses need specialist feeds, but on the other side of this coin is the truth that some horses – especially older ones – are just not 'good doers' or 'good keepers'. Whether from inborn deficiency or from age, their guts simply don't extract enough nourishment from hay and grass alone, and to stay in decent condition they have to be given buckets of extra, concentrated rations. (The horse can only take in so much food in a day: hence, in hard food, nourishment is concentrated into a small volume.) Temperament can also affect feeding needs: a highly strung or nervous horse can consume twice as much energy as a placid one, when exercised, and that energy has to be replaced.

Once again we are in an area where we have to find the balance between what is right for the specific horse, and the sometimes incompatible conclusions of experts; and judging what is best for a particular horse is often a matter of experience – an accumulation of observation of individual horses, the effects of various hard feeds on them, their available grazing, plus the application of one's own intelligence – and even experiment.

stables, fields and food

How to hang a haynet

A haynet with a fine mesh makes it harder for the horse to tug the hay out, and he takes smaller mouthfuls. This means the meal lasts longer, and the horse has something to think about while he's standing in his stable.

Haynets should be tied with the drawstring running through the lowest part of the mesh so that, when empty, they stay hanging just below head height. Then the horse can't get his feet tangled up in the net or drawstring.

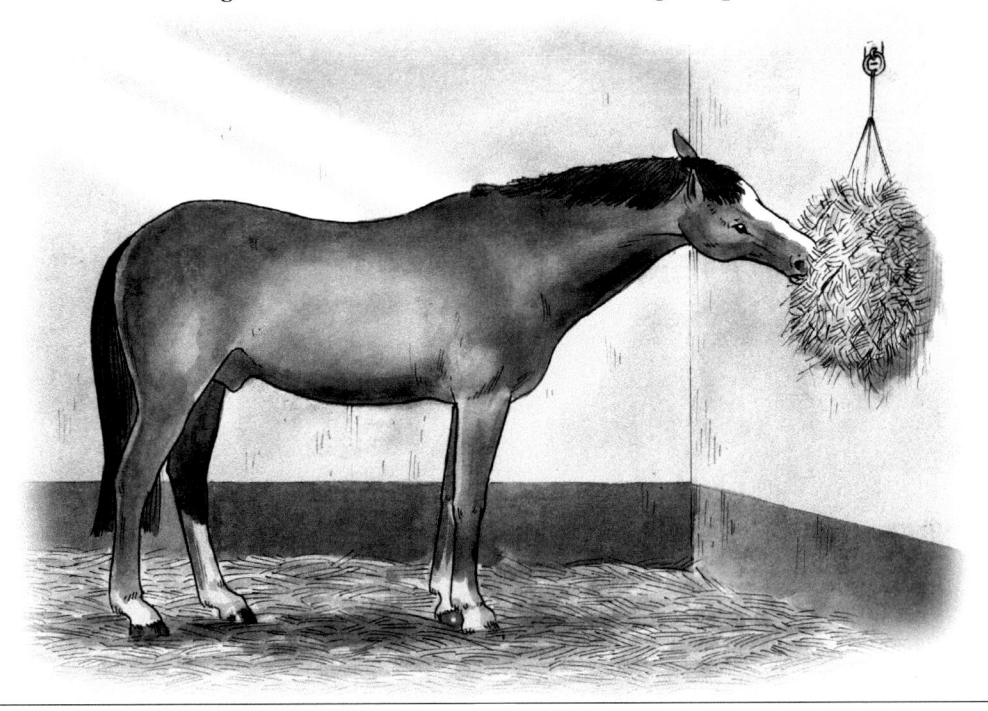

they have to carry), the climate they live in, and their temperament.

Factors like these make it difficult to give detailed advice on feeding. But when judging what to feed a particular horse, it helps to know the functions of the essential ingredients in the equine diet. Next to water (see below), the most vital ingredient in a horse's diet is fibre – found aplenty in forage food like grass and herbs and bulky foods such as hay (dried grass), the high-energy haylage (hay baled early, before it is completely dry, and wrapped or packed so that the sugars ferment slightly), straw and chaff (chopped hay or straw). All of these contain essential carbohydrates, and forage foods contain essential minerals and vitamins. Fibre helps to open up the horse's gut and gets the digestive juices flowing more efficiently, and buckets of hard food should always have a base of haylage or chaff to aid digestion. Grass is also a major source of water; fibre in general helps to retain water and electrolytes in the digestive tract, creating a reserve for periods of heavy work or hot weather. Fibre is digested by bacteria; this process creates heat, so feeding extra hay in winter helps to keep a horse warm. At least two-thirds of the diet of stabled horses in hard work should

stables, fields and food

consist of hay or grass. The better the fibre, the less hard food they need.

Proteins provide amino acids that build up body tissues, and help to make a horse fit and energetic. Good grazing, some hay and a modicum of grain such as oats or barley will contain 10-12 per cent protein, which is more than ample even for a horse in hard work. While traditionally it has been reckoned that protein should make up as much as 14 per cent of the diet, equine nutritionists now believe that as little as 8.5 per cent is sufficient. In fact, once fit, a horse fed more proteins than he needs will actually perform significantly more slowly than one whose intake is correctly judged.

Fats in food are ultimately converted to sugars and thus provide a horse with energy. Adding extra fat to a horse's diet (most prefer it in the form of corn oil) is a way of boosting energy, and many horse owners claim that a judicious mix of barley and corn oil will actually calm down tricky or nervous horses. But using fat as an alternative source of carbohydrate does bring complications in its wake. Using it as a direct substitute for grain feeds means the horse no longer gets the proteins, minerals and vitamins that are in grains, and so must be given them as supplements.

Both good grazing and proprietary feeds contain a correct mix of vitamins and minerals; if making up hard feeds from basic ingredients like oats, soaked sugar beet pulp, and so on, you may need to balance the results with additives. There are other occasions when vitamin and mineral supplements can be extremely useful. Grazing in many areas of the world is poor in the mineral selenium, for example; pastures may also lack potassium, iron, zinc and sulphur to varying degrees. Horses that have been undernourished as foals may grow up with an imperfect sense of balance, because of a lack of vitamin E. As a result, they may be reluctant to have their feet picked up, making the farrier's work extremely difficult. Adding vitamin E even to a grown horse's diet will help restore their sense of balance. Carrots - which many horses have to learn to like - contain vitamin A, and add succulence to feeds. Cut them lengthways, in short lengths, to avoid the risk of choking.

Soaking hay

If the hay that's available is dusty, it should be soaked in water before feeding to avoid the risk of producing coughing and other respiratory problems. Damp hay is also a lot tastier for the horse. Fungal spores in the forage, too, which would otherwise be breathed in to infect the lungs, are eaten without harm – but never feed a horse hay that is already mouldy. Soak the hay in water for an hour or so, until it is damp right through, then hang it up in a hay net until it has stopped dripping before giving it to the horse. Don't leave it for longer than eight hours, otherwise it will dry out again.

THOUGHTS ON FEEDING

Horses who spend time in stables need feeding - and not just because once indoors they're deprived of the nourishment of a meadow's fresh grass, herbs and minerals. Conventional stable designs don't allow horses much tactile social life, and without the stimulus of proper communication with their fellows, stabled horses soon become bored and lonely. Having access to bulk feed helps to keep the horse's mind occupied for fair stretches of time if it's fed in nets. This is because he has to work a bit to get at the hay, and this is better than nothing to think about at all.

Like some people, some stabled horses deal with loneliness and boredom through 'comfort eating'. This can be as problematic

stables, fields and food

Sweetening strange water

A horse arriving at a new yard, or out on the road at a competition, may be highly suspicious of strange water. Adding a bit of apple juice, runny honey or other sweet liquid will overcome the problem. The same ruse can be used if your own yard water is heavily chlorinated – most equines can't stand the smell and won't drink it.

as any officially labelled stable vice. Such horses can end up always trying to eat, in or out of their stable, when ridden or led, and become prime candidates for afflictions like colic and laminitis through eating too much too quickly. Leaving them without food for long periods only makes them anxious and even greedier when they do get fed. The best solution is to increase their exercise and give them low-energy bulk food (such as straw), but ration it out, little and often, throughout the time they're stabled.

But there's no reason why stabled horses who do get plenty of mental and emotional stimulation and physical exercise (whether through work with a rider or at grass with other horses) should not have access to as much hay or straw as they want. They don't spend all their time eating, and don't get fat, because they've so many other things to think about and keep them occupied; and the people who have to look after them spend less time filling hay nets and buckets, so everyone gains.

stables, fields and food

Feeding by the clock

Many horse experts advise absolutely regular feeding and maintain that horses love routine. This is true, but only of horses who spend more time in stables than out and/or do not have proper access to bulky foods such as hay. In these conditions, the equine digestive system responds to the routine set up by people, and highly regulated horses naturally become uncomfortable and restless, or will even develop vices, if not fed on time. Those fed hard food only to supplement thin winter grazing, or to bring them up to condition after illness or injury, should certainly be given their buckets at least twice a day – fed little and often – to maintain even nourishment. But some variation (within a span of a couple of hours) in feeding times will not distress horses physically or emotionally as long as they also have access to hay. They will learn from the start that buckets come at different times, and as a result be more relaxed at mealtimes. You will have more freedom in your daily schedule, and won't have to worry (or make special arrangements) if for any reason you occasionally have to feed early or late.

WATER

Horses need a certain amount of water in the gut in order to digest their solid food properly. They also sweat to keep cool in hot weather and when worked, and even medium-weight mares feeding foals may produce as much as 20 litres (35pts) of milk a day – liquid that has to be replenished at first opportunity. Equines should have constant access to water, whether in or out of their stables, and it should be clean – that is, clear – and not too salty for their taste (as water from wells can be). Less than clean troughs with murky water are a surprisingly common sight even in otherwise well-regulated yards. Water with as little as 5g per litre (five parts per thousand) of dissolved solids in it will impede both the growth and performance of the horse.

There is one occasion when it is not a good idea to let a horse have free access to water. That is when he's hot, sweaty and tired after working. Then, you should first let his breathing return to normal if need be, and give him a net of dampened hay to tussle with while you take his tack off, or a bucket with about 1 litre (2pts) of cool (but not too cold) water to drink. Chilled water can bring on colic in a hot and thirsty horse, so add some warm water to the bucket if necessary. After a quarter of an hour, when he has cooled down a bit, you can let him drink as much as he wants.

Generally you should offer a horse water before letting him eat, but whether you can persuade him to drink it is another matter. In any case horses prefer cool, not chilled, water (around 21–24°C/70–75°F). On wintry days, too, add a little warm water to make the supply palatable.

Horses can also be fussy about drinking water that tastes unfamiliar to them – what comes out of a tap at a showground, the riding club yard, or at the far end of a day's trail ride, for example. A simple solution is to add a dash of apple juice to the water, or a spoonful of runny honey. Some horses don't like the taste of chlorinated water. Adding an iron supplement will release the chlorine and restore the water's natural flavour.

There are also horses who just don't drink as much as they should. While on grass, a horse will need 27–54 litres (6–12gals) of water a day, and more in hot weather or if on dry feeds and in constant hard work. One reason for using buckets rather than an

stables, fields and food

automatic refilling system for equine water is that you can monitor how much horses are drinking. A neat cure for a horse that won't drink is to drop a large apple into his water. In trying to get at the elusive, bobbing thing the horse will inevitably sip some water. (The bucket needs to be thoroughly anchored so the horse can't cheat and tip it over to snaffle up the apple.) 'With time,' writes equine nutritionist John Kohnke, 'a smart horse will drink a 2 gallon [10 litre] bucket of water to obtain the apple.'

For reasons that are unclear, some horses dunk hay in their water while eating it. This is regarded as unacceptable behaviour by some people. It can make a mess of automatic water troughs, but a horse with two buckets of water will usually have the brains to dunk in one and drink clear water from the other. Hauling water buckets about and keeping them clean makes for more work for humans, but does ensure that you can keep an eye on the animals' water consumption, and that their water is always fresh.

Joining forces against flies

In hot weather when flies and other pestiferous insects are out in force, horses will pair off and stand nose-to-tail, swishing their tails to keep the buzzing things away from each other's faces. This is yet another example of how horses cooperate, rather than compete, and another reason why horses should not be left to lead solitary lives.

stables, fields and food

Good fence, bad fence

Barbed wire is always bad news in a field grazed by horses – they can easily cut themselves on it, and even a nick from rusty wire can bring on a deadly tetanus infection. Post and rail is best – and can take more punishment from the horses.

OUT AT GRASS

Whether horses are kept out all the time or only part time, their pasture needs as much thought and care as their stabling.

The first question is: how much pasture does a horse need? Like many questions about horses the answer is not straightforward, since the quality of the grazing, drainage and soil have to be taken into account. A horse grazing in the New Mexico desert may need 260 hectares (a square mile) or more, whereas a horse on a lush Virginia meadow will need only 0.4 hectares (1 acre). Paradoxically, you could keep 10 horses on 4 hectares (10 acres) of best pasture, but not one horse on 0.4 hectares (1 acre). This is because with the larger spread of land, you can move the horses around in the course of the year to rest fields, whereas over a year just one horse will trash the smaller patch.

Therefore, to manage paddocks properly, you need proportionately more land per head of horse. On pasture of average quality, reckon on needing 0.8 hectares (2 acres) per horse. It is always a good idea to have some grassland besides what the horses need so that you can set aside some fields for hay. Even horses that live out will need hay (and a salt lick) to supplement their grazing in winter, when the grass is not growing.

Regardless of the quality of the grazing (which you can improve by reseeding), there are four essentials to good pasture: shelter for the horses, good soil drainage, proper fencing and a water supply.

Shelter

This includes hedging or other tall, thick vegetation on the weather side of the field

stables, fields and food

Nothing like a good roll

No one knows exactly why horses roll: it may be the equivalent of a good stretch, or a simple expression of pleasure – many roll as soon as they reach pasture from the stable – or it may be to leave their scent on 'their' patch of ground. It was thought they covered themselves in mud to keep warm, but horses roll (often in the same place) in all weathers.

(the side in the direction of prevailing winds). Well-protected corners are better still, to reduce chill draughts in winter and provide shade in summer. In addition, there should be a field shelter large enough to accommodate all the horses likely to use the field. This too should have its back to the direction of the prevailing winds. Horses will use it as a haven from wind and rain in winter, and from flies in summer.

Drainage

Pasture should not develop standing pools of water from moderate rainfall or have areas that stay sodden all year, as grass growth will be suppressed (rushes often take their place, so you can see a long-standing problem at a glance) and horses' feet will suffer too. Fields may need to have land drains installed to cure these conditions; these are not expensive, and are a worthwhile investment. Ditches need to be kept free-running, clear of vegetation and other obstacles.

Fencing

Post and rail fencing is best for horses. Barbed wire is out because, apart from cuts and tears caused when horses play together, they will lean on it to get at the greener grass in the next field and nick themselves then, too. Horses are also quite strong enough to break through a wire fence if the urge takes them; properly installed rails offer far more resistance. Always place fencing between

stables, fields and food

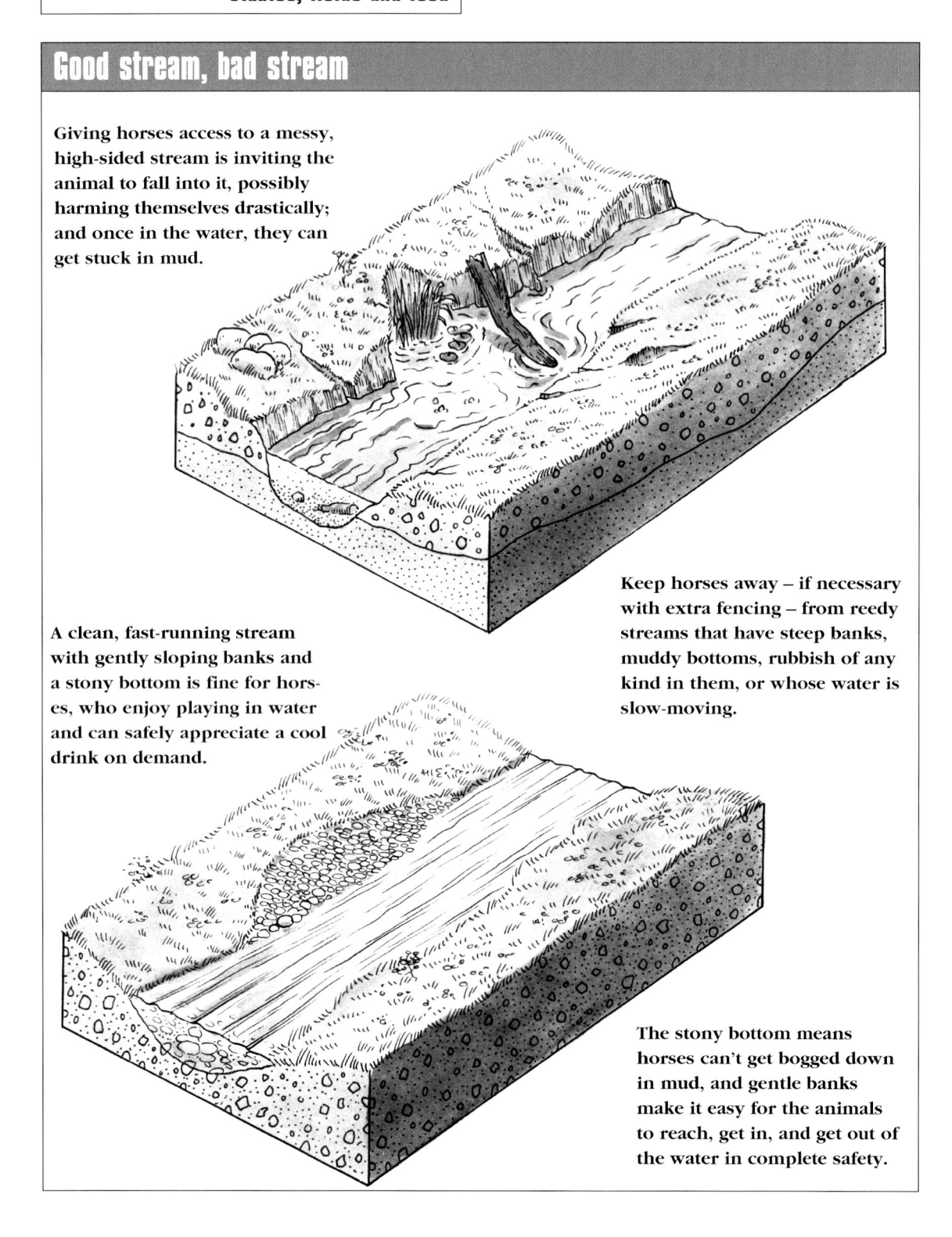

Good stream, bad stream

Giving horses access to a messy, high-sided stream is inviting the animal to fall into it, possibly harming themselves drastically; and once in the water, they can get stuck in mud.

Keep horses away – if necessary with extra fencing – from reedy streams that have steep banks, muddy bottoms, rubbish of any kind in them, or whose water is slow-moving.

A clean, fast-running stream with gently sloping banks and a stony bottom is fine for horses, who enjoy playing in water and can safely appreciate a cool drink on demand.

The stony bottom means horses can't get bogged down in mud, and gentle banks make it easy for the animals to reach, get in, and get out of the water in complete safety.

animals and ditches – if need be, double-fence. If you are using a mixed grazing system (horses with sheep, goats and/or cattle) then stock-proof, small-mesh wire may be needed below the lower rail. However, it is better, but more expensive, to add extra rails to the fencing, as horses can catch their feet in the mesh of stock wire. Horses lean and scratch on, stretch over and under, bump against and chew at wooden fencing, so check regularly for sprung nails and loosened posts. Even a foal tugging at a hay net enthusiastically can pull up a fence post. And some horses' ideas of amusement include testing the strength of fencing, no matter how stout.

Electric fencing (either battery or mains powered) can be extremely useful in dividing up larger fields – one section is grazed, while the remainder rests. Heavy-duty, thick-banded tape is best, attached to stout posts. Most horses will soon learn to avoid the mild shock this gives when touched, and after that it's often possible to use the fencing without the current turned on. Some horses, on the other hand, are impervious to electric fencing and will try to push under the tape, hence the need for stout posts. The tape can also be used with lightweight plastic posts to create a temporary fence, which allows a field to be grazed in strips; this is especially valuable in spring and early summer for horses in danger of eating too much lush grass at once.

Water supply

If you're depending on a stream to provide all or just a seasonal supply of water, be sure that it's suitable for horses (see illustration opposite). If need be, get at least a stretch of the banks cleared so that the animals have safe access to the water, and fence off the rest. Also, do find out if the water is both safe for horses to drink, and palatable to yours. If the land has either no or only seasonal natural running water, piping water to self-replenishing troughs will save much human labour involving buckets. Troughs must be kept clean and free of vegetation, algae, dust, soil and other contamination or the horses won't use them until desperate (if at all), and they will attract even more flies than usual. Water troughs should be placed in a cool, shady area of the field (although not under deciduous trees), and the valve system and ballcock should be covered, inaccessible to playful equines. Ponds and pools with shallow banks make acceptable equine watering holes if they clearly rise and fall with the water table and rainfall. This means the water is constantly being refreshed. Such

Sweats and salts

When a horse sweats he loses not only water from his body, but vital salts – called electrolytes – containing sodium, chlorine and potassium. If he's turned out onto good, herb-rich pasture after work, he'll soon replace these through normal grazing, and good pasture actually helps to retain both water and electrolytes in the horse's gut. Stabled horses and especially those continuing in work after sweating heavily – for instance when trekking or at a gymkhana on a hot day – will need to have these salts replaced immediately if they are to stay on top form. There are various proprietary rehydrating powders and solutions available, which are added either to drinking water or to feed: follow the instructions on the packaging precisely. Some horses need to get used to the taste of these salts; some need their water sweetened to accept them at all. Clean buckets thoroughly once the horse has finished his rehydrating feed or drink, as any salty or sweet moisture remaining will attract a cloud of flies.

stables, fields and food

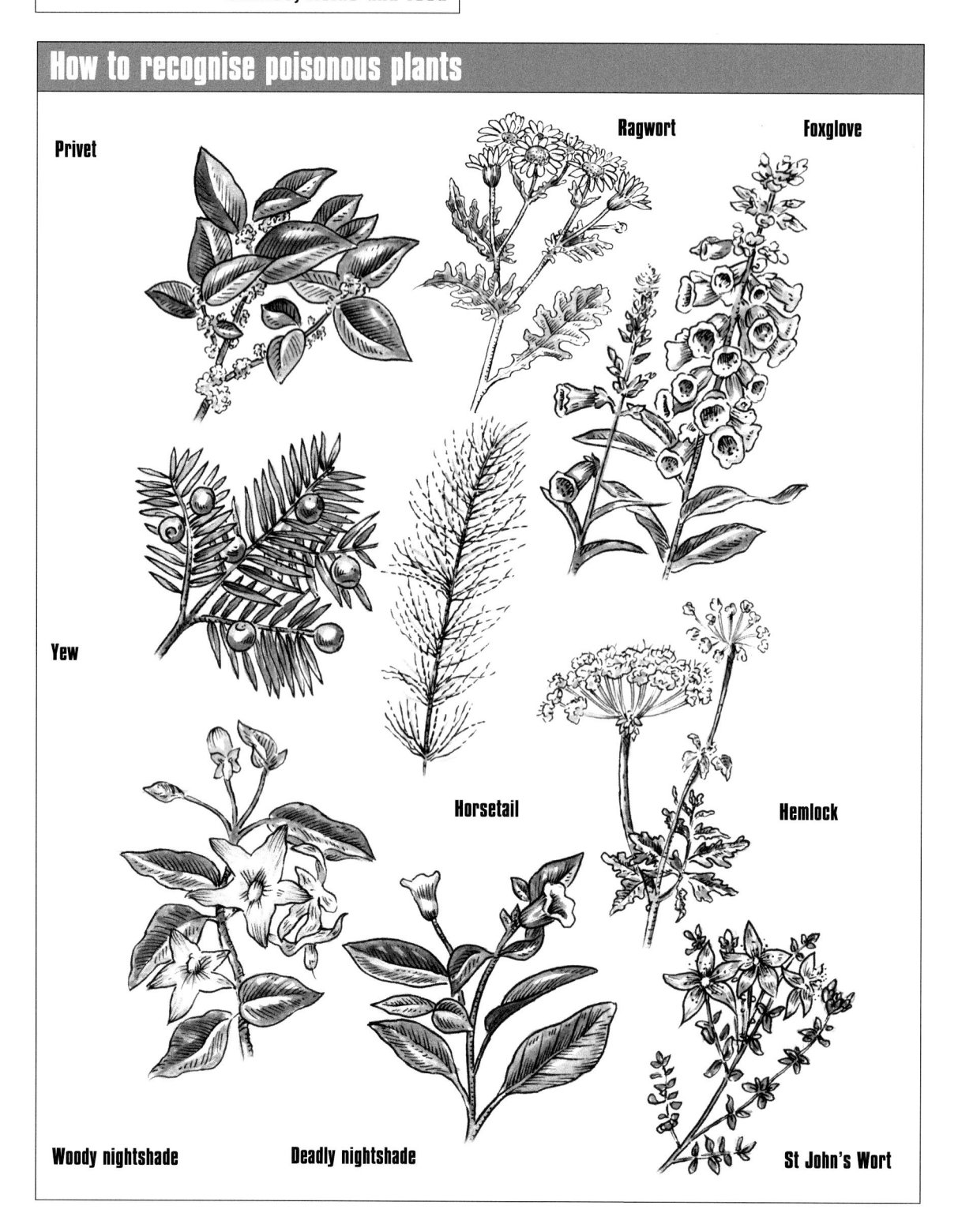

How to recognise poisonous plants

Privet

Ragwort

Foxglove

Yew

Horsetail

Hemlock

Woody nightshade

Deadly nightshade

St John's Wort

ponds are usually in rock. Stagnant ponds with muddy or sandy bottoms should be fenced off. The water is not good, and they are treacherous underfoot.

THE GRASS TO GROW

All horses love grass, but some grasses suit horses better than others. One of the commonest laments of pony owners is that their steed puts on weight so fast when out at grass that he has to be brought in, at worst for fear of laminitis, and at best so that he is not under undue strain when he's worked. Ponies have a special talent for putting on weight, but the problem can arise to some extent with all equines kept out, especially those not worked daily. On the other hand, being cooped up in a stable with nothing to eat is neither kind nor natural to the animal.

One reason horses, and most especially small ponies, get fat (or at least look extra bulbous) on lush spring grass is that there is a lot of water but relatively little nutrition in the grass. So to get the nourishment they need, they have to eat more of it, and bloat somewhat. Wild horses and those kept in the Russian tabun system fatten up on spring and summer grass in order to see themselves through leaner times in winter. At the same time, they are constantly on the move, as are horses in fields.

The conventional assertion that horses become unfit to work if allowed to stay out on grass is at least debatable. But if weight is a problem, the obvious solution is to give the horse more exercise. This doesn't have to be strenuous, to keep his weight down and his muscles well toned, but it must be regular. It used to be standard practice literally to starve overweight equines, leaving them in a stable for a couple of weeks with nothing but salty water to drink. Now, it is known that a horse's digestive system begins to break down if he doesn't eat for more than about five hours – to

his distress, while prolonged starvation results in fatty acids being dumped into the bloodstream and liver. The result is not unlike an overdose of cholesterol. The horse is unlikely to regain top condition, and in severe cases will die.

Another way to approach the problem of tubby horses is to look carefully at what kind of grass is on their pasture. Horses kept out certainly have suffered from acute laminitis (see 'Understanding Laminitis, p110') through eating too much rich grass. Horses have evolved to thrive on poor grasses (for energy) and a mix of herbs (which supply minerals and vitamins). Pasture laid down for dairy cows is particularly unsuitable for horses: it rarely contains herbs and is designed to increase the uptake of water. Seed mixes for grasses specifically suitable for horses are commercially available, and the producers will usually give helpful advice. Or you can consult public agencies – for instance, the County extension agent in the USA, or the Equine Services Department of the Ministry of Agriculture in the UK. Private consultants and nutritionists will also advise, but be prepared to pay.

Besides grass, a range of herbs is also essential to good pasture, and these may be few and far between in fields previously used by agribusiness. Herbs can be seeded in with grass but will flourish best in the highest, driest parts of the field. It's also essential to remove poisonous plants (see p108) from the paddock and from hedges.

CARE OF FIELDS

Horses graze unevenly, cropping some areas closely, but avoiding those patches where they leave their droppings. Mixed grazing is a useful way to even up a field. Cows put onto the pasture after horses will happily eat the long grass around horse droppings; and sheep following the cows will shave the field so that fresh growth

stables, fields and food

Understanding laminitis

Laminitis (also known as founder) is a result of congestion in the blood vessels that line the walls of the hoof. As the hoof cannot expand to accommodate the resultant swelling, it is extremely painful. The forefeet are usually the first to be affected. An early sign of potential laminitis is a hardening in the tissue of the crest, which is normally quite spongy to the hand. A horse with acute laminitis will stand, rooted to the spot with an agonized expression, with his forefeet stretched out and his hind legs tucked under him in an attempt to take weight off his front. He will be trembling and sweating profusely.

A common cause is a diet that's too rich in carbohydrates. It is not an affliction peculiar to horses kept out. It can be brought on as easily from overfeeding oats or barley as from lush grass. Lack of exercise and overfeeding in a stabled horse put it at risk. This is because circulation of the blood through a horse's hoof depends on the horse moving – on his feet hitting the ground, which pumps blood back up his legs. Laminitis can also arise from, among other things, excessive long, fast riding on hard surfaces, especially if the horse is overweight and unfit, and as a by-product of equine influenza; or, in mares, a difficult foaling, which can both disturb and weaken the heart and circulation.

In the worst cases, the pedal bone in the hoof breaks through the sole, and the animal must be put down. If the presence of laminitis is caught in time (usually within 10 days of its onset), the horse should become sound again. In more severe cases, the horse may survive but will be able to withstand only light work. If you even think you have spotted a horse with laminitis, call the vet and the farrier immediately.

comes through vigorous and nutritious, to the horses' benefit. Mixed grazing also helps to control the parasites that infest horses, since most won't survive being eaten by cattle or sheep.

For both fields and animals to flourish, grazing land should be rested for three continuous months of the year. To prevent weeds taking hold, fields should be topped – plants cut down to about 10cm (4in) in height – in spring and early summer, before weeds drop their seeds. This also encourages grass to grow more vigorously. When fields are rested they should also be harrowed: this breaks up and spreads the droppings,

stables, fields and food

which will then fertilize the soil, and removes dead grass, as well as evening out the inevitable dents and divots that hooves leave in the ground. Every three or four years it's worth checking the soil acidity to see if you need to apply lime.

COMMON AILMENTS

Whether kept in or out, and often through no fault of their own or their keepers, horses can become sick or suffer injury of some kind. Here are some of the most common conditions you may meet, and what to do about them. If in *any* doubt, call the vet. Some symptoms are very distressing, particularly when a horse reacts by thrashing about, but strive to stay calm and collected. Then you can concentrate on dealing with the real sufferer.

Azoturia

A muscular condition usually affecting the hindquarters. The muscles become cramped, feeling unusually hard to the touch and very hot, and the horse finds it difficult to move. Azoturia tends to occur after the horse has been ridden hard. If the condition comes on when you're out on a ride, don't try to keep him moving – this may destroy muscle fibres and even damage the kidneys; besides, he may collapse under you. Let the horse rest in a sheltered place, and get him home in a trailer or box. Call the vet. The cause is not known for certain. It was traditionally believed to be the result of feeding too much protein, but modern research indicates a build-up of calcium may be responsible. In either case, prevention is better than cure: never feed a horse more concentrated food than he needs for the work he is doing. On rest days and the day before a competition, for example, cut down on hard food. As a general rule, you should feed a horse for the work he has done, not for work he will do.

Chronic obstructive pulmonary disease

Also known as COPD, or broken wind, this is a chronic respiratory condition in which the lungs lose their elasticity, and infection sets in. Symptoms include a hollow cough that seems to come from the belly, a thick discharge from the nose, and the horse appearing to take two goes at breathing out. COPD can be caused by allergies (to fungal spores in hay, for example), overfeeding before exercise, or over-exercising an unfit horse. Take veterinary advice.

Colic

Abdominal pain, which can be caused by over-eating, drinking quantities of chilled water when hot, sudden changes of diet, eating mouldy hay, and worm infestation, among other things. Rate of breathing increases, and the horse may sweat; he becomes restless, kicks at his belly, and may lie down and roll violently. Don't let him eat or drink. The condition is often self-righting after about 20 minutes. If he does not calm down, call the vet, and try to walk him about quietly.

Influenza

An extremely infectious viral disease, the most severe forms of which can be fatal or lead to pneumonia. The horse develops a high temperature, cough and nasal discharge and loses his appetite; his eyes may become highly inflamed. The horse should be isolated, and the temperature of other horses on the yard taken. Keep the patient warm in a cooler rug, away from draughts, and bandage his legs for extra warmth. Give small, frequent feeds of soft food. Call the vet. To prevent infection, have horses immunized annually.

Lameness

Pain in the hooves or limbs is clearly apparent if it comes on when riding, as you

stables, fields and food

Shelter in the lee

Horses will turn their well-upholstered backsides into the wind to protect their more vulnerable parts from the cold. Good thick hedging, especially on the weather side of a paddock, provides welcome extra shelter against foul conditions – and adds variety to the diet, as horses will browse the leaves. But hedges won't keep a horse in like fences do!

can feel the horse's step become uneven. In that case, check at once for stones or other objects lodged in the feet. (It really is a good idea to take a hoofpick when you ride out.) Check for heat and swelling in the whole leg at the same time. If nothing can be found in any hoof, walk the horse home (or arrange to have him transported, if he's severely lame). Possible causes are multifarious: a bruised sole from a stone that's since worked free; an old wound in the sole that is festering; a nail driven into or near sensitive parts of the hoof when being shod; a cracked hoof; a sprain; or the onset of a more serious affliction such as laminitis or navicular disease. In these cases, get expert advice from your vet and/or farrier. But don't fret unduly. Many minor, common causes of lameness can be treated quickly, easily and permanently.

Mud fever (scratches) and cracked heels:

These are skin diseases seen mostly in horses kept in cold, wet, muddy conditions, when skin on the feet, legs and belly become infected by bacteria, scabs form and lock the microbes in. An early sign is heat in the hooves; get the horse indoors, dry him out thoroughly, and keep him in until the heat has subsided. If necessary, clip affected parts and wash scabs off with warm water, dry thoroughly, and apply antibiotic cream or powder. The vet should treat severe cases.

Navicular disease

A form of arthritis in the navicular bone of the hoof. Symptoms include initial lameness when worked, which wears off as the horse warms up, and the horse standing with one foot forwards. This disease is possibly hereditary in horses with small feet and upright pasterns, but can be caused by shoeing such horses inappropriately, or extended work on hard surfaces. Must be treated by the vet.

Parasites

Not ailments but virtual inevitabilities are infestation by parasites such as worms and bot flies. There are half a dozen or so parasites that commonly affect horses. Most interfere with the digestive process and prevent nutrients being absorbed, and can variously cause colic, diarrhoea, obstructions in the bowel, loss of condition, and ulcers.

Large redworms migrate in the walls of blood vessels, and feed in the colon. Small redworms live in the small colon. Whiteworms (ascarids) hatch in the colon, then migrate via blood vessels to the liver and lungs; they are coughed up, swallowed, and then live in the small colon. Tapeworms develop from eggs carried by mites living on grass; eggs hatch in the large colon. Pinworms live in the large colon; females lay eggs around the anus, which causes itching and severe rubbing by the horse. Bot flies lay their eggs on the horse's limbs and these are ingested by the horse. The larvae hook onto the stomach wall and remain for 7–9 months, causing ulceration and perforation; they are eventually passed out with droppings to pupate; after 1–3 months, the adult flies begin to emerge.

Various proprietary worming pastes are available, although none deals with all these parasites; they must be given regularly to ensure they are effective. Bot fly infestation can be reduced by combing the eggs off the horse with a serrated knife during general grooming (see Chapter 4). Fields in which only horses graze should have droppings removed regularly. Most parasites go from pasture to horse and back to pasture again at various stages of their existence, and the trick is to break this cycle.

Photosensitivity

Extreme susceptibility to sunburn in horses with pale areas of skin, caused by eating plants such as St John's wort (*Hypericum perforatum*). Pale-skinned horses should in any case have equine sun-blocking creams applied before being exposed to bright sunlight; fields must be scoured of harmful plants. Treat as for human sunburn.

Sarcoids

Wart-like skin cancers, which can appear on any part of the horse. Extremely problematic, as little is known for certain about causes, transmission, prevention or treatment. In some horses the affliction never rises above one or two growths; if these are not in contact with tack (so they do not spread through injury), the horse is unaffected. In others, growths may be widespread (in the thousands), large, and debilitating, treatable only by euthanasia. Sarcoids are probably caused by a virus, possibly spread by flies, researchers speculate, and as the effect on individual horses is unpredictable one horse with one sarcoid may cause havoc in a yard. Or may not. No treatment is universally effective or without risk: failure of one treatment generally results in more

stables, fields and food

aggressive and numerous growths. At the first appearance, insist that your vet consults experts immediately.

Sweet itch
An intensely irritating skin disease caused by midge bites to the crest, withers and croup; hair in these areas is lost as the horse rubs himself constantly on trees or posts to relieve the irritation; in severe cases, the skin becomes ridged and oozes a yellow liquid. Washing and drying well and applying a soothing lotion treats mild cases; otherwise consult your vet. For prevention, keep horses in at dusk and dawn, when biting insects are most active.

Strangles
A highly contagious respiratory disease, most common in horses under six years old. Inhaled bacteria affect the nasal passages, enter the lymphatic system and create an abscess in the jaw. Symptoms include high temperature, nasal catarrh and difficulty in eating. Eventually the abscess bursts, and the horse recovers. Isolate the horse, keep him warm, and use eucalyptus ointment to keep air passages open. Treat the burst abscess as for a normal wound. This is one of the few equine diseases best left to run its course (about six weeks). Antibiotics may prolong or worsen it. Be sure to disinfect all tack, feed buckets, and any other equipment in contact with the horse.

Tetanus
The same disease that is also known as tetanus or lockjaw in humans, tetanus is caused by bacteria entering wounds, particularly puncture wounds from rusty metal. The horse runs a temperature, stands with nose, tail and hind legs thrust out, and the jaws may become locked. Immediate veterinary treatment is crucial to avert death. All horses should be vaccinated against tetanus and given annual boosters.

Thrush
A fungal infection of the frog of the hoof, detectable by its uniquely repulsive smell and the ragged appearance of the frog. Causes are lack of pressure on the foot, standing in unclean stables, and failure to pick out feet. Clean the frog and foot with medicated soap and water, then dry thoroughly. Dress with antibiotic lotion. After a few days apply Stockholm tar (held in place with cotton wool). Completely clean out and disinfect stables.

Avoiding a fight over food

stables, fields and food

Weatherbeat (rainscald)
A skin condition similar to mud fever (see above), but affecting the back, flanks and hindquarters, especially of horses living out in persistently wet conditions. Wash and dry affected areas and treat with antibiotic ointment.

Wounds
Treat as human wounds – wash with cold salt water, dry, and sprinkle with antibiotic powder if more than skin-deep. Most minor wounds are best left to heal themselves. If the horse gets a puncture wound and is not up-to-date with tetanus immunization, watch the animal carefully. Wounds so deep that bone, ligament or tendon shows, or if blood spurts violently (meaning a cut artery), need urgent veterinary attention. Do not worry about bleeding otherwise, as long as you have cleaned the wound: the blood will soon clot. Protect a large or long wound with a dressing, and try to keep the horse out of flies' way until a scab is fully formed.

A group of horses kept out will get into a tussle over supplementary rations of hay, and the one who's lowest in the social scale can end up getting very little to eat. Avoid this by putting out several heaps of hay – at least one heap more than the number of horses. They will mill around for a while, sorting out who's to feed at which heap, but will soon be quiet, and end up with fair shares all round.

116

CHAPTER FOUR

Partners

Riding involves much more than sitting on a horse and getting used to doing several things at once. Here is a guide to what to do before, after, and while you ride.

The heart of this chapter is about riding, but before you ride you need to groom the horse - and afterwards as well. Both you and he also need to be properly attired. Then you're ready to start riding.

Grooming a horse, even lightly, isn't just a matter of making him neat and gleaming, although there's nothing wrong with that. It puts you in intimate contact with this large, warm creature, so that you know every centimetre of his body, immediately pick up on even minor injuries or ailments, and get a feel for his condition, fitness and moods - which can be a good clue to any internal pain. In turn, he becomes acquainted with you and used to you handling him, which builds up the mutual trust and tolerance between you.

GROOMING BEFORE GOING OUT

Always groom a horse before putting on his tack and riding him, even if you're going no further than the arena. Most importantly, you'll need to clean out his feet, a task made much easier if the horse has been trained to lift them for you (see 'Picking out feet').

Begin brushing off mud and stains with a body brush, following the lie of the coat. cleaning the brush by scraping it across a curry comb after every five or six strokes. Use a dandy brush if he's caked with mud - but not on his face. If the weather is cold, and the horse is wearing a rug, fold it back halfway and clean up his front; then fold it forward to clean up his rear half. Make absolutely sure there is no mud or muck at any point where tack will touch the horse. Finally, clean the eyes and nostrils with a damp (not running wet) sponge. Use a separate, dedicated sponge for the dock of the tail, and unless you trust the animal absolutely, stand to one side to use it.

If the horse lives out, this is as much grooming as he'll need before and after being worked. His skin should be in good fettle and you don't want to remove the natural oils from his coat, as they keep him warm and dry. After riding, get mud off with the dandy brush, using a body brush only on the mane, tail and face. Sponge him on the body only in hot weather and/or after work, when he may have sweated, particularly under the saddle.

GROOMING AFTER WORK

After working the horse, as beforehand, check his feet first and remove any accumulated mud, stones and so on. Next, use a dandy brush to clean mud, sweat or scurf from unclipped parts of the coat.

Now, go to work with the body brush. Flop his mane onto the side away from you and brush down his crest. Then take a lock of the mane at the head end and brush out the ends to clean and disentangle them; then sort out the roots. Work your way along the mane in the same way. Be gentle, but be thorough. When brushing the body, too, keep up a firm pressure, which horses prefer to over-tender treatment. You'll know if you put on too much pressure, because the horse will lean back into it. Always brush in the direction the coat lies, and start at the poll and work back and down (neck, body, then legs), first on one side, then the other. Keep the brush clean with a curry comb. Brush out the tail, starting at the top with the ends of a few hairs at a time and then cleaning and straightening the roots, as you did with the mane. When this is done, use the body brush carefully on his head. You should be able to do this with the head collar off, steadying the horse's head with your free hand; if he shuffles about too much (particularly when grooming in the open), buckle the collar loosely around his neck. Complete the whole process by sponging his eyes and muzzle and the dock of the tail. Throughout, talk amiably to the horse, and stroke him – your sense of touch will sometimes tell you better than your eyes if he's got an odd lump, cut, abrasion or other tender spot that needs attention, and will always tell you more about the state of his muscles.

Washing or, worse, shampooing a horse is an intolerably lazy way of grooming, is no way to keep his coat in good condition and, unless the weather's very hot indeed, risks giving him a chill. Washing removes the oils in his coat and soaks it right through to the skin, which rain will not. Unclipped horses in their winter coats should never be washed. This is not, however, the same as sponging down or sprinkling a very hot horse with water to cool him off after hard work. Then, you should first let his breathing and pulse come back to normal. Lightly sponge or sprinkle him with lukewarm water, particularly in his armpits and high up under his hind legs, and then take off the water with a sweat scraper. Lead him around until he's dry – put a rug on him in cold or windy weather – before turning him out into the field or putting him back in the stable.

BEFORE RIDING: RIDING GEAR AND TACK

Riding gear

Before riding, you'll need to change into riding clothes. The absolute essential here is a safety helmet or skull cap with a securely fitting strap. This really can save your life. Footwear is important too: boots are better than shoes since they give more protection to your ankles, and they should have a definite heel to stop them sliding through the stirrups.

After that, there are any number of conventions about how to dress, depending on the kind of riding you do, but the greatest wear and tear on you will be on your legs and seat. Whatever covers your nether regions should not have an inner seam, or you'll end up feeling very sore, especially if you ride in an English saddle. Jodhpurs are designed for painless riding; you can also buy seamless jeans for Western riding.

Tack

The horse's equipment for riding breaks down into three basic parts: the bridle and reins, the saddle and the stirrups. There are many variations in tack and its fitting and, as ever, a plethora of strongly held opinions on every aspect of the subject. Only the

partners

The basic grooming kit

A basic grooming kit includes all the items as shown below, however, it will almost certainly expand to suit your own needs. The esssential items are: bucket (A), sponges (B) for face and body, water brush (C). sweat scraper (D), dandy brush (E), body brush (F), plastic curry comb (G), metal curry comb, (H) and the all-important hoof pick (I).

essential elements of English and Western tack are considered here, along with some of the additional gadgetry you might see used on a horse.

Hogging the mane

Hogging means clipping off the whole mane. Polo ponies, Norwegian Fjord horses, Icelandic ponies and some cobs and Western American horses are traditionally hogged. Some very hairy horses that are worked hard are more comfortable clipped, even in summer, and hogging can look very elegant.

English Tack

If you're learning the English style of riding, your horse will probably wear a simple bridle with a snaffle bit. It consists of a headpiece, which fits behind the horse's ears, a browband to prevent the headpiece slipping back, a noseband, which fits around the nose, a throatlash, and a bit, with a pair of reins fastened to the bit rings at one end and buckled together at the other.

The saddle will usually be a standard general purpose (GP) saddle. Attached to it will be stirrup leathers and stirrups, and a girth. In its original form the saddle was little more than something from which to hang the stirrups; indeed some people teach children to ride with just a saddle pad rather than a conventional saddle, so that they learn the feel of a horse from a very early age. Beneath the saddle is a numnah, made from sheepskin, cotton or some type of synthetic material; this protects the horse's back and keeps the saddle clean. The girth holds the saddle in place and may be made of leather or of some form of fabric, which is sometimes elasticated.

Stirrups are attached to adjustable stirrup leathers that hang from the saddle. Stirrups aren't just metal loops to keep your feet from flapping about and stop you falling off. Carefully adjusting your weight in them is part of controlling what the horse does. Make sure they are wide enough for your feet to move in and out easily: you should have a gap of about 1cm (½in) each side of your boot.

There are different styles of saddle for different sports and disciplines – dressage, showjumping, and so on – but if you're buying your first saddle, it's best to choose a general purpose one. There's little point in buying a dressage saddle only to find that you love jumping, or vice-versa. There is little to be said either for buying a new leather saddle. First, they are very expensive and, second, it takes a long time for the leather to soften to a comfortable point. Used leather saddles are widely available, but do make absolutely sure the one you choose fits your horse (see 'Fitting a Saddle And Bridle'). If you can't find a suitable used leather saddle, you could try a synthetic one. These are

partners

Equine anatomy

The skeleton is the essential framework of the horse, which is powered by the muscles. This diagram shows clearly how the horse is actually structurally weak along its back. Yet the rider sits over the lowest part of the spine, at its very weakest point. For this reason, it is not sensible to work horses until their bones are fully developed, hard and strong. Excessive work can irreparably damage the skeletal structure of a young horse.

Muscles in the horse, as in all mammals, are connected to bones by tendons. The blood supply to the tendons is relatively poor, which means that when damaged they heal slowly. Warming the horse up before work and cooling down afterwards avoids that damage. The most important muscles in the horse for the rider are those on which she sits: these must be strengthened through a careful fitness programme to let the horse carry weight easily and without pain.

How different bits work

A selection of standard bits.

A: A loose ring french link. The double jointed action of the french link is softer than that of the single jointed snaffle.

B: An eggbutt snaffle. It has the same action as the loose ring but the smooth side joints prevent possible pinching.

C: A kimblewick. This is a single rein pelham and is commonly used on strong ponies.

D: A vulcanite pelham. This puts pressure on on the poll (not the mouth) to lower the head, and should be used with two reins.

E: A bridoon and a curb. The bridoon acts like a snaffle, while the curb bit encourages the horse to soften through the poll.

F: A cowboy snaffle. This acts primarily on the poll and can be used by anyone, from beginners to professionals.

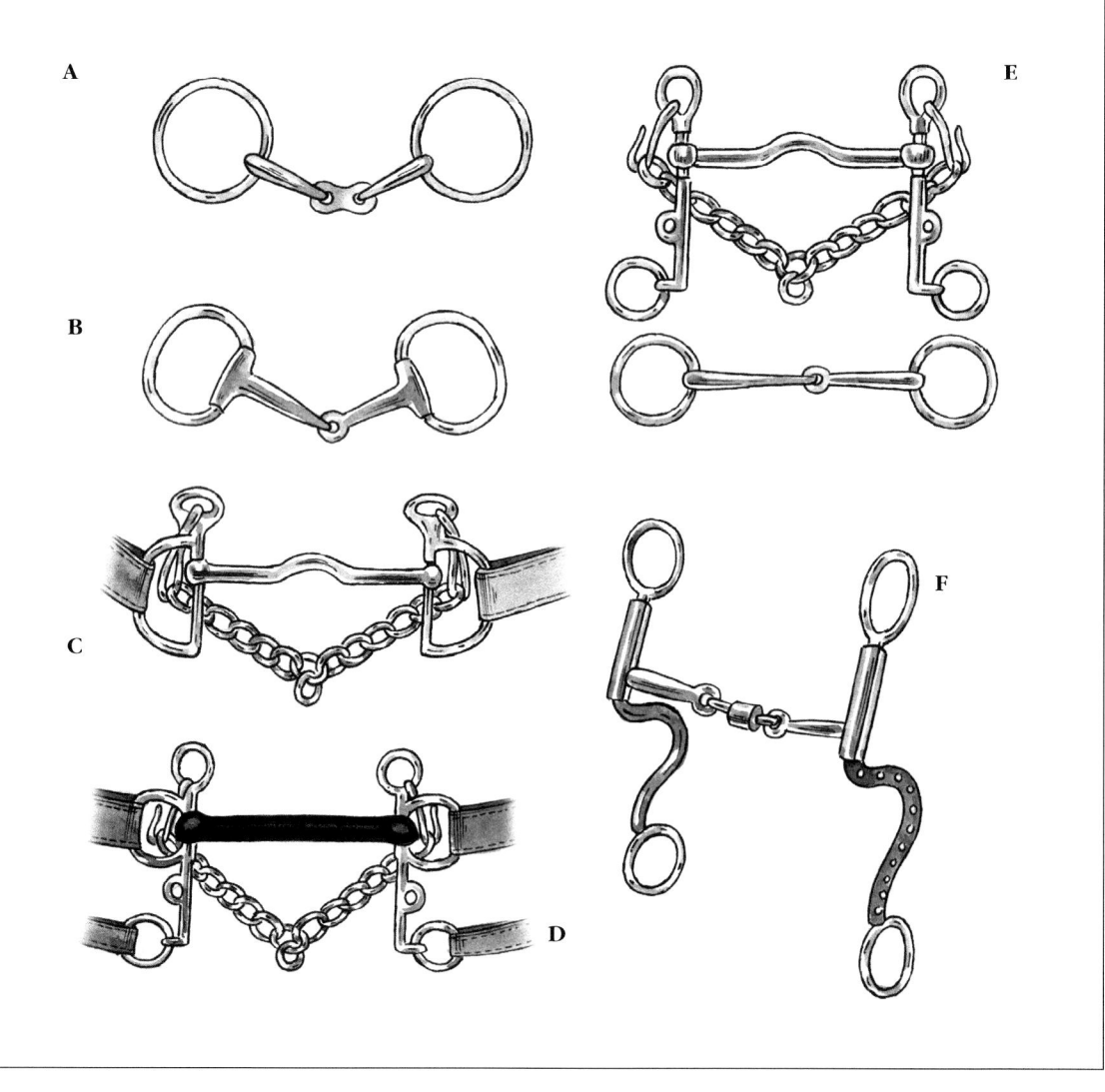

relatively cheap and easy to clean, and in some the size of the tree can be adjusted so the saddle will fit your horse even if he changes shape. Some modern saddles (both leather and synthetic) have an airbag system instead of the traditional flocking (stuffing) in the saddle panels; in some the airbags can be inflated or deflated as your horse changes size. The great advantage of these systems is that they spread the pressure of saddle and rider evenly along the horse's back. But be warned: some horses who've been ridden in a saddle with air suspension will then refuse point-blank to work in a standard flocked one.

Western Tack

If you're learning to ride Western style, the bridle your horse will wear will be much the same as an English one, but may not have a noseband or a throatlash (and some have neither). Western riders favour the cowboy snaffle bit, which is usually used with two pairs of (double) reins. Western reins are not joined as English ones are, so that they can be dropped and hang down to the ground without risk of the horse getting tangled in the loop.

The saddle will probably be a standard Western trail saddle, usually of plain leather (tooled leather is mostly reserved for the show ring). Western saddles were designed for cowboys who spent all day on horseback, and they differ from English saddles in a number of ways. The most obvious is the horn (extended pommel) at the front, used in roping, and the deep, chair-like seat. Instead of a numnah will be layers of blankets, with their number and thickness adjusted to ensure the best fit of the saddle on the horse. Although heavier than an English saddle, the Western type is less tiring for the horse, as the weight of both saddle and rider is spread over a larger area of his back. On the other hand, a Western saddle doesn't give such close contact as an English one, so the

rider's awareness and control of the horse are less subtle. Western stirrups are somewhat different in style from their equivalents on English tack - they are broader, deeper and padded - but they fulfil exactly the same functions.

Cleaning Tack

Whatever sort of saddle and bridle you use, the most vital thing to get right is their fit (see 'Fitting A Saddle And Bridle'). It's also most important to give it proper care. You should clean your tack every time you use it, not only to remove dried sweat and mud and nourish the leather, but also to check wear and stitching: you don't want to be cantering across a field and suddenly have a rein break or a girth give way. You don't need to take tack apart every time you clean it: just removing the sweat from the bridle will reduce the risk of your horse getting sores. When you clean tack, always swap over your stirrup straps. Few people have legs of exactly the same length, so the straps tend to stretch to different lengths from constant use. Swapping them over helps to keep them even.

Numnahs, saddle blankets and girths too should be washed or cleaned regularly. This is when fabric girths come into their own. It's vastly less arduous to hurl one into the washing machine than to scrub away at a leather girth.

THE TROUBLE WITH GADGETS

Some people will always try to take a short cut with horses. They will try to force a horse to do something instead of ask him, and insist that something is done now, rather than wait until he becomes strong enough to do what is wanted. (Rarely will they consider that the horse isn't cooperating because he is in pain, or just being ridden badly.) This is when riders resort to gadgets - additional, usually restrictive, bits of tack.

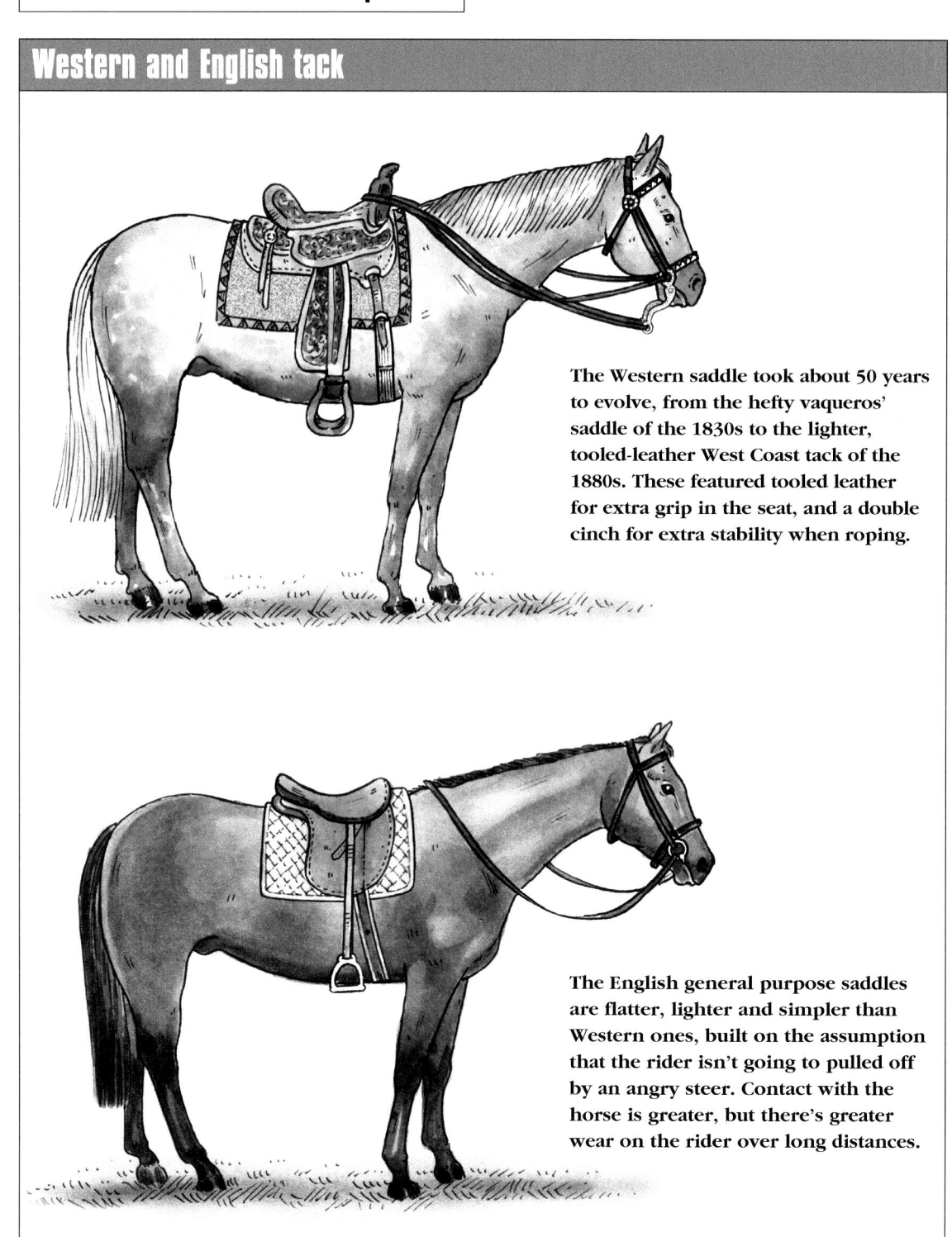

partners

Western and English tack

The Western saddle took about 50 years to evolve, from the hefty vaqueros' saddle of the 1830s to the lighter, tooled-leather West Coast tack of the 1880s. These featured tooled leather for extra grip in the seat, and a double cinch for extra stability when roping.

The English general purpose saddles are flatter, lighter and simpler than Western ones, built on the assumption that the rider isn't going to pulled off by an angry steer. Contact with the horse is greater, but there's greater wear on the rider over long distances.

Among the most common gadgets are draw reins. These are attached to the girth and pass up through the bit into the rider's hands, so that they pull the horse's head down towards the girth and make him appear collected. However, if the horse doesn't have sufficient neck muscle to maintain the shape, the strain eventually causes the line of the neck to break between the fourth and fifth vertebrae. The neck isn't actually broken, but comes to an ugly point where weak muscle tissue has collapsed. Once this has happened, it cannot be made right: the damage is irreversible. Draw reins, in short, are best avoided.

Martingales are not usually classified as gadgets, but they too can have a negative effect on the horse if misused. A martingale consists of one strap that buckles around the horse's neck and another that attaches to the girth at one end, passes through the neck strap, and either attaches to the noseband (standing martingale) or divides into two and attaches to the reins (running martingale). The running martingale is commonly seen on showjumpers, to stop the horse raising his head above the level of the rider's hand. To fit correctly, the ring on the end of each strap (when not on the rein) should reach to the top of the withers. Then the martingale will not obstruct the line of the rein and will come into play only when absolutely necessary. Too often the martingale pulls the rein down, creating a kink in it. This is unhelpful for both horse and rider as it blocks the mouth-to-hand connection between them. Standing martingales are more rarely seen, except on polo ponies, who all wear them (more from convention than necessity). They are used mainly on horses who throw their heads so high that they can hit their riders in the face, or on habitual rearers. If your horse does either of these things, it would be better to get his back and teeth checked, than simply strap his head down.

Gadgets should only be used kindly, as a temporary measure, with expert guidance, and for the horse's benefit. They are no substitute for correct training, intelligent riding and proper horse care. It is always better to ask why a horse is behaving in a certain way, than to ask how you can strap him down to stop him doing it. A horse who seems to be making trouble for his rider is usually only doing his best to tell her that something's wrong.

THINKING ABOUT RIDING

The best way to learn to ride is to sit on a bareback pony or small horse as early in life as possible, and learn, as only open-minded children can, how to adapt your body to the horse's movements. If you take up riding later on, it is still best to start by riding bareback on a placid animal (with someone on the ground guiding the direction and speed of the horse). The overwhelming advantage of starting like this is that it teaches you to ride from your seat and the legs; the reins, when you get some, are a luxury. Unfortunately, such is the litigious nature of the age, riding schools and instructors are very unlikely to let you get on a bareback horse, for fear of being sued should you fall off and be injured. Indeed their insurance companies probably forbid it. What follows, then, assumes that you're starting with a tacked-up horse, equipped with saddle, stirrups, bridle and reins.

There are scores, if not hundreds, of books that try to teach people how to ride. Few of them entirely agree, and some give advice so dissimilar they might have been written by people living on different planets. Even fewer approach the most remarkable fact about riding – that horses allow people to sit on their backs at all – from the horse's point of view. No book can deal with the idiosyncrasies of individual horses and riders – that is why one needs an instructor. Standard phrases for basic manoeuvres, such

partners

as 'allowing with the rein', 'letting your weight down through your legs', and so on, don't mean much until you know what they feel like, and getting your body to carry them out is more like acquiring a knack than a matter of following step-by-step instructions. Yet, despite these drawbacks, there is some use in reading about how to ride.

For, while there's no substitute for the real thing, you may find some essential principles of riding only in books, because surprisingly few riding instructors communicate them before getting down to nitty-gritty details. Some instructors have been around horses so long they've forgotten them; some think they're too obvious to mention; some have never heard of them; and some instructors regard horses (and their pupil riders) as slaves to be driven. If your instructor falls into the last class, find another one, someone who is prepared to discuss basic principles with you as well as focus on the details.

The approach taken here is consistent with everything else in this book. If you ride a horse so that everything you ask him to do – from letting you get on his back to the most complex and spectacular dressage display – seems natural to him, he will cooperate with you to the best of his ability, even when you really challenge him to stretch himself. Together, you will become a great partnership. This not only means knowing what's right and natural for the horse: it calls for great self-discipline,

Styles of stirrup iron

The heavy-duty rubber band on 'Peacock' safety stirrups (top left) flicks off to let the foot escape easily if the rider comes off the horse. Bent-leg or Australian stirrups (bottom) also allow an easy escape. Standard stirrup irons are shown at top right.

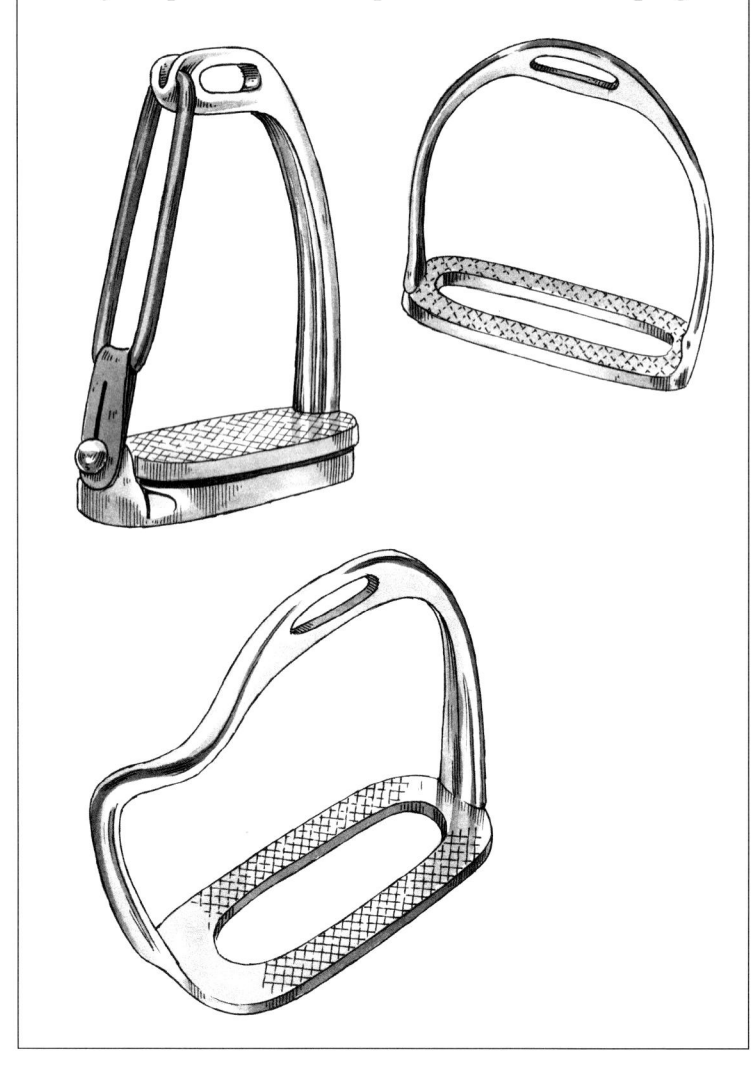

partners

Grooming with a body brush

Grooming with a body brush before or after work (cleaning it as you go with the curry comb in your spare hand) not only lifts scurf and dust out of the horse's coat, but gives you the opportunity to check for wounds, bites and abrasions. Horses like the attention, too, and so this necessary job helps to strengthen the bonds between him and you.

consistency and practice in you the rider, along with some imagination, because what's right for the horse is sometimes not obvious or intuitive to a human being, until you begin to get a feel for the horse's way of doing things.

Take, for example, the use of the reins. Horses, in their saintly way, will always

partners

try to do as they're asked. But they can only work within the limits that nature has imposed on them. If you pull on the reins, they will try to stop. (If they're already standing still, they'll step backwards, even though they don't like doing it.) If you press in with your legs and push forward with your seat, they'll go forwards. Novice, which generally means a bit nervous, riders tend to do all these things at once, usually without realizing it. People tense up and hang on to things when they feel in physical danger, and nearly every beginner is afraid of falling off a horse – the ground usually seems a very long way off. So the reins become a source of security. Your legs are doing the same as your hands – hanging on for safety's sake. At the same time you're almost certainly clenching your buttocks, creating a forward movement in your seat. The poor horse is utterly confused: asked to stop at the front, and driven forward from behind. Whatever he does, he will be deeply uncomfortable, physically and psychologically (unless he just tries to buck you off to relieve his confusion). Some people ride like this all the time, and as a result, besides creating deep-seated muscular problems in the horse, they hatch emotional chaos in him too.

This is one reason why, if you can't start bareback, you should learn to ride from the seat, with long stirrups and loose reins. Once you can get a horse to follow your wishes by using your seat and your legs, perhaps with some help from your voice, the reins become no more than gentle reinforcements, reminders, of what you want. You still have to learn not to grip overmuch with your legs, but if you get your posture right in the first place this won't be too difficult. Above all,

Fitting a saddle and bridle

Always find an expert to fit a saddle to your horse. Initially it should be fitted without a numnah or saddle blankets. There are several points to look for when choosing a saddle. They include:

- The saddle tree must be the correct width. You should be able to fit your fingers between the pommel and the horse's withers once seated. If the tree is too wide, the pommel arch will sit on the withers; if it is too narrow, the arch will pinch the spine.
- There should be a clear channel between the saddle and the horse's spine.
- There must be no weight on the loins.
- The saddle should lie flat on the horse's back: it should not tip at either the pommel or the cantle.
- The panel stuffing should be equal on both sides and it should sit squarely on the horse's back.
- To check the fit of a bridle with a single-jointed snaffle bit, first put the bit in the horse's mouth, and then pull the mouthpiece straight. There should be about 5mm (¼in) of bit protruding either side of the mouth. Once connected to the bridle, the bit should make the horse 'smile', although it should not cause the corners of the mouth to wrinkle.
- The throatlash should be loose enough to allow a full hand's width between it and the side of the cheekbone. It must not be too tight, or it will restrict the movement of his head or, in the worst instances, his breathing.
- The browband should be loose enough to avoid rubbing on the horse's ears, but shouldn't sag in the centre.
- The noseband should allow two fingers between it and the nose. It should lie midway between the end of the cheekbones and the mouth.

partners

Putting on a bridle

Putting on a bridle becomes quick and easy with practice.
1: Gently ask the horse to open his mouth and then slide the bit inside.
2: Thread first one ear, then the other through the bridle.

3: Do up the throatlash and noseband.
4: Pull out the forelock from under the browband and check that bridle is fitting snugly, but not too tightly, on the horse.

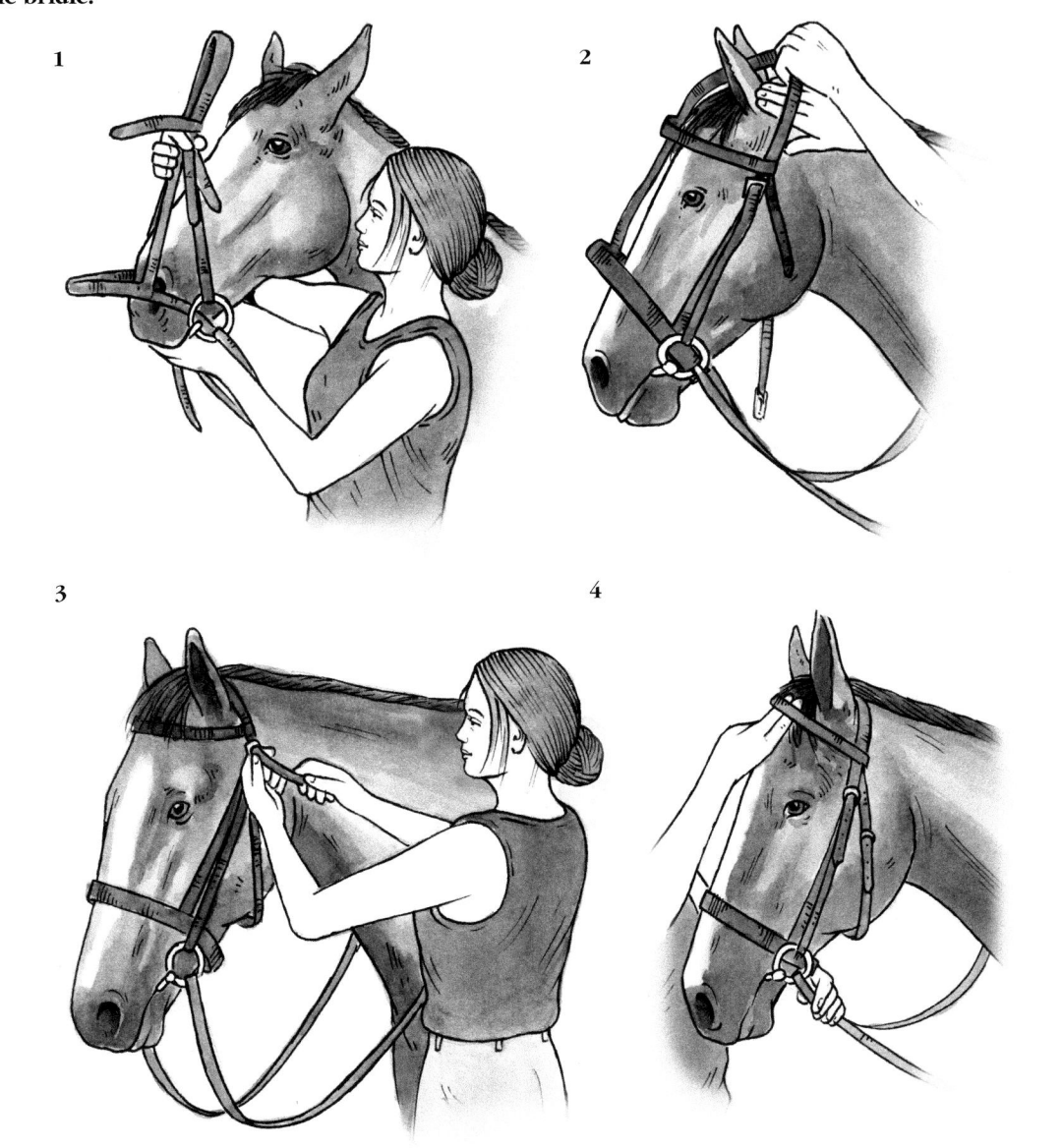

1

2

3

4

partners

Saddling up

First smooth down the coat, front to back (the direction it lies). Next, hold the numnah over the withers and slide it down and back into position (just behind the withers) so that the coat remains lying flat and unruffled underneath it.

Then lift and place the saddle straight down on the numnah. It's better to be a fraction too far forward, to keep the coat flat when you make a final adjustment. Finally, attach the girth on one side, and tighten from the other.

don't worry about falling off. The ground really isn't that far away. If you do come off, unless you're completely out of luck the damage to your pride will be a lot worse than any injury to your body. Even then you can console yourself with the old horseman's adage: you can't call yourself a rider until you've come off a horse at least seven times.

MOUNTING

First of all, you have to get on your horse. You may need a mounting block or a leg-up from someone else to help you into the saddle, or you may be able to mount from the ground, depending on how big you and your horse are; but the basic technique is the same. You should practise how to mount from both left and right sides of the horse; there's no basic difference in the technique, just a difference in each individual's preferences. This is how to mount from the left.

Stand at the saddle, at about 45 degrees to the horse. Gather up the reins in your left hand so that the horse is discouraged from moving, and hold them over the withers. Put your left foot in the stirrup. Lightly grasp the far side of the front arch of the saddle, and think of it as a reassurance, or guide, not a prop. Then spring off your right foot so that you launch yourself both forward and across the horse. Don't pull on the saddle as you leave the ground. Instead, use your right arm to help you reach a point of balance over the horse. You should end up, momentarily, with your head somewhere beyond his neck, and your backside approximately over the saddle. Then let yourself down as gently as you can into the saddle. Find the right stirrup and get the bar on the ball of your foot. Then take up the reins in both hands. You're aboard.

This method is not quite the same as the guidance you may see printed in conventional books, but it puts less strain on the horse and involves less risk of shifting the saddle off-centre. After you've been riding for 10 minutes or so, check that the girth is still tight enough, and adjust it if need be. To do this, move your leg forward, the foot still in the stirrup, and lift the saddle flap to gain access to the girth strap. This is also an opportunity to shorten or lengthen your stirrups if you need to. Move your leg back slightly (again, keeping the foot in the stirrup) so that you can reach the buckle easily.

DISMOUNTING

Eventually you'll need to get off your horse. To get off on the horse's left side, first take both feet out of the stirrups. Gather up the reins in your left hand and let it rest on the pommel of the saddle. Swing your right leg up and behind you and follow its arc with your right arm so that your centre of gravity is, as far as possible, still over the saddle before you slip to the ground. Bend your knees as you land. If you find this too tricky, try lowering yourself down onto the saddle as you swing your right leg over the back of the horse so that you end up balanced on your stomach; then slide lightly to the ground. As in mounting, the point is to be kind to the horse by keeping your weight squarely on or over him as much as possible before you descend. Once off, run up the stirrups (see 'Leaving Your Horse Tacked Up'), and lead the horse with one hand grasping the reins under the bit.

SITTING ON YOUR HORSE

When you're sitting on a horse, you shouldn't feel as if you're sitting at all. If your body is correctly positioned and your deportment is right, the sensation is more like standing in mid-air, supported by your seat, with a horse conveniently placed between your legs. This feels rather strange to begin with, especially if your first inclination is - like most people's - to think of the horse as

Leaving your horse tacked up

For all sorts of reasons you may need to leave your horse tacked up for a short time; whenever you do so, bear in mind that if he can get tangled up in the reins, then he will. To avoid this, leave the reins lying on the horse's neck, and draw them together under his jaw. Put a couple of fingers between them and twist them until they form, in effect, a single unit (not too tight against the neck). You'll end up with a twisted rein and a gap where your fingers are. Hold the gap open, undo the throatlash on the bridle and put one end through the gap, then fasten the throatlash again. Now the horse won't be able to put his foot through the reins, or chew them.

Next, put a head collar over the bridle, checking you are not causing the horse discomfort, and hitch him up. Loosen the girth, too, for his comfort, and check that the stirrups are securely run up. To do this, push the stirrup up the inside of the leather until it is at the top, then tuck the leather through the stirrup to hold it in place.

partners

Lessons on the lunge

When starting to ride, it's useful to have your horse held on a lunge rein. You don't need to worry about steering the horse, and can concentrate on your basic riding position.

a mobile armchair. But this position is more comfortable for the horse, and for you in the long run, and gives you more control over him than any other way of riding.

This is the way to set yourself up. Your head should be in line with your hips, which should be in line with your ankles. The stirrups should be set long, at such a height that you can move your legs back and forth and in and out easily, but not so long that you lose all sense of pressure in your feet. This means your legs should be more straight than bent at the knee (compare the two illustrations), with the ball of each foot resting on the stirrup bar, and your heels down. This position also helps to keep pressure from your thighs, knees and calves off the horse without effort. Your legs should be resting against his sides, but not pressing against them. Keep your spine straight, but don't puff out your chest or your balance will go out of kilter, and you'll be sending confusing signals to the horse.

To take up the reins properly, first hold your hands out as if you were going to shake hands with someone. Then close your fingers over the reins so that, as they run up from the bit, they lie flat between your index finger and your thumb. Keep your thumb uppermost, on top of your loosely closed fist, and the flat of the rein parallel to the horizon. The length of rein between your hands should feed out between your third finger and your little finger. Now adjust your arms. Keep your

partners

elbows in by your sides, but not so close in that the reins touch the horse's neck. Adjust your grip so that your forearm and the rein make a straight line from your elbow to the bit. Now loosen the reins a little, either lengthening them or moving your elbows forward slightly. (Your elbows should now be a little forward of your midriff.) You should be able to feel the horse's mouth, but should be putting only fractional pressure on it. Remember that a competent – not even expert – rider will be able to give aids to the horse (i.e. tell him what to do) in a way that's almost imperceptible to someone on the ground. The weight of the reins and the steadiness with which you hold them are enough to let the horse know you're in charge, and minute and gentle pressure from one side or the other is enough to point him in the right direction. After all, he's done this before, even if you haven't.

Remember too that the reins are not a steering device like the handlebars of a bike, or a set of handbrakes, or a contraption to help you balance. They're there to confirm the intentions you signal with your legs, seat and voice, not as the principal guide to the steed. It's perfectly possible to ride brilliantly without reins at all. Above all, reins are not a grab-handle for emergencies or a support to keep you on horseback. Except in a few special circumstances, and certainly

Walking slow and loose

After work in the arena or at the end of a hack, let you horse stretch and relax in a slow walk to help him cool down gently.

when you start riding, if you ever get really worried about falling off, hang on to the pommel of the saddle (or the horn, on a Western saddle) for security. Even clutching on to the horse's mane is better than hauling on the reins.

You'll need someone – such as your instructor – on the ground beside you to achieve the correct riding posture. You'll know you have it right when you really do feel as if you're standing in mid-air, supported by your seat. Then, having got yourself in position, hold yourself there while slowly letting your muscles relax. Start with the neck, and release your shoulders, arms, hips, legs and feet. This is important, because when you start to walk the horse, your pelvis should be following the horse's movements – up and down, back and forth, side to side – so closely that it has almost become part of the horse, as if it were buttoned on. It can't do that if you're tense and, besides, the tension in your body will transmit itself to the horse. Once you're relaxed, try to fix in your mind what your body feels like. Then you'll be ready to walk the horse.

WALK ON!

Just as when leading the horse from the ground, say 'Walk on!' in an authoritative but encouraging voice. At the same time, give a distinct nudge forward with your hips, press in with your calves, lean forward fractionally, and 'allow' with the reins. This means taking off what little pressure you have on the reins, and you have to learn the feel of it. Besides, if you do everything else right, your elbows will more or less automatically come forward as you start the walk. If they don't, you're using the reins as a handle, and you need to relax yourself again. As soon as he's moving, take the pressure off your calves, and sit up straight.

The walk is a four-beat gait, in which the horse moves both legs on one side first, then the legs on the other side; for example, left hind leg, left fore leg, right hind, right fore, and so on. As his feet lift and fall, his back goes up and down and from side to side, and this creates what feels through the reins like a fore and aft movement of his head. You need to move your hands back and forth in time with his head, to maintain a steady contact on his mouth with the reins, no matter how loosely you're holding them. It is the change in the feel of the bit that he interprets as a signal, and at the moment you just want him going steadily and quietly in a straight line.

The difficult part (until you get the knack) is letting your pelvis follow the movement of the horse while keeping everything else in place – and resisting the temptation to grip with the legs. This isn't easy, but it will come in time. For now, you need to get your seat in tune with his movement. This makes you much easier for him to carry, as you shift your balance in harmony with the changes in his balance, and it makes riding vastly more comfortable for you. Once again, it's the changes you make in your seat and legs that direct the horse, and these are far more important (and more comfortable for him) than directing him with the reins. So by letting your pelvis follow the horse's natural movements, you give him a consistent base from which he can sense any deliberate variations in the pressure of your seat. He can then interpret these accurately and without confusion, and will do exactly what you ask.

To stop the horse – which you'll have to do sooner or later – you also have to do several things at once. Sing out, firmly and distinctly, but not aggressively, 'Whoa!' As you do, press your thighs in against his flanks. You'll feel yourself rise slightly in the saddle as a result. Keep this going – sit up really tall from the waist. As your upper body rises, you'll feel your bottom go back and as if your weight is magically going down your legs. At the same time, repeatedly close up and release your fingers on the reins as if

partners

How not to sit on a horse

These are common mistakes made by learners. The rider here isn't sitting square on the horse, so one arm is too straight, the other too bent, and the horse's head is pulled too far down and back. The rider also isn't balanced – feet are too far forward, and head and shoulders too far back – so the horse is having to drag himself along from the front.

squeezing a sponge, quickly alternating this action from one rein to the other. Don't pull on them. The little extra pressure that comes from closing your hands on the reins is all the message he needs. Take the pressure off, and release your thighs, as soon as he starts to stop.

Apart from anything else, you'll have noted that when you put pressure on with your calves, the horse responds by moving forwards (or faster); putting pressure on with your thighs slows him down.

TURNING LEFT AND RIGHT

Turning corners and going around bends involves essentially the same techniques whatever pace you're keeping. Besides doing it correctly, there is also a totally

partners

wrong way to do it, as well as a logical, but still wrong way. It's worth looking at these first, as they're very easy to confuse with the right way when you're learning.

The horse is an 'into pressure' animal. This means that if you lean on a horse, he will lean back on you. So if a horse inadvertently stands on your foot when he's facing you, it's pointless trying to shove him directly back – you have to prod him in the side. A green horse has to be trained to move away from the pressure of the leg. This is done

Correct riding posture

Here the horse is properly collected – his head perpendicular to the ground and his hindquarters working neatly underneath him, all because the rider is in the right position and therefore balanced. Head, shoulders, hips and ankle fall one beneath the other; shoulders are back, and reins and forearms form a straight line – all without tension.

A basic fitness plan

Any horse that's to be ridden has to be fit enough not just to carry his rider, but to do the work he's asked to do without strain or injury, safely. For example, building up suppleness in the joints and hardness in muscles takes weeks, even if the horse is not going to work hard. The following guide assumes he will be working hard at the end of the programme, that is, he'll be able to hunt, event, do moun-ted games, and trek or cover one of the less demanding endurance courses for about three days a fortnight. Even if you're interested only in a daily or weekly hack, or similar light work, the fitter the horse is, the better he'll do any work. At the same time, you don't want him overfed for the work he does. If he's generally kept in, he'll pop with energy; if he doesn't use that up, because he's either stuck too long in his stable or not worked enough, he'll become miserable and fractious, and anything but easy to handle. Increase feed to build up muscle and provide energy for the kind of work the horse is actually doing, and no more. Once fit, he'll need to be ridden regularly to keep him contented, not just to keep him up to par. This doesn't mean working him every single day: in both getting the horse fit and when he's in work, you should give him at least one day a week off.

The first stage in getting your horse fit should take three to four weeks; for a very unfit horse, extend this to six weeks. Start by hacking for 20 minutes at the walk, and increase this by two or three minutes every day you go out. At the end of the first week you should be out for nearly 40 minutes, and 55 minutes at the end of the second week. By the end of four weeks, you should be taking the horse out for 11/2 hours. (For a horse that starts out really unfit, continue for two more weeks until you're doing two hours daily.) At the start of the third week, trot the horse gently on the flat for a few minutes a couple of times during your ride; by the end of week four, you should be able to spend a total of a quarter of an hour trotting up hills. Don't overdo the speed, or trot for too long at a time: keep a careful eye on how much he puffs and sweats. And don't forget to vary your routes – the horse will get fed up faster than you will, if you make the same old journey every time.

Over the following three weeks, add some schooling to the walk-and-trot hacking routine. The whole should now amount to a couple of hours' work a day, six days a week; you can split this into two daily sessions. During the schooling, with the help of your instructor, concentrate on softening and suppling exercises, so that you tone up the horse's back and neck muscles. Remember to give him a few minutes' rest at least every quarter of an hour – more frequently for a young horse. In the final week of this stage, add some slow cantering on the flat for a few minutes, either in the arena or when riding out.

In the last stage, when riding out, increase the amount of cantering. Start with about 400 metres (1/4 mile), and over the next three weeks increase the distance day by day to about 1.5km (1 mile). At the end of this time you should be able to cover 1.5km (1 mile) at a strong canter (not a gallop) a couple of times a week. Take it at a gentler pace on other days – although some slow uphill work is a good idea – and continue to mix hacking and schooling. No two horses are quite the same, so don't be afraid to ask more experienced riders for advice if you're unsure what to do. The main thing is to increase the demands you make on the horse gradually, and to remember that every horse has his limit.

by adjusting the seat and hinting with the reins, so that his wish to stay balanced is stronger than his instinct to push back into pressure, and he associates particular kinds of pressure as a cue to move in certain ways. You can turn a horse to the right by putting your right foot forward of the girth and your left foot behind it, and pressing in with them: he'll lean into both and duly pivot in the right direction, but he won't make a turn that's smooth or comfortable, and his hind legs won't follow neatly and naturally in the track of his fore legs.

Note how that way of turning doesn't call for any use of the reins. The worst possible way to turn a horse (again, let's say to the right) is to pull on the right rein. This twists the horse's neck, locks up his shoulder muscles, causes you to lose contact with his mouth with the left rein, and doesn't offer him any guidance from the seat or legs. He turns right only to release the discomfort. Since misuse of the rein in this way is so common and, to be fair, perhaps seems the most obvious way to do it, this is the first thing to get right.

What you have to do is 'allow' with both reins. Then, don't pull on the right rein, but open it up - move your right hand out and forward, so that it makes an arc, as if swinging like a pendulum from the horse's mouth. This creates a slight but not uncomfortable pressure on the outside left of the horse's mouth, which he releases by turning his head to the right. Having allowed with both reins, you should have created enough slack in the left rein to let him do this without restraint.

At the same time, you should be using your seat and legs to do the real work of turning his body. If you turn your own upper body very slightly to the right, you will inevitably put extra weight on your right seat bone (but don't twist your pelvis - this will send weight down the wrong leg). You can also do this more subtly by thinking you've grown an extra centimetre on your right side at the waist. This sends weight down your leg in the same way as when coming to the halt, but this time on one side only. Now stretch your right thigh down, so that your right stirrup comes out from the girth, and press down on the ball of your right foot. Slide your left leg behind the girth, and put pressure on with your calf. The horse will move away from that. You now have him bent gently around your right (inside) leg, inexorably turning around it to the right. His apparently bent quarters will now follow through so that his hind feet step into the track of his forefeet - a tidy, elegant and entirely painless turn. To go to the left, do exactly the same using opposite reins, legs and seat bones.

GOING INTO TROT

Once you're comfortable riding the horse in walk, making turns to left and right, and confident that you can bring him safely to a stop when you want to, you're ready to try riding at different gaits (speeds) - the trot, the canter and the gallop.

The trot is a two-beat gait. The horse moves his legs on the diagonal, that is his right hind leg and left fore leg move forward together, followed by the left hind leg with the right fore. As he drives himself forward from the ground with one set of legs, he rises into the air as the other diagonal pair comes forward for the next pace, to land almost simultaneously. In English riding, most trotting is done by 'posting', or 'rising' in response to the horse's movement, in order to take weight off the horse's back at the moments when his feet are off the ground. You shouldn't actually rise straight up, but move the pelvis gracefully forward out of the saddle and back into it, while your head and shoulders should stay on the same plane. Some people take years to get this right, so don't worry if you don't get the hang of it instantly.

partners

To move into the trot from the walk, squeeze with the calves and, in a brisk, encouraging tone, call 'Trot!', while allowing with the reins and leaning forward fractionally. All this needs to be done with a bit more oomph than when you set the horse off walking. Keep the reins soft – you don't want to jab him in the mouth with the bit, even accidentally. If you've got the knack of letting your pelvis absorb the horse's movement at the walk and become one with it, you should be able to feel (as well as hear)

Rising to the trot

In the rising trot you should tip the pelvis forward slightly and be swinging it up and forward out of the saddle, so that your head and shoulders don't bob up and down. Keep the reins shorter than at the walk, but don't increase the tension on them. Don't hang on with your legs once you're up to speed – the horse will just speed up more!

partners

when he rises off the ground. You should absorb that upward thrust, and glide forward with it, just clearing the saddle, then flow back into the saddle with the pelvis tipped slightly forward and your shoulders a little ahead of upright as well. This should bring you lightly back into the saddle ready to be lifted comfortably up and forward by the motion of the horse on the next pace. The trick here is to be directed by the horse's body (so you naturally tip forward a little), not try to sit upright and heave yourself up and down in the stirrups. Doing this makes your whole body bob up and down inelegantly, and puts a downward thrust onto the animal just when he needs you to lighten his load. Besides

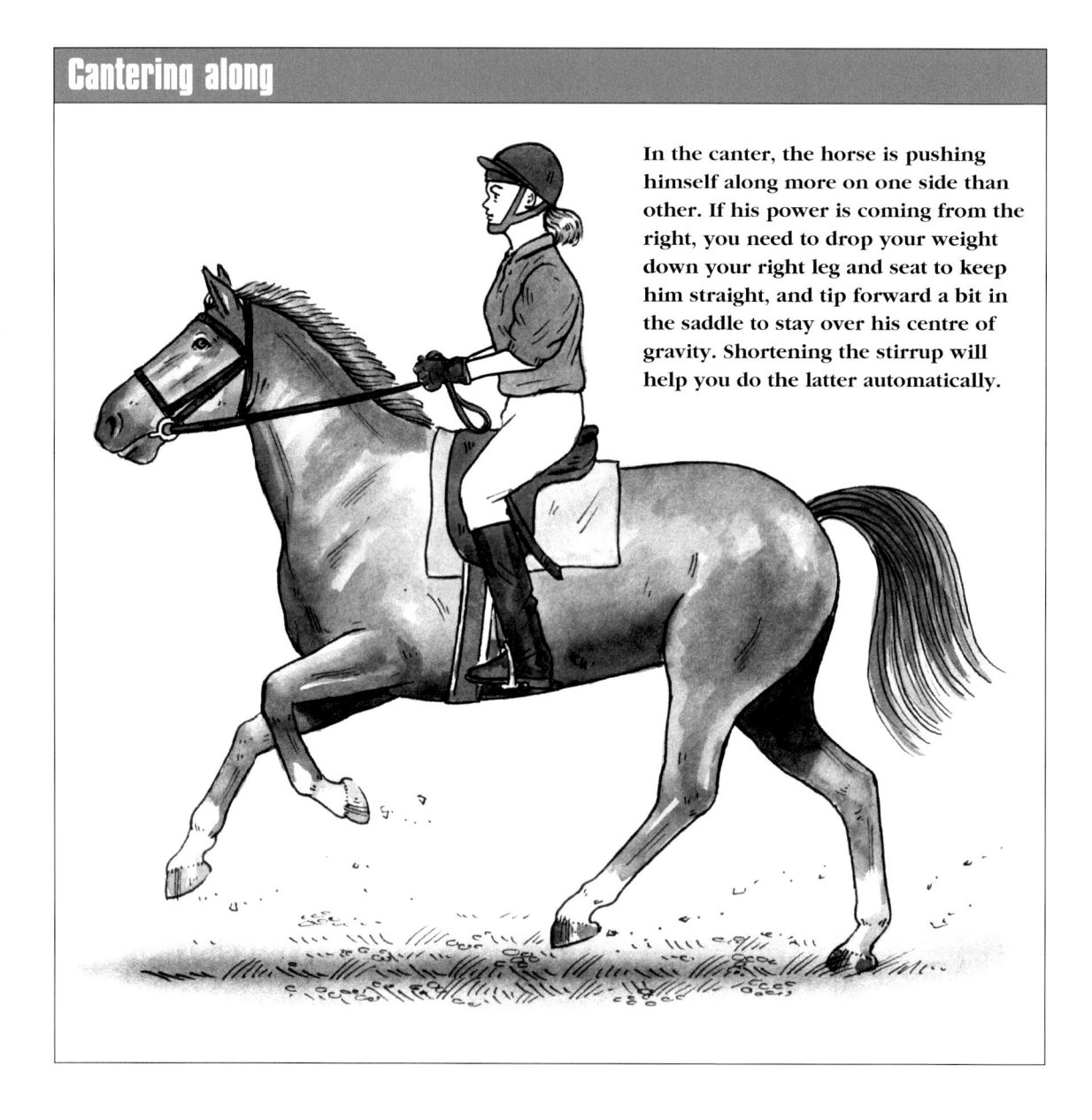

Cantering along

In the canter, the horse is pushing himself along more on one side than other. If his power is coming from the right, you need to drop your weight down your right leg and seat to keep him straight, and tip forward a bit in the saddle to stay over his centre of gravity. Shortening the stirrup will help you do the latter automatically.

which, you end up banging up and down on the saddle, which is painful for both you and the steed. It's easy to let the pelvis tip back as you come back into the saddle, too, which is also painful for both of you. Don't be persuaded by traditionalist instructors that keeping your pelvis upright at all times is a good idea: you can now see why not.

The sitting trot is the only kind of trot for anyone riding in a Western saddle, since you can't glide forward out of it without engaging in some agony as you encounter the horn. Essentially what you do is follow the horse's movements in the same way as when rising to the trot, lightening his load when he's in suspension (in the air), but without losing contact with the saddle. The important thing is never to think of the sitting trot as sitting still - you'll just bounce all over the saddle. Remember how, in the walk, you let your pelvis move both back and forth and up and down, tipping at different angles with the undulations of the horse's back. In the sitting trot you need to follow the horse in the same way, while at the same time trimming your weight to keep you both in balance.

If you go into the trot when, for instance, the horse's left hind leg and right fore leg are coming forward, then you should move your left hip forward enough to feel your left seat bone pivot on its front edge. As you do this, you flex your back forward as the horse rises, so that your weight (and balance) are keeping pace with his; meanwhile, your back is bending to absorb the upward thrust in his hindquarters. By the time he touches down your spine should be straight again. Then, as the right hind and left fore legs come forward, flex your back again and this time rotate your right hip; then straighten up again.

When learning both rising and sitting trot, it's a good idea to do just a few paces at a time at first while you pick up the horse's rhythm, and increase the number of paces as you get the hang of what to do. If you get your seat, timing and balance right, your horse will naturally collect - have his head down and his hind legs underneath him - and won't need holding in place through pressure on the reins. You will feel him soften and relax as the two of you come into harmony. Once you have mastered the gait, you can shorten the reins a little so that when you want to slow, turn or stop, your aids on the rein will be clear.

At first, coming back into walk from trot may be bumpy, but will become smooth and swift as you and the horse adjust to each other. From the sitting trot, close up and release your fingers on alternate reins, as when going from walk to stop. Don't pull back. Put pressure on with your thighs. At the same time, progressively slow the flexing and straightening of your spine. The horse will keep his quarters under him and his head down, and adapt to your new rhythm by adjusting his balance under you, until finally he's walking.

From the rising trot, close and release your fingers on alternate reins and simply progressively slow your forward movement from the saddle, and close your thighs as you come back to it. Again, he will adjust to your new rhythm in order to stay balanced.

In both these downward transitions (changes of pace), release the pressure from your hands and legs as soon as he responds, and put your body back into walking mode - sitting upright, pelvis moving as if part of the horse. Now here is the really subtle part. Having asked for a walk, you need to alert yourself to the horse's own sense of rhythm as he responds to your aids, so that in turn you respond correctly to him. Ultimately, you will both make the change in a single flowing movement, with the result that the horse exudes the same aura of energy in the walk as he had in the trot. Achieving this, known technically as riding forward into a slower gait, is a matter of lots of practice and concentration. For now, learning to get in time and in tune with his reactions is an invaluable first step in feeling your way into what's going on in the flesh and bones and brain beneath you. Once you learn to identify with the horse in this way all the time, you should be able to do almost anything as a rider, because you and your mount will be thinking and moving as one.

In coming down from trot to walk the commonest mistake is for the rider to sit down and upright into the saddle, in one go, keeping too much pressure on the reins. This tends to pull the horse's head up, while you give him a bang in the back, putting him off his stride completely. He may just grind to a halt. At best he'll jog – a kind of frustrated or half-hearted trot that's remarkably uncomfortable for you, the rider. By cueing him in the way described here, you create a smooth transition using the seat and legs (as your weight acts on his sense of balance) and don't confuse him by misapplying the reins.

THE CANTER

Like some people who always take stairs three at a time, horses like to get uphill slopes over with as soon as possible, and naturally canter up them. Learning to canter on a short, clear uphill section of one of your hacking routes is thus a good idea. The horse is going at a pace that makes sense to him, and when he gets to the top he's ready to stop and look around. While he's doing what comes naturally, you can get used to the new gait, and you needn't worry about him running away with you. Some people find cantering a trifle alarming at first; some take at once to its long stride, exhilarating rhythm and floating sensation. If you get yourself in tune with the horse from the start, and set off right, you'll be among the latter, and have no problem enjoying the countryside flying by for a while.

The canter is a three-beat gait, and there is a slightly sideways feel to it. The horse goes into canter by pushing off on one hind leg or the other – let's say the left. The left fore leg and right hind leg follow through and hit the ground together, and then the right fore leg touches down. As that leg leaves the ground, the left hind leg comes forward, so that, briefly, the horse has no feet on the ground. Curiously enough, this is known as leading off the right fore leg, despite the initial launch coming from the left hind. To the rider it feels as if the horse is leading with the whole right side of his body, hence the slightly skewed feeling to the gait – although in the general excitement of doing this for the first time you can be forgiven for not noticing it just yet.

If you're going to learn cantering on a short slope, first shorten your stirrups by a hole or two. As you put your heels down, this will make you tip forward slightly, so that you stay perpendicular to the horizon as the horse goes uphill. If for some reason things get bumpy, the shorter stirrups also make it easier for you to lift forward out of the saddle a bit – easing things for the horse, too. Before setting him off, shorten your reins a little too. Remember, this doesn't mean increasing the pressure on them.

An experienced horse – the kind you should be learning on – will recognize the aids you give and will go effortlessly from walk to canter. For your part, you must make the aids from your legs and seat crystal clear. To lead off the right fore leg, do the following. First, drop your right knee a little so that your weight is shifted slightly onto your right seat bone. The stirrup leather should be hanging vertical alongside the girth. This leg will support his right side and keep him on track. Sing out 'Caaan-ter!'. That last note should come as the horse's left hind foot touches the ground. (You'll need your instructor to call out the footfall sequence until you get the hang of it.) Simultaneously,

partners

Inner conflict for the horse

Sitting correctly and using your seat and legs as your main riding aids will let the horse collect himself naturally. Here, pulling on the reins and driving with the seat are giving the horse conflicting messages – stop, and go forward, at the same time. Confusion reigns, throwing the rider into a skewed posture that gives even less control.

give a slight nudge with your hips, lean forward a fraction and allow with the reins, and move your left leg back to put a brief, distinct pressure on his side, a handsbreadth behind the girth. This is his signal to go.

Once he's off, keep your legs steady and in place – right leg straight down, left one just behind the girth. The canter is (and feels like) a series of leaps, and the human's natural reaction to flying through the air is to tense the back and the hands. Tense hands will check the horse, and tensing your back will make you bump on the saddle. Let your pelvis absorb the flowing movement of the bounding horse and concentrate on keeping your weight right, your legs in place and

partners

Full gallop

The gallop calls for short stirrups, a short rein, and a bit of air between you and the saddle. The horse is actually pulling himself along with his forelegs, so all this is necessary to keep you leaning forward and over his centre of gravity. If the horse is bolting, keep the reins low so that you can get his head down as soon as possible.

your heels down, and your reins not too taut. This lets the horse get on with the gait with as little interference as possible. You can then get used to the feel of the canter, and how to both maintain it and adjust to it.

The horse's natural inclination at the top of a slope will be to stop and look around. You don't want him to do this (he's not in charge), but you can take advantage of it to show you're in charge. At the top of the slope bring him down to the walk as you learned from the trot, and keep him going gently for a dozen paces before you stop.

THE GALLOP

It's unlikely that you'll be called on to do much galloping while you're learning to ride. Still, there's always the chance that a horse will bolt under you, and it's as well to know what to do, to stay on until he calms down and is ready to take notice of you again. (This rarely takes very long.) For a deliberate gallop, as for a hard canter, you would ideally shorten your stirrups. If you can't, you have to make the best of standing up in the stirrups, keeping your backside clear of the saddle, and leaning forward, with the reins fairly short. The horse hauls himself along from the front when he gallops, and this position keeps you both in balance. Keep your legs in gentle contact with his sides so that you can put pressure on with your thighs and slow him down when you want to.

If the horse is running away with you, remember that you're generally less likely to get hurt by hanging on than by trying to bail out, and that he's unlikely to go at full tilt for very far. Keep your reins low so that you can get his head down as soon as possible, but don't pull back on them. If there's space, try to turn the horse so that he's running in a circle, and then tighten the circle into a spiral until he's got nowhere to go. At the first real sign of slackening, put the brakes on firmly (as when stopping from the walk, but more powerfully). But, if you possibly can, keep him going at a trot or walk before you stop completely – you need to remind him that you're in charge, and you'll stop when you say so.

TROUBLESHOOTING

At some point, you will encounter some stroppiness from a horse when riding. Some of the most common manifestations of equine awkwardness are bucking, rearing and napping (refusing to accept your aids and go forward as he's asked). All have a multitude of possible causes. The horse might be in pain; he might be bored with what he's doing and want to be rid of you; he might not want to leave his friends at that particular moment, and nap at the yard gate; he might be testing the mettle of an unfam-iliar rider; he might buck once in a blue moon from high spirits or consistently nap because he's lost confidence in himself. To sort out a persistently evasive horse, you have to look at all aspects of his existence, from the possibility that he needs a visit from the dentist or masseur, to the fit of his tack, the company he keeps, and his programme of work. Even if his problem is deep-seated, you still need to keep him under control long enough to get off him in your own good time, and you do that in the same way you handle the occasional reaction to a fright or momentary discomfort.

Shoeing

Most horses worked on roads and very hard ground need shoeing. A few breeds have extremely hard feet and may not need shoeing at all. Shoeing is expensive – a good farrier is priceless – and shoes need to be checked or changed every month or so when the horse is in work. Don't shoe, therefore, if you don't have to. When you do, have the horse shoed hot – that is, the shoes are put on while the metal is hot so each one can be fitted precisely to the shape of the individual hoof.

Ask friends, neighbours and anyone else you know involved with horses who is the best farrier in your area, and grill them as to why they make a particular recommendation. There are no universally recognized professional standards for farriers, so their skills vary, and their views can be as much subject to fashion as they may be the seasoned product of generations of wisdom. Until you know your farrier extremely well, take a second or third opinion before agreeing to fancy or remedial shoeing.

partners

Bucking

The horse flips his rear end in the air, and both hind feet come off the ground. If this is intended to get you off, and not just a flash of passing exuberance, he'll try to get his head down between his legs. This is one of the rare occasions when you need to keep his head up: open the reins by moving your hands further apart and then pull up and back. You also need to make it harder for him to lift his rear end, so sit as far back in the saddle as you can, and lean back too. At the same time drive him forward hard with your calves or a series of kicks from the heels so that he can't pause long enough to pivot on his fore legs. Keep him moving once the bucking has stopped.

Rearing

The horse stands up on his hind legs. This is a hair-raising experience, because he can so easily topple over backwards, with calam-itous consequences to himself and his rider. This possibility is increased because one's instinctive reaction is to hang on to the reins – which only pulls him back

Lifting the feet

Horses instinctively dislike having their feet trapped or picked up: they're flight animals, and a restriction on their feet could, in the wild, mean the difference between life and death. Therefore, you have to approach the subject carefully. In essence, you have to reassure the horse that no harm will come to him if you pick up his feet – you have to get him to trust you. Training a foal usually takes two people – one to do the picking up, the other to reinforce the reassurance, and should establish the routine for life. At first, you should keep each hoof off the ground for no more than a couple of seconds, increasing the time by a few seconds daily until the foal not only stops resisting, but willingly takes up the weight of his foot for you and lets you hold it as long as you want.

A trained horse is no less instinctive than a foal, so the routine has to be the same every time. Start at the front, and stand at his shoulder. Give his crest a good scratch and natter to him. Then run your hand down his shoulder and stroke his leg firmly, going further down with each stroke until you are in a well-balanced crouch. Take the pastern in your hand so that the coronet is under your little finger. Get your upper arm just under and behind his knee to give leverage if you need it. Say, loud and clear, 'Give it up!' (Some horses will respond to just 'Give!') and sweep the foot back and up off the ground. You can then rest it on your knee, or switch it to your other hand for support, if you need to, depending on what you're doing – checking for thrush, or picking out the hoof, for example. Bear in mind that some horses never learn actually to lift their feet, even though they give them up without a murmur, and some horses (such as Shires) have very large and hefty ones.

When you've done at the front, run your hand firmly along the horse's side as you step along it and then, as before, stroke your way down to the hind foot, and pick it up as before. Put your upper arm under and behind the hock if you need extra leverage. Some manuals suggest that you can stay on one side to pick up both the horse's hind feet. Don't. It's not only compli-cated but, unless you entirely trust the horse, you risk getting kicked. Start again on the other side at the front and work back.

partners

Right and wrong ways to turn

The horse pictured at left is being asked to turn right by having his head pulled to the right. This twists his neck painfully and locks up his shoulder muscles, while you lose contact on the left rein. He will turn, but only to release the discomfort in his neck, shoulders and mouth, and the results are ungainly (his feet will be all over the place) as well as unnatural.

Giving the correct aids to make a horse turn are virtually imperceptible. This rider has put weight down her right leg and is opening up the right rein, giving the horse a firm 'pole' around which to walk. She has also turned fractionally to the right in the saddle. The horse will turn to get her seat square again. Meanwhile, she is maintaining contact with the left rein.

partners

Picking out feet

First, be sure your balance is good and the hoof is resting comfortably in your weak hand (supported on your leg if need be). Always use the hoof pick in your strong hand, and always pick out mud, muck and stones away from your body. Start at the heel in the seat of the crown and work out to the toe. The frog is the most sensitive part of the hoof, so be very careful when cleaning it – and alwasys make sure that it's clear of gunge before and after riding. Strip out everything that's stuck on the sole between the wall of the hoof and the frog, so that the hoof comes down square onto the ground. Never skimp on this job. At the same time, check that there are no loose nails or lifted clenches (bent down nail ends driven through the wall of the hoof) that need attention, and check for signs of thrush.

further. Don't let go of the reins, but lean (or lie) down on the horse's neck and try to get your forearms down and around it. Shove or pull the horse's neck sideways to put him off balance and get his front feet down, and ride him forward. If he persists in rearing, get your feet out of the stirrups and slide off him.

Napping

The horse will halt, twist and turn, or start going backwards to avoid going forward. Not to be confused with shying, which usually involves a clearly visible 'threat', such as a bag blowing across the road, when the horse simply moves his body to one side, and tilts his head, usually without warning. He will normally hesitate just before napping (and before bucking, too) and, in both cases, if you catch this hesitation in time you can often drive him forward through it. Don't ever beat him: just use the aids forcefully - that might include a few sharp taps with a whip - and make encouraging and reassuring noises. Give him lots of strokes as a reward when he responds properly. If you don't catch the hesitation and he starts to nap, try riding him around in a tight circle a few times, with lots of downward pressure on your inside leg. By doing this that, he'll probably lose concentration and stop worrying about why he napped, and accept that you're in charge – while you will have got him moving. Once you sense that he's absorbed in what he's actually doing, you can straighten up and keep him going forward.

Who's grooming whom?

It's not exactly unknown for a horse to bend around and start nibbling at the clothes on your back when you're attending to his feet. He may well do the same when you're grooming him. This can be a mild distraction but, unless he nips or bites, don't mistake it for naughtiness or him giving you some attitude. It's much more likely to be his way of showing real appreciation. In the field, horses groom one another, and best friends do so most often. You should take this gesture as a compliment. Don't punish it – he's telling you that you're one of his best mates.

FINALLY...

Riding a horse is like keeping a horse – the way to do either with the least trouble for both of you is to approach it from the horse's point of view. This isn't to recommend spoiling the animal: it's to recognize that most horses, almost all of the time, want to please; and if things make sense to them they will respond to your wishes with amazing grace, pleasure and panache. No horse looks well ridden when he's forced into place against his nature or in opposition to his mechanical structure. Likewise, no horse that's badly kept, with few opportunities to socialize and on the wrong diet, will be happy. But a well kept horse is not only happy, he's the easiest kind to ride, well mannered and eager to learn. For best results, your approaches to keeping and riding your horse both have to come from the same direction.

partners

The hoof close up

A hoof is actually a huge toenail, and without feeling. The sole is sensitive to pressure, but the softer frog at the base is extremely tender, and should be cleaned with great gentleness.

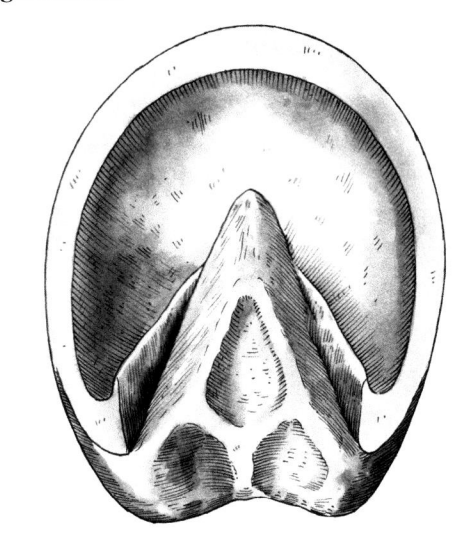

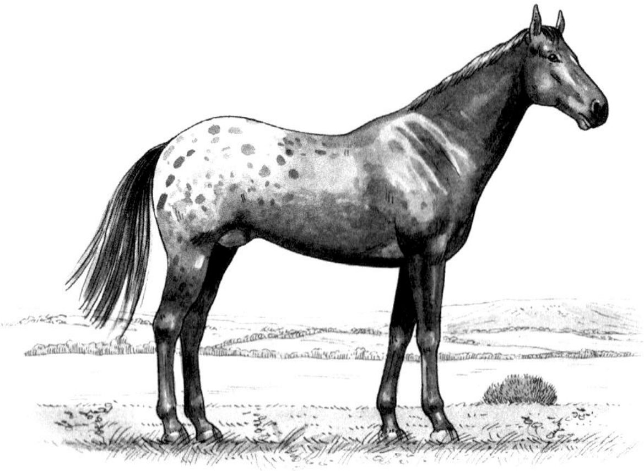

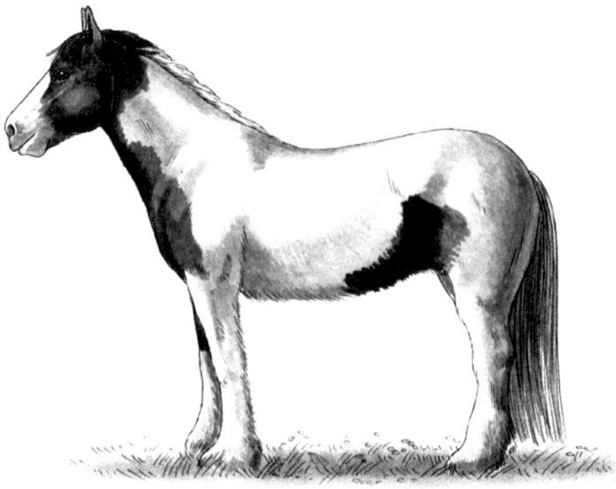

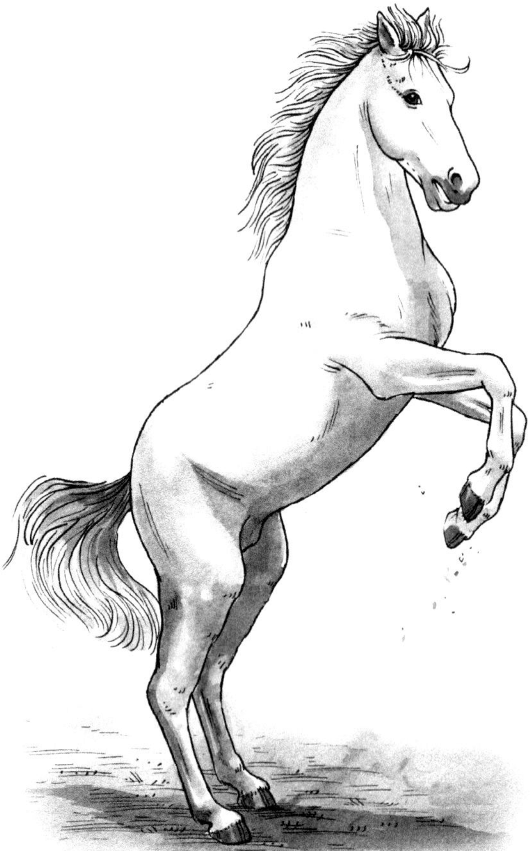

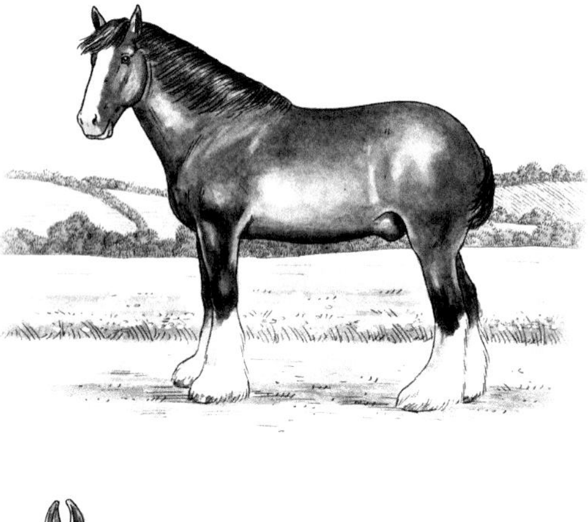

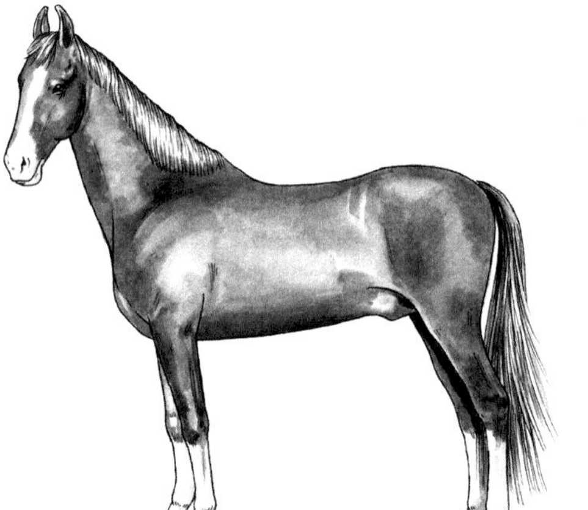

CHAPTER FIVE

Choosing a Horse

Some of the world's finest breeds of riding horses, with summaries of their history, talents, strengths, weaknesses and – perhaps most important when you're starting out – their manners and temperaments.

Here follow snapshots of 50 or so breeds that are worth considering if and when you decide to buy a horse for riding. Inevitably, only a selection of the world's horses have been included. There are many excellent European Warmbloods, for instance: they don't all appear here, but there is a brief overview of Warmbloods in general. Some of the horses described here are very rare breeds, and some are phenomenally expensive; but there's no harm in dreaming occasionally.

Breed societies set the standards for their horses' shape, proportions, musculature and size (known as 'conformation'); some also specify colour. The societies keep a record (the 'stud book' or breed register) of foals whose dam and sire are the same breed ('pure-breds'), and most will register, as 'cross-breds', foals who have only one parent who is a registered member of the breed. Some societies have closed their stud books, which means that to be accepted for registration all a foal's forebears must have been registered pure-breds. A few societies insist on testing stallions for strength, looks and character before allowing their offspring to be registered as pure-breds.

Most of the horses described here are breeds, not types. A type can be of any breed – for example, a hunter is a type of horse whose conformation makes it particularly suitable for hard, all-weather riding and jumping. Some types are classified by colour, and there are also societies devoted to these. Palominos, for example, with

choosing a horse

their pale golden coats and light manes and tails, are found in many breeds, and may be registered both with a breed society and with a national palomino society.

Equines also fall into two general categories decided largely by size - horses, which are over 14.2 hands (147cm/58in) high at the withers, and ponies, which are shorter than that, and usually also have rounder bodies and shorter legs than horses.

When you're choosing a horse, remember that these creatures are as individual as people or cats. One breed may deserve a reputation for being pushy, and another for being docile to the point of sleepiness. But the way an individual horse has been backed, trained, ridden and handled - or even fed - may have turned the one you fancy into something quite different from the usual run of the breed. Most awkward horses are like that because they're unhappy, but given love, patience and respect will sooner or later make a great partner.

Horses are not fools, and can be very playful. They're so sensitive to mood and body language that some people are convinced they're telepathic. And they like to form close bonds. Some are one-person animals - when you try out a horse he may initially resent the fact that you are not his

Akhal-Teke

One of the great Russian hotbloods, this desert horse is built to live in extreme climates, and is a champion endurance mount.

owner, and 'misbehave'. As far as the horse is concerned, he needs to find out whether you're compatible with him, just as much as you need to determine whether or not he is the right choice for you.

After casting around a bit, you will probably find yourself wanting to have more horses, and more breeds, than you've time, space or budget for. That's when the fun begins. That's the world of horses!

AKHAL-TEKE

Originally developed in the Akhal oasis region of Turkmenistan by the Teke nomads some 3000 years ago, the long, lean and graceful Akhal-Teke is one of the world's oldest distinct breeds. Desert conditions produced a horse that could thrive in extreme heat, dry cold and drought. Fresh grass was available only a few months of the year, so Akhal-Tekes had to adapt to a manmade diet, traditionally of grain stirred with mutton fat, butter and eggs; it is this that gives them their legendary stamina. Surprisingly for such a tough horse, the skin is thin as an Arab's, with silky hair; the tail is short, and some individuals have little or no mane. Unique to Akhal-Tekes is the extraordinary metallic sheen of the coat. Akhal-Tekes are naturally gentle and very observant, with a quick intelligence. Those who know them say that, if you listen to your Akhal-Teke, 'he will teach you many things.' Temperament varies from very cool to hot and highly expressive, but these horses will become mulish and bitter if treated harshly. Bred as war horses, Akhal-Tekes are renowned for their courage. They tend to bond very closely with a good owner – and show a corresponding wariness towards strangers. The heavier 'massive' strain is often easier for beginners to handle; the lighter types take an experienced rider to bring out their best performance.

- **Colours:** Golden dun, bay, chestnut; some black or grey

choosing a horse

- **Height:** 14.3-15.2 hands (150-157cm/59-62in)
- **Gaits:** Walk, trot, canter, gallop
- **Recommended for:** Endurance riding especially; dressage, eventing

ANDALUSIAN

The Andalusian is one of the most ancient horse breeds: cave paintings 25,000 years old show horses remarkably like modern Andalusians. As a war horse in classical times, it terrified foes with its natural ability to raise its fore legs very high. The modern breed was largely founded by Carthusian monks in the late Middle Ages. Its courage and cunning are still on show in the bullring. Until the 1960s, the Andalusian and the Lusitano were treated as identical in all but colloquial name; the official Spanish term *Pura Raza Española* (meaning 'the pure Spanish breed') covered both. Official rivalries then separated the registries, although the horses remain unchanged. Andalusians are lively-eyed, very strong, elegant and extremely agile. Their rounded, high-stepping action – which some call flashy – and short back let them collect easily to perform the most spectacular *Haute Ecole* dressage moves – the 'airs above the ground', in which they proceed on their hind legs or leap into the air. Even in classical times, the horse was known for its kind, trustful demeanour. Commentators on today's Andalusians call them 'eminently trainable and athletic', with a 'generous kind temperament ... a good ride for amateurs', 'trainable; generous with presence' and 'renowned for their ability to learn and their superb temperament'.

- **Colours:** Grey; some bay; more rarely, black or roan
- **Height:** 15.1-15.3 hands (155-160cm/61-63in)
- **Gaits:** Walk, trot, canter, gallop
- **Recommended for:** Dressage primarily; jumping, driving, pleasure

choosing a horse

Appaloosa

Sporting a stunning variety of patterns in their coats, Appaloosas have become one of America's favourite breeds, and have made a mark in a huge variety of equestrian sports.

APPALOOSA

The unusual spotted pattern on the coat is the Appaloosa's most distinctive feature; this horse also shows more white of the eye when calm than others do, and has mottled skin and, very often, vertically striped hooves. Appaloosas are descendants of the Spanish Jennet, the horse brought to the Americas by the Spanish conquistadores from the fifteenth century onwards. They reached the Pacific Northwest from California by way of Russian merchant seamen, who sold the horses to the Ni Mee Poo (Nez Percé) tribe; they both prized them for their own sake and used them in their sophisticated breeding programmes. White settlers called them 'a Palouse Horse' – diminutive, 'Appalousey' – which became 'Appaloosa'. When the Ni Mee Poo were forcibly relocated by the US Army in 1877, their horses were dispersed and the characteristics of the breed were in danger of disappearing; but in 1938 a band of enthusiasts dedicated themselves to preserving the Appaloosa. It is now one of the most pop-ular breeds in the USA, and can be found taking part in most equestrian sports. Today's Appaloosas are compact, strong, athletic and nimble animals, well muscled and with very hard hooves, with great stamina. They retain the character the Ni Mee Poo prized: gentle, even tempered, with an eager-to-please outlook.

- **Colours:** Five basic coat patterns (blanket, marble, leopard, snowflake and frost). No greys or pintos may be registered
- **Height:** 14.2–16 hands (147–163cm/58–64in)
- **Gaits:** Walk, trot, canter, gallop
- **Recommended for:** Trekking, trail riding, Western stock horse events, jumping, dressage; a good family horse

ARABIAN

The Bedouin tribes of the Arabian peninsula established the Arabian breed at least 18 centuries ago, and jealously guarded the purity of its bloodlines, devoting as much care to memorizing their horses' genealogies as they did to remembering their own families'. Arabians were bred for desert life and lightning-fast guerrilla warfare – and for intelligence and beauty. Europeans first saw this light, delicate, yet brave and sturdy animal when the armies of Islam swept into Spain in the eighth century, and it immediately captured their imagination. But it was not until after the eleventh century, when Christian crusaders first brought Arabian horses home as war booty,

Arabian

'It's a divine wind that blows between a horse's ears,' says an old Arab proverb; and the Arabs bred horses of amazing grace, yet indomitable strength, resolution and stamina.

that they had any real impact on European breeds. Today, all light horses show some Arabian influence: and two of the three foundation sires of the Thoroughbred line were Arabians. After a brief myopic lapse in the 1980s when some breeders produced celebrity fashion accessories that were really too hot to handle, Arabians have settled again into affectionate, tractable, if still distinctly lively horses. At least as interested in people as in other equines (which can occasionally be bothersome), they bond very closely; foals are virtually fearless and very hard to spook. Today's Arabians make good all-rounders, and absolutely excel at endurance tests, but do demand confident, not domineering, riders.

- **Colours:** Grey, chestnut, bay, roan; occasionally solid black
- **Height:** 14.2-15.1 hands (147-155cm/58-61in)
- **Gaits:** Walk, trot, canter, gallop
- **Recommended for:** Endurance primarily; dressage, jumping, driving

AZTECA

Development of the Azteca breed began in 1972 with the express intention of creating a national horse of Mexico. The Azteca is a mixture of Andalusian and Quarter Horse, with some Criollo blood, and an official breeding programme ensures that the horse remains true in the future. It was designed as both a working horse for the *charro* (Mexican cowboy), able to work with cattle and adapt to the *charro*'s intricate reining techniques, and as a sport horse. The result is a warmblood with huge courage and intelligence, combining the Andalusian's nobility, agility and natural collectedness with the strength, speed, docility and built-in 'cow sense' of the Quarter Horse. Aztecas have the densest bones of any horse, and hooves as hard as iron. They mature slowly, and should not be ridden until well into their fourth year. They are easy to train and never forget their lessons. Aztecas have a mellow, sociable and sensible disposition and relate exceptionally well to people. Prospective owners should be prepared to be entertained by a very alert and inquisitive animal. Such are the byproducts of the Azteca's acumen and eagerness to learn.

- **Colours:** All solid colours; grey and black predominate
- **Height:** 14.3-16 hands (150-163cm/59-64in)
- **Gaits:** Walk, trot, canter, gallop
- **Recommended for:** Cattle work, *Haute Ecole* dressage, jumping, pleasure riding; great potential for polo

BARB

This fiery, almond-eyed horse is also known as the Spanish Barb, and is distinct from the few remaining original pure Barb horses surviving in desert regions of North Africa. The Spanish *conquistadores* introduced the Barb, then known as the Spanish War Horse, into the Americas in the sixteenth century. This had a conformation perfectly geared to perform the strenuous, balanced leaps and kicks that were used to terrify (or kill) an enemy. Inevitably, some of these horses escaped; in due course some were domesticated, and brilliantly ridden, by native Americans. After the Spanish withdrew from North America in the nineteenth century, frontier settlers regarded the 'native' horses in the old Spanish territories as unappealing, and they were confiscated, cross-bred, castrated or slaughtered. The pure Spanish Barb, already vanished from Europe, was in danger of dying out; but since 1972 strenuous efforts have been made to back-breed the original Barb. These are hot, spirited horses, with unlimited endurance and stamina, surefooted (with very hard feet), and real sprinters over short distances. They generally call for a skilled rider to bring out their best, but they are willing and

Barb

With intelligence to match their innate fire and grace, Barbs need an experienced rider to bring out their best. Treated kindly, they respond with immense affection and loyalty.

choosing a horse

Basuto Pony

Phenomenally strong for their size, Basutos are now undergoing a revival as superb, easy-to-keep, supremely sure-footed long-distance mounts in their native South Africa.

intelligent, with a temperament of 'fire and feather' – fierce in war, gentle at home.

- **Colours:** All colours; bay, black and buckskin predominate
- **Height:** 13.2–15 hands (137–152cm/54–60in)
- **Gaits:** Walk, trot, canter, gallop
- **Recommended for:** Trail riding, endurance, ranch work

BASUTO PONY

The Basuto is usually called a pony, but (like the Caspian) it is actually a small horse. Its direct ancestor is the Cape Horse, which was developed in South Africa between the seventeenth and nineteenth centuries from Persian, Arabian, Thoroughbred and American stock; recent research suggests, surprisingly, that Basutos are of predominantly Thoroughbred blood. From the 1830s on, Cape Horses were stolen from or abandoned by settlers in Basutoland (now Lesotho) and adopted by the local people. They rode the horses at the gallop over the roughest and steepest terrain, but took little interest in their care in the coldest and most mountainous region of southern Africa, which boasts little good grazing. The survivors of this treatment were pony-sized, self-reliant horses with immense hardiness, strength and stamina, capable of great speed – and as fearless as their riders. The Basuto has a reputation as the most surefooted of all horses. During the Boer War the British Army acquired over 30,000 Basutos, and found them fast, reliable, easy to train and ride, and brave. They also found they made superb polo ponies. After a decline in numbers during the twentieth century, Basutos are now being revived and are in demand as riding ponies, particularly for trekking.

- **Colours:** Bay, brown, grey, chestnut
- **Height:** 12–14.2 hands (122–147cm/48–58in)
- **Gaits:** Walk, trot, canter, gallop; also the triple (a fast, three-beat trot) and pace
- **Recommended for:** Trail riding, trekking, endurance, flat racing, polo

BUDENNY

In 1921, after the revolution and civil war in Russia, the population of the Don horse was severely depleted, and the Red Army needed a new horse for officers. This would need to be willing to work hard, amenable to being kept in herds, equable, very brave, and fast as well as full of stamina – for a cavalry charge at the end of a long march might cover 5km (3 miles). Revolutionary hero and cavalryman Marshal Budenny (pronounced *bood-YAW-nee*), whose ambition was to create the perfect cavalry horse, oversaw the breeding programme. His work was complete when the Budenny was officially recognized in 1948. The best results came from a cross of Anglo-Don mares and Thoroughbred stallions; the Thoroughbred gave the Budenny elegance and agility; from the Don it gained substantial bone and an undemanding nature. The Budenny is a large, kind, quiet, patient and intelligent horse although, it is said, some may be 'a bit difficult' with strangers. But it has bags of spirit, courage and enthusiasm as well as great speed, stamina and jumping ability. The Budenny makes a superb all-round competition horse, excelling at both endurance riding and flat racing, and goes well in harness too. Its toughness and gallantry make it a good steeplechaser.

- **Colours:** Chestnut predominates, often with a golden cast; bay and black less common.
- **Height:** 15.2–17.2 hands (157–178cm/62–70in)

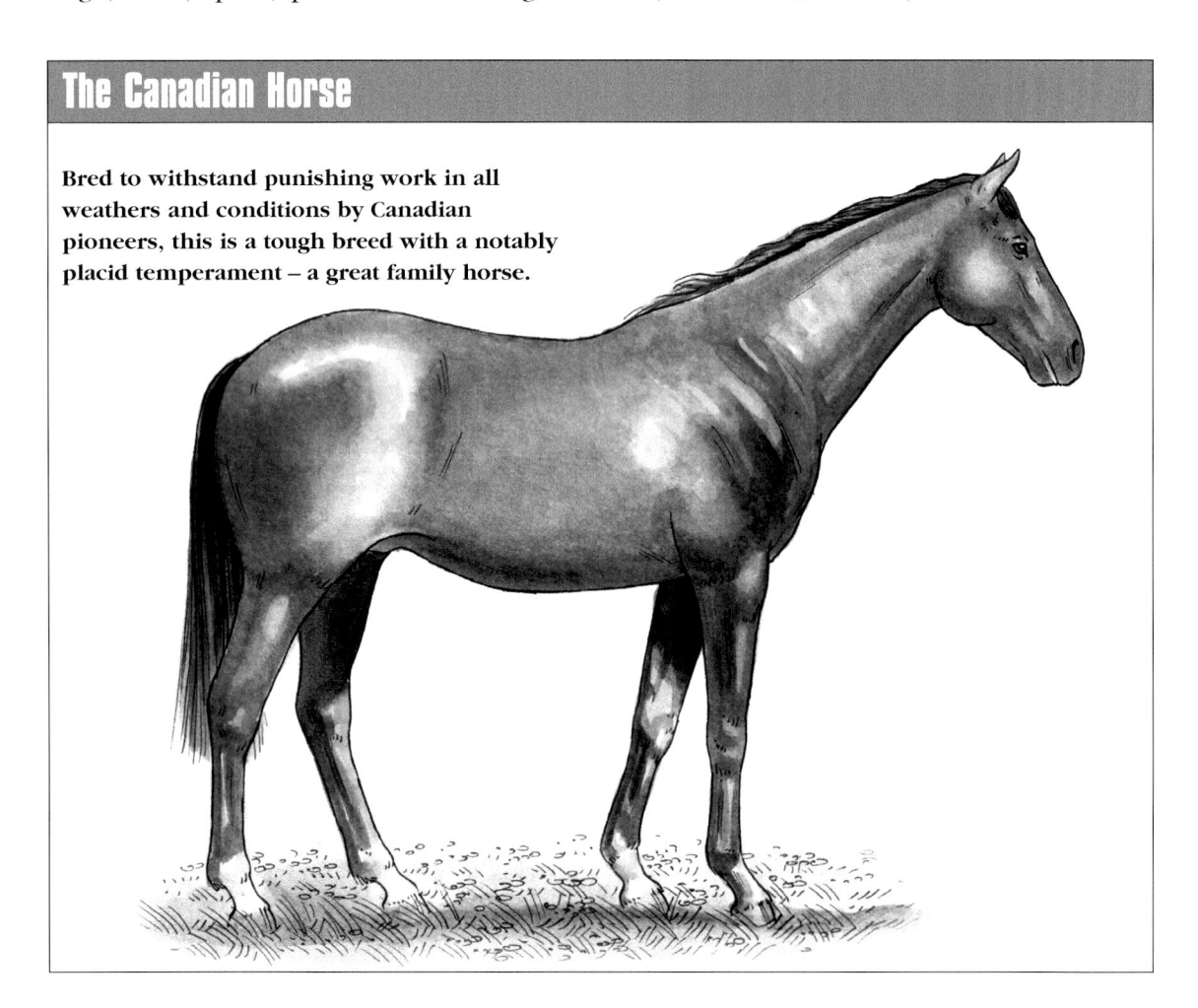

The Canadian Horse

Bred to withstand punishing work in all weathers and conditions by Canadian pioneers, this is a tough breed with a notably placid temperament – a great family horse.

- **Gaits:** Walk, trot, canter, gallop
- **Recommended for:** Most equestrian sports, notably endurance, jumping, steeplechasing

THE CANADIAN HORSE

Known as the 'little iron horse', the Canadian is the rugged descendant of Andalusian, Breton and Norman horses sent to French colonists by King Louis XIV in the seventeenth century. Owners drove their horses hard while feeding them only straw and a little grain, and leaving them in the open to fend for themselves against marauding insects in summer and violent blizzards in winter. Natural selection made the Canadian exceptionally hardy, and reduced its size. One historian wrote: 'Small, but robust, hocks of steel, thick mane floating in the wind, bright and lively eyes, pricking its sensitive ears at the least noise, going along day and night with the same courage, wide awake beneath its harness; spirited, good, gentle, affectionate, following his road with the finest instinct to come surely home. … Such were the horses of our fathers.' But by the 1880s, export to the USA, especially during the American Civil War (1861-5), cross-breeding, the introduction of large draught horses to Canada and then the start of mechanized farming, had all put the breed at risk. First the federal then the Quebec government sponsored a revival of the breed between 1907 and 1979. Canadians are economical to keep, and are bright, kind, notably lacking in nervousness and easy to handle.

- **Colours:** Usually black or dark bay; also chestnut, brown and lighter bay
- **Height:** 14-16 hands (142-163cm/56-64in)
- **Gaits:** Walk, trot, canter, gallop; some are pacers
- **Recommended for:** All equestrian disciplines, farm and ranch work, hunting; a good family horse

choosing a horse

CASPIAN

At first sight a Caspian could be taken for a very small, long-legged pony, or even a foal. But it is a very small and very well-proportioned horse. Caspians simply do not grow very much after their first six months. They were (re)discovered in Iran in 1965, when only 50 or so animals were still surviving around the southern Caspian Sea. Seven mares and six stallions were used in a breeding programme to try to ensure the Caspian did not become extinct, and despite war, politics and natural disasters, Caspian studs now exist in the UK, USA and New Zealand as well as in Iran; but there are still only about 1000 animals worldwide. The silky-coated Caspian may be the ancestor of the Arabian (which in miniature it resembles) and hence of most light horses, and may be the descendant of the tiny prehistoric Persian horse, seen pulling the royal chariot on the seal of Darius the Great, around 500 BC. Among their unusual features are very dense, hard, oval hooves that rarely need shoeing, and their habit of browsing on twigs, leaves and shoots rather than grazing. Having lived for thousands of years among mountains, they are extremely nimble and jump superbly. Caspians are inquisitive and affectionate, fast, intelligent learners and very good around people.

- **Colours:** Bay, grey, chestnut; occasionally black, buckskin
- **Height:** 10-13 hands (102-132cm/40-52in)
- **Gaits:** Walk, trot, canter, gallop
- **Recommended for:** Child's first horse

CONNEMARA PONY

The tough but handsome Connemara Pony arrived in Ireland in the fourth century BC with invading Celts; it is the country's only indigenous horse. A few Andalusians, escaping from a wrecked vessel of the Spanish Armada, may have added to the breed. The

choosing a horse

Caspian

One of the friendliest horses, the diminutive, bright-eyed Caspian is famed for nimbleness and jumping ability. Very rare, but a great first mount for children if you can find one.

temperament. Although they are sharp to ride, they have a generous and steadfast character, and they bond very well with humans.

- **Colours:** Grey and dun most common; some black, bay, brown; occasional roan, chestnut, palomino, dark-eyed cream
- **Height:** 12.2-15 hands (127-152cm/50-60in)
- **Gaits:** Walk, trot, canter, gallop
- **Recommended for:** Showjumping, cross-country, eventing, endurance; dressage

CRIOLLO

The 'creole' horse is found all over South America: it is known as *Criollo* in Argentina and Uruguay, *Crioulo* in Brazil, *Costeño* and *Morochuco* in Peru, *Corralero* in Chile, and *Llanero* in Venezuela. The Argentines first established a standard for these horses, which are descendants of what were probably Andalusians and hardy Garranos and Sorraias brought to South America in the sixteenth century. Living wild on the Argentine pampas, and gaining some Thoroughbred and Percheron blood along the way, they developed into small, immensely resilient animals with a high resistance to disease. The Criollo was, and is, the favoured mount of the *gauchos* (cowboys of the South American pampas), who revered horsemanship and chose the most difficult horses on which to demonstrate their talents. The breed standard was based on the *gaucho*'s working demands – a tireless horse that needed little food, and had all the agility and responsiveness necessary for controlling cattle. The Criollo tends to be

Irish left the ponies to fend for themselves in the wild, rock-strewn Connemara landscape, and caught mares when needed for work. A mare, not a stallion, would be taken because she could also give a foal each year, and this would be sold to supplement a subsistence farmer's meagre income. Poverty meant that any animal not up to the farmer's hefty demands was rapidly replaced; when breeding became more organized, only the toughest had survived. Even so, by the 1920s random cross-breeding threatened the purity of the Connemara, and it was re-established from a dozen top-quality ponies that were left to breed in the wild again. Inured to mountain life and poor natural food, the Connemara is adaptable, hardy, and an amazing jumper: at the 1939 New York Open Championships, for example, a 13.2 hand (137cm/54in) Connemara astonished spectators by clearing 2.2m (7ft) fences. Connemaras are renowned for their gentle

choosing a horse

a one-person horse but, having established trust, will fearlessly do anything its rider asks. And it really is tireless: in the 1920s one pair travelled the 19,300km (12,000 miles) from Buenos Aires to New York and back, and lived to the ripe old age of 40.

- **Colours:** Mostly dun, but more than 100 colours are recognized. Mule or zebra stripes appear with some colours.
- **Height:** 13.2-15 hands (137-152cm/54-60in)
- **Gaits:** Walk, trot, canter, gallop
- **Recommended for:** Trekking, trail riding, endurance

DON HORSE

First systematically bred in the eighteenth century, the Don horse was the product of semi-wild steppe horses and the Cossack way of life. This semi-nomadic people of southern Russia grew, from the fourteenth century on, from communities of fugitives from serfdom, and lived largely on the spoils of mounted raids. Karabakh, Turkmenian and Persian horses contributed to the breed. As one writer puts it, 'The Don Horse evolved from the Cossacks' need for reliable horses for mounted combat. And, perhaps in turn, the Cossack life became viable thanks to the distinguishing features of their horses: speed,

Criollo

The Criollo breed was developed from the hardy and fearless horses of the gauchos, the cowboys of the Argentine. A truly great trail horse, capable of boundless loyalty.

choosing a horse

agility, physical and mental strength and stamina.' Don horses were bred to survive freezing winters and drought-filled summers, and are famously tough, frugal animals. From the eighteenth century, Cossack 'hosts' became part of the Imperial Russian Army, and the Don became a favourite Russian cavalry mount, although (despite its broadness) it is not a comfortable ride. Only a few hundred Don horses survived the combined onslaughts of World War I, the Russian revolution and civil war. From 1921 on, a concerted effort was made to preserve the breed. Today the Don is used as a sport horse, outperforming all European breeds at endurance events. Good-natured, calm, reliable, easily managed yet energetic, the Don has highly expressive eyes.

- **Colours:** Chestnut, bay, often with gold metallic sheen; grey
- **Height:** 15.3–16.2 hands (160–168cm/63–66in)
- **Gaits:** Walk, trot, canter, gallop
- **Recommended for:** Endurance, driving

ESTONIAN NATIVE HORSE

Once numerous all over its native country, the pony-sized, adaptable Estonian Native Horse survives today on the Baltic islands of Saaremaa, Hiiumaa and Muhu. The total herd numbers only about 1000. The breed

Royal Friesian

The Friesian is instantly recognizable for its long mane and tail, which traditionally are never shorn, and its invariably black coat. Calm and reliable: a horse for all the family.

gave way in the first part of the twentieth cen-tury to the Tori, itself now reduced to fewer than 100 pure-bred horses, and which was developed using Estonian Native mares. A long-lived animal (one mare is known to have lived for over 47 years), the Estonian Native is easy to keep, full of stamina and highly resistant to disease, with a willing and undemanding temperament. It is still used for light farm work and as a mount for tourists, and makes a good, solid, affable first pony for children.

- **Colours:** Chestnut, bay, dun, grey
- **Height:** 12.2-14.3 hands (127-150cm/50-59in)
- **Gaits:** Walk, trot, canter, gallop
- **Recommended for:** Child's first horse, pleasure riding, light draught work

ROYAL FRIESIAN

One of the great driving horses, and one of Europe's oldest breeds, the stately black Friesian hails from the Netherlands, where it has been a familiar sight for some 2000 years. Friesian soldiers rode these horses into battle against the Roman legions; when no longer needed for warfare, Friesians worked the land, were fine carriage horses, and ran in the world's first trotting races (invented in Holland in the eighteenth century). Friesians contributed too to improving such breeds as the Shire, Morgan, Swedish Warmblood and the Orlov Trotter, and to reviving the Kladruby. As with so many other breeds, the advent of machinery and the automobile almost brought about the Friesian's demise. Devotees rescued it, and the Friesian revived further during World War II when a shortage of fuel made the horse once more a practicable means of transport. Although not large, the Friesian is a striking horse, with its ceremonious air, high knee action, feathered fetlocks and immensely long, luxuriant mane and tail, which traditionally are left uncut. Outwardly a coldblood but counted a warmblood, the Friesian combines a huge capacity for hard toil with great intelligence and a genial, unflappable and kindly temperament; easy, patient and docile to handle, it soon pops with energy and suppleness when put to work. In 1954 the Friesian was awarded the title 'Royal' by Queen Juliana of the Netherlands.

- **Colours:** Solid black only
- **Height:** 14.3-15.3 hands (150-160cm/59-63in)
- **Gaits:** Walk, trot, canter, gallop
- **Recommended for:** Driving, endurance, jumping, dressage; excellent family horse

HAFLINGER

Known affectionately as the 'Tractor of the Alps', the Haflinger hails from the Tyrol mountains straddling the Austrian-Italian border. Haflingers are probably descended from a mixture of local breeds and Arabian-type horses brought to the region in the sixth century. They gained their striking colouring – chestnut with a flaxen mane and tail – only in 1874, from an Arab-Haflinger stallion named Folie. Haflingers are pony-sized, but all horse: 'A prince in front' – referring to their refined heads – 'and a peasant behind', as the Tyrolean saying goes. Phenomenally powerful, tireless and very surefooted, they were bred to haul logs, plough fields, pull carts and carry packs in steep, uncertain terrain. While able to survive on scant rations, they are very long-lived, often reaching 35 or more. Haflingers served with mountain troops in both world wars, and still work with the Austrian Army and on farmland that machines cannot reach. In the USA, the Amish community use them for ploughing and driving. Haflingers' uncomplicated, cooperative nature and steady nerves combine with a long stride and smooth gait to make them a popular and versatile pleasure horse. They have proved

choosing a horse

to be excellent mounts for people with communication and learning difficulties.

- **Colours:** Chestnut, ranging from honey blonde to dark chocolate; flaxen or white mane and tail
- **Height:** 13.3-14.3 hands (140-150cm/55-59in)
- **Gaits:** Walk, trot, canter, gallop
- **Recommended for:** Driving, dressage, trekking; an excellent family horse

HANOVERIAN

This warmblooded horse is one of the world's most prominent riding horses. It was originally the inspiration of King George II of England (also the ruler of Hanover), who in 1735 directed the Celle stud in Lower Saxony to produce a coach horse that was also suited to agricultural work. In the nineteenth century it was developed into a military mount, while after World War I the breeders' stated aim was a horse good on the farm 'yet possessed of enough blood, nerve and gaits to be usable as a bold riding and coach horse'. After World War II it was crossed with Thoroughbreds to create a sport horse with an ideal conformation and temperament for athleticism. Hanoverian breed societies keep a tight grip on the quality of their animals; not all foals born to Hanoverians are deemed acceptable for continuing the line. The modern Hanoverian has a powerful, strong-limbed body; ideally, movements should be big, yet light and springy. It is a particularly willing, cooperative and trainable horse, with a calm and level-headed temperament.

Haflinger

Long a warhorse and tireless Alpine worker, the Haflinger is now finding a new role as a pleasure mount thanks to its terrific strength and stamina and amiable disposition.

- **Colours:** Most colours; chestnut used to be dominant
- **Height:** 15.3-17.2 hands (160-178cm/63-70in)
- **Gaits:** Walk, trot, canter, gallop
- **Recommended for:** Dressage, showjumping, cross-country, eventing

HOKKAIDO

Horses were not widely used in Japanese agriculture until the late nineteenth century (when the government encouraged it), but they were central to the warrior Samurai culture and the Shinto religion: some shrines still keep a sacred white horse. Horses were ridden by aristocrats, and otherwise used as pack animals. All Japanese breeds are small, and some have been reduced to tiny herds – for example the Misaki, with fewer than 90 head, the Noma with fewer than 50, and the Miyako with a mere score or so of animals. The most numerous (over 3000 head) and

choosing a horse

Hokkaido

These hardy, immensely sure-footed little Japanese horses are very easy keepers. Despite the tough life they traditionally lead, they are known for being easy-going and obedient.

widespread is the Hokkaido, known as 'Do-san-ko' ('child of Hokkaido'). These horses were originally imported from Honshu in the seventeenth century by fishermen, who used them in summer and left them to fend for themselves in winter. They survived the harsh climate – and grew very tough – by living mainly on bamboo grass. Some are now bred on stud farms, but many are still left to overwinter unassisted. The Hokkaido is reported to be easier and more comfortable to ride than a Thoroughbred, and visitors to Hokkaido can ride them on wildlife trails. Like so many other equines left to look after themselves in very poor conditions, they amaze with their amiable and willing attitude to humans.

- **Colours:** Most solid colours; many roan
- **Height:** 12.2-13 hands (127-132cm/50-52in)
- **Gaits:** Walk, trot, canter, gallop; many are natural pacers
- **Recommended for:** Trail riding, packing, hacking

ICELANDIC PONY

This tough, long-lived and idiosyncratic horse arrived in Iceland with the Vikings in the ninth century, and has not been cross-bred there since. In a country with few roads, many earthquakes and an unforgiving landscape, it is still used for draught work and personal transport – notably for the annual sheep round-up. There are around 80,000 of the breed in Iceland, and about 270,000 people, and they are increasingly popular abroad.

The Icelandic's toughness is maintained by letting foals live free with the herd for their first four years, with winter grazing supplemented with a daily dry salt herring and some hay. The result, says one expert, is 'a spirited and forward-going horse with much respect for the rider, [and] the landscape creates a sure-footed and muscular horse, toughened by harsh weather and wide-open spaces.' Another says: 'The hardships that they have survived have given us a horse that is not afraid to face the world.' Icelandics are strong, cheerfully amiable creatures who suit both adults and children. They have a fluid and seemingly effortless running walk called the *toelt*, which is supremely comfortable; and an exhilarating flying pace that will power them along at up to 50km/h (30mph). They also have a strong homing instinct. Ride out on an Icelandic, turn it loose at your destination, and it will happily make its own way home. Icelandics

Icelandic Pony

Very distinctive in appearance, with their long, flowing, fine-haired manes, Icelandic ponies also boast a very comfortable ride – and a useful, unerring homing instinct.

have a thoughtful, independent streak, and call for education, not domination.

- **Colours:** All colours except appaloosa; most common are duns and chestnuts
- **Height:** 12-14.2 hands (122-147cm/48-58in)
- **Gaits:** Walk, trot, canter; also *toelt* and flying pace
- **Recommended for:** Draught and pack work; trail riding, endurance; most forms of pleasure riding; child's second pony

IRISH COB

Also known as the Irish Tinker or Gypsy Horse, the Irish Cob developed from the Celtic horse which arrived in Ireland in about 400 AD, with some Norman heavy horse blood being added in the eleventh century. Traditionally used as a draught horse by tinkers and Gypsies, the muscular Irish Cob also served as a farmers' mount. A remarkably tolerant and generous disposition combines with trustworthiness and physical solidity to make an animal that anyone, of any age, can take for their first ride on horseback. Irish Cobs get on extremely well with people, and are unaggressive with other horses. But beneath the Irish Cob's slightly sleepy exterior, feet 'like hairy milk pails' and barrelish shape lies an animal that, once stimulated, is capable of either

choosing a horse

the most delicate dressage movements or a thundering bold gallop. Irish Cobs are intelligent and inquisitive and enjoy learning, although they often need some initial motivation. Novice riders find them eminently sane and steady: if in doubt, Irish Cobs will simply stop and wait for clear instructions, rather than take off, and they are generally slow to spook.

- **Colours:** Most piebald or skewbald (some tri-colour); dun, palomino and all solid colours are also found
- **Height:** 13.2–15.2 hands (137–157cm/54–62in)
- **Gaits:** Walk, trot, canter, gallop
- **Recommended for:** All equestrian sports, hunting, driving; a good family horse; an excellent adult learner's mount

IRISH DRAUGHT

Despite its name the Irish Draught is not a traditional 'heavy horse', but a muscular, moderately sized, free-moving and well-balanced animal that performs as well in dressage and showjumping as it does in eventing or at pulling a farmer's cart. It is a distant descendant of the Norman heavy horse, which arrived in Ireland in the eleventh century, with an influx of Andalusian blood in the sixteenth century. It found a role as a war horse for centuries, then was valued as a combination of agricultural worker, smart riding horse and hedge-hopping hunter; but it came into its own as a sport horse with the invention of showjumping in Ireland in the late nineteenth century.

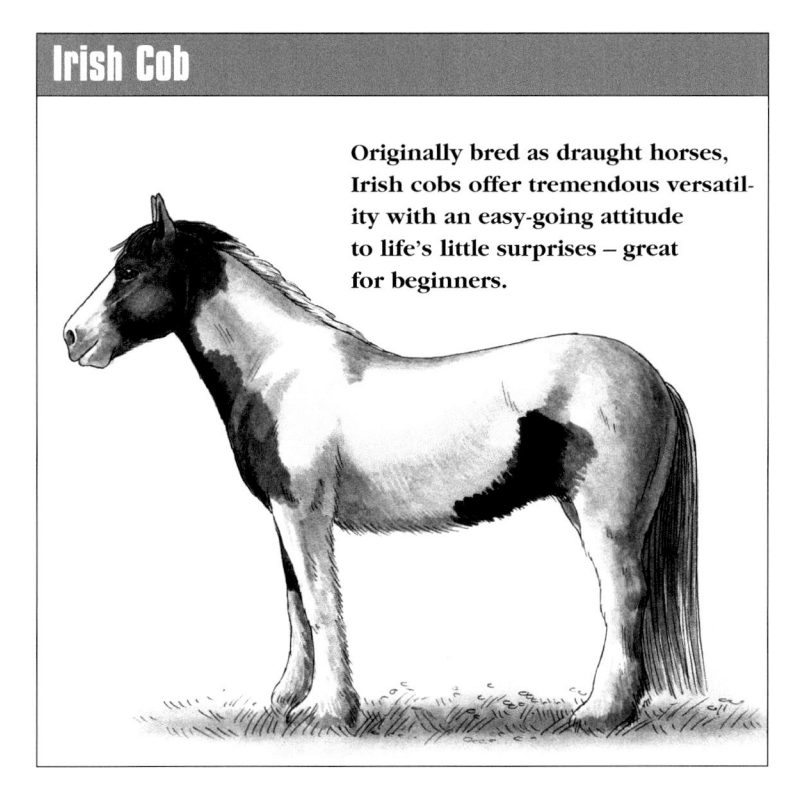

Crossed with the Thoroughbred, it founded the celebrated line of Irish hunters. The Irish Draught's fortunes have waxed and waned with Ireland's, and it has teetered on extinction several times: there are only some 2000 pure-breds in the world even today. This is a sturdy, willing, hard-working and intelligently alert breed with a sane, kindly demeanour. If not quite as forgiving as Irish Cobs, Irish Draughts make great mounts for those looking for a powerful galloper and jumper with a dependably sensible outlook.

- **Colours:** All solid colours; dappled grey most common
- **Height:** 15.1–16.3 hands (155–170cm/61–67in)
- **Gaits:** Walk, trot, canter, gallop
- **Recommended for:** All equestrian activities

Irish Cob

Originally bred as draught horses, Irish cobs offer tremendous versatility with an easy-going attitude to life's little surprises – great for beginners.

KABARDIN

The Kabardin is a classic Russian mountain horse – surefooted, good-natured and bright, as well as strong, reliable and immensely courageous. Reputed to be the world's best mountain horse, Kabardins come from the Caucasian range, where for centuries they have been in the service of nomadic peoples as pack animals and fast mounts. In original form, they were the product of steppe horses crossed with Karabakhs, Persians and Turkmenians. In the 1920s some Thoroughbred blood was added to produce larger animals for the military. They remain an 'extreme' breed nonetheless, capable of enduring appalling climatic conditions on meagre rations, and thrive at altitudes above 1800m (6000ft). They will cross torrential icy waters without a murmur; one was even ridden to the peak of Mt Elbrus, at 5642m (18,510ft) the highest peak in the Caucasus. They also have a gift for finding their way safely and accurately through fog, mist and darkness, and if they do get lost will find their way back to their own herd. These are not fast horses (although in 1946 a Kabardin covered 250km [155 miles] in 25 hours), but they are survivors, and their obedience and tractability are probably more the product of intrepid determination than innate kindliness. As any Kabardin herdsmen will tell you, these horses should be treated with great respect.

- **Colours:** Dark bay, cherry bay; black is rare
- **Height:** 14.1–15.2 hands (142–145cm/57–62in)
- **Gaits:** Walk, trot, canter, gallop; some are natural pacers
- **Recommended for:** Endurance, driving; not a beginner's horse

KISBER FELVER

Developed as a superior cavalry horse at the Kisber stud in Hungary at the end of the nineteenth century, the Kisber Felver is known as 'the world's most beautiful sport horse' and 'the heavenly horse'. Essentially the product of very careful crossings of the indestructible Felver, the Trakehner and the Thoroughbred, the Kisber Felver resembles a large-boned Thoroughbred, but has the far less excitable, balanced temperament of the warmblood breeds. Despite its short history, the Kisber has had a chequered existence. In 1945, half the foundation stock was taken as war booty by the Soviet Union, and disappeared without trace. About 150 head were rescued by General George S. Patton (a passionate horseman) for the US Army and taken to the USA, only to be sold off unannounced two years later. Fortunately many were traced by those who understood their value, but there are now only about 2000 of the breed worldwide. The Kisber Felver is notable for more than its stunning looks. It is good with people, kind and intelligent, with plenty of stamina and energy. Inquisitive and brave, it will take on any new challenge, and consequently learns well.

- **Colours:** All solid colours, including palomino and buckskin
- **Height:** 15.3–17 hands (160–173cm/63–68in)
- **Gaits:** Walk, trot, canter, gallop
- **Recommended for:** All equestrian sports, especially jumping and cross-country

KUSTANAI

Work on developing the Kustanai breed was begun at state-owned studs in western Kazakhstan in 1887, the aim being to inject the speed and grace of the Thoroughbred into the tough but not notably fast native Kazakh steppe horse. As a group, steppe horses are incredibly hardy, and live out all year round, grazing un-attended in huge herds or 'tabuns', and surviving winter temperatures that can drop to -40°C/F.

Blessed with determination and a very keen sense of smell, they can find food beneath snow 1m (3ft) deep. The new breed was recognized as early as 1890, but development continued until 1951. The results were popular and successful: by 1980, there were over 40,000 Kustanais. Originally, two types were produced, a saddle horse with a high proportion of Thoroughbred blood, and a steppe horse coming from crosses among Kazakh, Don, Stralets and other breeds, with only a little Thoroughbred. The modern Kustanai combines the best qualities of the two types: it is a massive animal, with the steppe horse's

choosing a horse

powerful legs, deep chest and powers of tireless endurance. It also has plenty of zip: over a 1.6km (1 mile) sprint, it has reached more than 56km/h (35mph), while in a 24-hour ride it has covered nearly 286km (178 miles). Steppe horses are fiercely loyal to their owners, and don't take at once to strangers: their trust has to be earned.

- **Colours:** Bay, chestnut, reddish grey, brown
- **Height:** 14.3-17 hands (150-173cm/59-68in)
- **Gaits:** Walk, trot, canter, gallop
- **Recommended for:** Endurance, cross-country

Kisber Felver

One of Hungary's most celebrated cavalry horses, the Kisber Felver is now very rare. They are reckoned to have the virtues of the Thoroughbred, but none of its drawbacks.

LIPIZZANER

In 1580, the Hapsburg Archduke Charles (brother of Maximillian II, who founded the Kladruby breed) set up a stud at Lipizza, now in Slovenia, to produce a fast, light cavalry horse. Spanish stallions (a mix of Berber, Arab and Iberian lines) were crossed with native Karst horses: the breed settled in its current form at the beginning of the nineteenth century. Today's Lipizzaner is striking for its crested neck, powerful shoulders, large kindly eyes, alert ears and proud bearing, and it is most famous as the star of the Spanish Riding School in Vienna. Lipizzaners are almost always white (technically, light grey), although they are born dark; their bright coat comes through when they are six or seven years old. There are only about 3000 Lipizzaners worldwide, and their rarity, good looks, remarkable talents for *Haute Ecole* dressage and romantic background all make for a high market value. One commentary notes: 'The Lipizzan is a loyal, obedient animal. In the paddock, they often seem world-weary. However ... when being ridden, they display a fiery temperament. Finally, when approached on the ground by a friendly person, they immediately become docile and obedient, without losing their

Lipizzaner

Made famous by the Spanish Riding School of Vienna, the stunning good looks of the Lippizaner are matched by its intelligence, athletic ability, and willingness to please.

pride.' They are fine, highly individual, intelligent and self-possessed mounts for accomplished riders of all ages.

- **Colours:** Grey; very occasionally bay
- **Height:** 14.2–16 hands (147–163cm/58–64in)
- **Gaits:** Walk, trot, canter, gallop
- **Recommended for:** Dressage; driving; not a beginner's horse

MANGALARGA MARCHADOR

The national horse of Brazil, the Mangalarga Marchador is much admired for its special gaits, the *marcha picada* and *marcha batida*, and is not to be confused with the Mangalarga of other countries, which has only the standard gaits of walk, trot and canter. The Marchador has been compared to the Swiss Army knife for its capacity to do so many things so well, but definitely not for its sharpness. This a gentle, even-tempered, hugely willing animal with great patience and stamina, and is very comfortable to ride. Its primary, and continuing, purpose was to provide an easy mount for farm managers who spent hours at a time in the saddle, but it is a worker's horse too, with fine 'cow sense'. It has also become an accomplished competitor in cutting, endurance riding, trail and pleasure riding, jumping and polo.

The *marcha picada* (meaning 'light touch') is the smoother of the Marchador's two special gaits, and can be kept up for long distances. It is a broken pace, which creates little vertical movement, with moments of triple support when three of the hooves touch the ground at the same time. The *marcha batida* ('hit') is like a broken trot: the legs move in diagonal pairs, with transient triple support; in this gait, the horse is always in contact with the ground.

- **Colours:** Grey, bay, chestnut
- **Height:** 14.2–15.3 hands (147–160cm/58–63in)

choosing a horse

- **Gaits:** Walk, trot, canter, gallop; marcha picada, marcha batida
- **Recommended for:** Endurance, trail riding, cross-country, polo, pleasure riding, Western events

MARWARI

The Marwari of India is instantly recognizable by its unique ears: crescent-shaped, touching at the tips when pricked, and capable of rotating (not just flattening) through 180 degrees. In its native Rajasthan, the majestic Marwari is a horse of legend, famed for its prowess in battle and the homing instinct that would bring a wounded warrior to safety. The Marwari horse actually derives from Turkmenistan and Kathiawar lines, and its ancestry, free of inter-breeding, can be traced over 10 generations. Its history goes back until at least the twelfth century, when it adapted to desert life. It then became a war horse for the Rajputi aristocracy and warrior caste, and was numbered in tens of thousands; it declined under British rule and in particular when the Indian Government withdrew financial support from those struggling to preserve the breed. Since the 1990s efforts to revive it have been successful; and Marwaris are now even bred in the USA. The Marwari's swivelling ears give it unusually sharp hearing, and its *revaal* pacing gait – which has the action of a smooth walk, but at the speed of a canter – makes long-distance travel fast and comfortable. Unswervingly loyal, the Marwari is known for its intelligence, willingness and quickness to learn. Marwaris enjoy performing and have a talent for the local form of *Haute Ecole* dressage, which they 'dance' at Rajputi festivals.

- **Colours:** Bay, chestnut, brown, palomino, piebald, skewbald
- **Height:** 14–17 hands (142–173cm/56–68in)

choosing a horse

Marwari

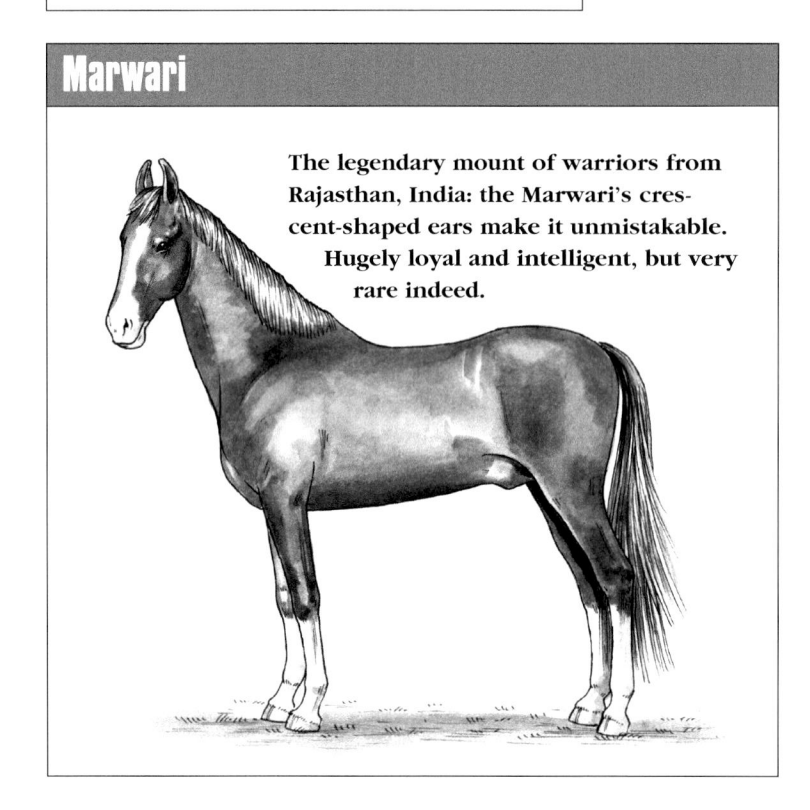

The legendary mount of warriors from Rajasthan, India: the Marwari's crescent-shaped ears make it unmistakable. Hugely loyal and intelligent, but very rare indeed.

- **Gaits:** Walk, trot, canter, gallop; *revaal*
- **Recommended for:** Dressage, trail riding; very scarce

MISSOURI FOX TROTTER

The defining feature of the Missouri Fox Trotter is its fluid, four-beat, diagonal 'fox trot' gait. It achieves this by way of a sliding trot with the hind legs while the fore legs walk. This means that there is at least one hoof on the ground at all times, so that there is no jarring, as when a horse comes out of free fall in a standard trot. Thus, there is no need for the rider to rise (post) to the trot. The Fox Trotter can keep the gait up for hours, creating a smooth, comfortable long-distance ride at 8-13km/h (5-8mph). The breed was developed from the 1820s onwards, from a number of American horses; it was needed by farmers in Missouri's Ozark mountains, where days might be spent in the saddle in treacherous terrain: and besides being comfortable the Missouri Fox Trotter is immensely surefooted with plenty of stamina. It was also, inevitably, used for light haulage and to pull the family buggy. The advent of cars and tractors did not affect the breed too badly, as cattle ranchers in the region had found they made excellent, intelligent cow horses; while today they are a favoured mount of US Forest Service Rangers, who have to go where vehicles do not reach. Fox Trotters have an amiable, gentle disposition and are easily trained.

- **Colours:** All colours, including pinto, white, roan and buckskin
- **Height:** 14-16 hands (142-163cm/56-64in)
- **Gaits:** Flat-footed walk, fox trot, 'rocking chair' canter, gallop
- **Recommended for:** Trail riding, endurance, trekking; a good family horse

MORGAN

In 1790, schoolteacher Justin Morgan of Randolph, Vermont, USA, was given a yearling colt named Figure as part repayment of a debt; the colt became a stallion of stunning looks, gentle manners and great spirit, strength and speed. Figure was much in demand at stud in his 31 years, and nearly all today's Morgans can be traced back to him. Figure's descendants in turn made great contributions to several other famed American breeds, such as the Saddlebred, Standardbred, Tennessee Walker and Quarter Horse. The Morgan is celebrated as a horse that can do anything, and it has certainly excelled at international level in disciplines and sports

choosing a horse

as diverse as driving, jumping, dressage, cattle cutting and cross-country endurance. It has also been used widely in therapeutic riding and riding for the disabled, thanks to its steady temperament and markedly comfortable gaits. This versatility is in part due to the Morgan's compact and muscular build, which makes it easy to get a balanced seat and a properly collected horse, and in part to its inherent trainability and ability to adapt quickly to changing circumstances. A good Morgan can think for itself, without taking itself out of the rider's control.

- **Colours:** Bay, black, brown, chestnut, grey, palomino, cream, dun, buckskin
- **Height:** 14.1-15.2 hands (145-157cm/57-62in)
- **Gaits:** Walk, trot, canter, gallop
- **Recommended for:** All equestrian activities; good with children

MUSTANG

The term 'mustang' has been applied to all kinds of feral horses in North America: the word derives from the Spanish *mesteño* or *mostrenco* meaning 'wild' or 'stray'. The assumption is that these are descendants of horses brought to the Americas by Spanish colonists from the fifteenth century on – and famously ridden by native Americans – but the wild horse of the western USA and Canada contains a rich mixture of other breeds. French horses from Louisiana and Michigan, Old Friesians that plodded away from the US Army, and any number of pioneer and cowhands' animals have added to the mix over the centuries. But a handful of Mustang herds have remained pure: the Siffleur herd of southern Alberta and the Sulphur Springs herd of Utah are examples. In the USA, Mustangs can be adopted through a Bureau of Land Management programme; in Canada, their protection is in private hands. They are, of course, incredibly tough, having survived for so long on desert and mountain land that no settler could use. These animals require a slow and gentle approach to gain their trust, but can be immensely rewarding; they have an even temperament and are quick to learn. Some have been used in therapeutic programmes for psychologically damaged children, as well as in prisoner rehabilitation schemes.

- **Colours:** All: no other breed shows as many colours

Morgan

Reckoned by many to be the quintessentially American horse, the Morgan is one of the USA's oldest breeds, and has proved equal to to the demands of every equestrian pursuit.

choosing a horse

Norwegian Fjord

Patient, intelligent and calm, Norwegian Fjords are excellent mounts for those with limited experience of horses, but will also rise to great things for accomplished riders.

- **Height:** 14-16 hands (142-163cm/56-64in)
- **Gaits:** Walk, trot, canter, gallop; some are natural pacers
- **Recommended for:** Endurance, Western sports, ranch work

NORWEGIAN FJORD

The Fjord horse, with its unusual two-tone mane and 'primitive' dun coat, has been in Norway for at least 4000 years, and domesticated for 2000: it was the horse of the Vikings. It is believed to be related to the primitive wild horse of Asia, the Przewalski, and all today's western European draught horses probably carry some Fjord blood. The Fjord horse has a thick coat to see it through Norway's bitter winters, yet despite the rigours of the climate it will thrive on hay and water alone and is renowned for its strength and stamina. The Norwegian Fjord has gaits that are smooth and comfortable to ride, and it has terrific powers of endurance. Its mild manner and willingness to work make it an ideal family horse, ridden or driven as easily by the novice or youngster as by the knowledgeable adult. One American breeder says: 'They are an ideal horse for those with little horse experience wishing to buy a good, gentle-natured horse. They do not frighten easily, and react calmly in a bad situation, waiting patiently until someone comes to help.' Another warns: 'Fjords are known for being tolerant. However, they are animals, and will try to get the upper hand if they can.'

- **Colours:** Brown dun; more rarely, red dun, grey, pale dun, gold or yellow dun
- **Height:** 13.1-14.2 hands (135-147cm/53-58in)
- **Gaits:** Walk, trot, canter, gallop
- **Recommended for:** Draught work, general riding, driving; good with children

OLDENBURG

The Oldenburg developed by Count Anton von Oldenburg in the mid-seventeenth century was a large, black, proud carriage horse that became something of a model for its kind. Since then Oldenburg breeders, who are mostly neighbours in Lower Saxony, Germany, have constantly adapted the breed in the light of changing circumstances, and in the 1960s made the strategic decision to attempt to develop an ideal, all-round sport horse. They also decided, rather shrewdly, to include in the breed any horse of suitable conformation, performance and temperament - providing themselves with a comprehensive gene pool from which to redevelop their own horse. The strategy has certainly succeeded - Oldenburg bloodlines now include most major European breeds as well as the Neapolitan, Tartary and Barbary blood that went into the original. This high-stepping horse is still large, but compact and consequently athletic, and frequently competes in world-class jumping, dressage and eventing as well as in driving. The traditional Oldenburg docility, tractability and trainability have been carefully retained, along with a taste for hard work, a kindly eye and an elegant outline.

choosing a horse

- **Colours:** Black, dark bay most common
- **Height:** 16.1-17.3 hands (165-180cm/65-71in)
- **Gaits:** Walk, trot, canter, gallop
- **Recommended for:** Showjumping, dressage, eventing, driving

PASO FINO

The Paso Fino is one of many descendants of the Spanish horses brought to the Americas by the conquistadores, and is the national horse of Puerto Rico. The official description of 'the horse with the fine step' runs: 'a light horse of great grace and style and with definite, but controlled, spirit ... gentle at hand, but spirited under saddle'. The breed standard also explains its particular gait: as 'essentially a broken pace, a lateral, not diagonal gait. The sequence of the hooves is: right rear, right fore, left rear, left fore; the hind foot touching the ground a fraction of a second before the front foot. ... The motion of the horse is absorbed in [its] back and loins giving the rider comfort. This gait is performed at three speeds with the collection of the carriage decreasing as the speed increases.' The three speeds are *paso fino*, *paso corto* and *paso largo*. The corto is the more relaxed form, and most Paso Fino horses prefer it to walking. In the *paso largo* these horses have been known to reach 51km/h (32mph). The Paso Fino, while willing to learn, is a hotblooded horse with 'hidden fire', and will tend to zip if it gets the chance, so training and handling must be gentle but firm and unambiguous.

- **Colours:** All colours, including palomino, grey, roan, pinto
- **Height:** 13-15.2 hands (132-157cm/52-62in)
- **Gaits:** Walk, trot, canter; also *paso fino*, *paso corto*, *paso largo*
- **Recommended for:** Trail riding, trekking; good with cattle

QUARTER HORSE

There are two basic types of Quarter Horse: the short, square and muscular stock, bred for ranch work, and the lean, long-legged running type, bred to sprint. The general appearance is of a very muscular Thoroughbred. There are many sub-strains within the breed, most of them deliberately bred to provide a Quarter Horse to suit a particular speciality. This diversity is partly a result of the breed's longevity. It was originally a cross between Spanish horses, maintained by the Chickasaw Indians, and more refined English horses, and first appeared in Virginia and the Carolinas in the 1690s – making it the USA's oldest breed. Before long it was being celebrated as a phenomenal sprinter over the quarter mile (400m) – hence its name. (The current record is around 20 seconds.) But it also proved to have its Andalusian ancestors' innate 'cow sense', and the speed, balance and agility to match. It became a favourite for working with cattle, and was further refined as such in the southwestern states. Another reason for the Quarter Horse's adaptability is its intelligence and its ease of handling: this is an even-tempered, good-natured and tractable animal that is willing to apply its nimbleness and its muscle to most tasks.

- **Colours:** Mostly sorrel; most other solid colours and duns
- **Height:** 14-16 hands (142-163cm/56-64in)
- **Gaits:** Walk, trot, canter, gallop
- **Recommended for:** All equestrian sports and disciplines, ranch work, general riding; a good family horse

BRITISH RIDING PONY

Sometimes awkwardly called the Riding Pony (Breeding) and more elegantly and accurately known as the British Riding Pony, this breed was deliberately developed in the UK to create a pony with the proportions of a horse. It has been called (by an Englishman) 'in terms of proportion and quality ... the most nearly perfect equine in the world'. In the 1920s a number of visionary breeders banded together to cross small Thoroughbreds and Arabians with Welsh and Dartmoor ponies. The British Riding Pony has the silhouette of a Thoroughbred, with the delicacy of an Arabian, but the dimensions of a native British pony. Riding Ponies also have the independent temperament of British ponies, particularly the Welsh, which can sometimes have more mountain weather and rock in their souls than any spirit of benign cooperation, and the potential explosiveness of the Thoroughbred. They do not respond to violence; in confident hands and with the right approach, however, they can perform brilliantly, for they are surefooted and very willing to learn if convinced it is in their own interests. Challenging, but potentially hugely rewarding, these are animals for riders as alert and intelligent as their mounts.

- **Colours:** All solid colours
- **Height:** 12.2-15 hands (122-152cm/50-60in)
- **Gaits:** Walk, trot, canter, gallop
- **Recommended for:** Young rider's or beginner's first or second pony

SADDLEBRED

The American Saddlebred has a long history: its precursor was the American Horse, an all-purpose product of crossing Rhode Island Narragansett Pacers with early Thoroughbreds in the seventeenth century. At the beginning of the nineteenth century, after further crossing with Thoroughbreds, Morgans and Standardbreds, the Saddlebred emerged as a breed in its own right, in the southern state of Kentucky. The Saddlebred was a favoured mount in the Confederate Army during the American Civil War (1861-5); this conflict was devastating to the

British Riding Pony

An elegant mixture of Thoroughbred good looks and British native ponies' shrewdness, the Riding Pony is tremendously rewarding in experienced and affectionate hands.

southern states and, it is said, the breed was probably saved by Union General Grant's order that defeated Confederate soldiers should keep their horses. The Saddlebred is born as a three-gaited horse (walk, trot and canter) with a natural ability to learn the slow, diagonal, four-beat 'stepping pace' and rack (the equivalent of a gallop) in which the legs are lifted high off the ground. Bred as an all-rounder, the Saddlebred is still used to work cattle, but has a stunning presence in the show ring, as a harness horse and as a pleasure mount. It has plenty of stamina and strength and is spirited and sensitive. As one writer notes of the breed: 'A distinguishable trait is high intelligence. Alert and curious, Saddlebreds possess personality, making them people-oriented.'

- **Colours:** All colours; most bay or chestnut
- **Height:** 15–16.3 hands (152–170cm/60–67in)
- **Gaits:** Flat-footed walk; 'primp' walk; stepping pace; trot; 'rocking chair' canter; rack
- **Recommended for:** All equestrian sports and disciplines

SELLE FRANÇAIS

The Cheval de Selle Français (French Saddle Horse) is unusual in being a warmblooded sport horse with plenty of trotting-horse blood in its background. It was developed after World War II from Normandy Trotter-Thoroughbred crosses and several local French breeds. The Selle Français was recognized in 1958. Some

Arab blood has been introduced since, although generally the horse still largely resembles a big-boned, well-muscled Thoroughbred. With so many contributions to its makeup, the conformation of the Selle Français does show considerable variation. The breed has excelled in showjumping at international level with a string of Olympic champions, but also has a fine record in dressage and eventing. Some consider the Selle Français to be 'the epitome of what a sport horse should be' – athletic, strong, with elegant looks, intelligent and tractable. This is indeed a large, strong, bold horse, with a powerful intelligence but also with a mind of its own to match. Fans of the breed call this 'that little spark that distinguishes the superstars from the rest of the class', and point to the Selle Français' otherwise kindly and forgiving nature, its attachment to humans, and almost canine desire to please.

- **Colours:** All colours, but chestnut most common
- **Height:** 15.2-17 hands (157-173cm/62-68in)
- **Gaits:** Walk, trot, canter, gallop
- **Recommended for:** All equestrian sports and disciplines, especially showjumping; not a horse for beginners or inexperienced riders

SHETLAND PONY

Originating in the harsh climate of a group of islands off northeast Scotland, the immensely strong and hardy Shetland was originally used as a pack and ploughing animal, and later as a pit pony in the English coalfields. Today it is typically used as a children's first pony, and has a reputation as a kindly and tolerant creature. But Shetlands can also be bad-tempered and aggressive, and highly defensive of what they consider their territory. The stocky, bulbous profile, alert eyes and lush mane and tail do appeal to children, however, and their broad seat, surefootedness and reassuring proximity to the ground form a highly stable, confidence-building platform for very young riders. Shetlands respond well to affectionate treatment and even by equine standards are markedly nosey, which translates into a great willingness to learn. In the 1970s, breeders in the USA introduced Morgan and Hackney blood into the breed to create a higher-stepping action and more agility for the show ring; these American Shetlands are larger than the original

Selle Français

Exceptionally willing to please, this talented French breed has lately become a world star in all equestrian disciplines. A bold horse with real class – not for inexperienced riders.

choosing a horse

breed, and purist devotees tend to regard them with mild disdain.

- **Colours:** All colours, except spotted; changes with seasons
- **Height:** 7–10.2 hands (72–107cm/28–42in)
- **Gaits:** Walk, trot, canter, gallop
- **Recommended for:** Child's first pony; driving

SHIRE HORSE

The Shire Horse is one of very few draught horses included here, because it, or more often the Shire-Thoroughbred cross, is proving increasingly popular as a riding horse. The Shire is massive – it is the world's tallest and heaviest horse. Standing at up to 19 hands (193cm/76in) and muscled to match, this one-tonne horse can haul five times its own weight. The Shire is probably descended from the medieval Great Horse that carried metal-clad knights into battle and the joust. It seems to have developed into its present form during the sixteenth century in the English Midlands, with some addition of Friesian and Flemish blood. It gained its hairy ('feathered') fetlocks, which drain water away from the hoofs, through deliberate breeding in the seventeenth century. The tolerance and placidity needed for carrying knights or hauling canal boats remain characteristic of the breed, although Shires don't lack willpower, as some heavy horses seem to. Shire crosses are less quiescent, and can be pushy, even wilful, and so need a strong, firm but unaggressive rider. In compensation, they are supremely comfortable – cantering one is rather like sitting on a flying armchair – and if in doubt tend to halt or quietly find a haven, not spook or bolt.

Shire Horse

One of the great draught breeds, the Shire has now become a popular riding horse. Needs strong riders, but is sensible and hard to spook. Despite its size and weight, the Shire can move with tremendous grace and delicacy in the right hands.

- **Colours:** Black, bay, less often grey
- **Height:** 16–19 hands (163–193cm/64–76in)
- **Gaits:** Walk, trot, canter, gallop
- **Recommended for:** Draught work, hacking

TENNESSEE WALKING HORSE

The Tennessee Walking Horse was developed informally by bluegrass farmers in the late nineteenth century. They used Narragansett Pacer, Thoroughbred, Standard-bred, Morgan and Saddlebred lines to create a saddle horse whose 'running walk' made it a notably comfortable but speedy form of personal transport. Both the flat-footed walk and the running walk involve the horse overreaching with the hind feet by up to 45cm (18in), in a diagonal, regular gait, keeping the rear hooves

choosing a horse

low to the ground. At the walk the horse may reach 13km/h (8mph); in the running walk it can hit 32km/h (20mph), but the rider still feels as if 'she were gliding through the air as if propelled by some powerful but smooth-running machine'. At the same time the Tennessee Walker will nod its head, swing its ears or even snap its teeth in rhythm. These horses also canter – really a collected, relaxed gallop that lifts off from one hind leg, giving a floating, 'rocking chair' feeling to the rider. Since the 1970s the Tennessee Walker has been finding a role as an all-purpose sport and pleasure horse, and has become one of the most popular breeds in the USA. Apart from its quick and easy ride, and its versatility, this is in large part due to the Tennessee Walker's affable nature. It is an even-tempered breed, and easy to train; good for young riders and those with creaking joints.

- **Colours:** All colours
- **Height:** 14.3–17 hands (150–173cm/59–68in)
- **Gaits:** Flat-footed walk, running walk, 'rocking chair' canter; also easily trained to the rack, stepping pace, fox trot and single-foot gaits
- **Recommended for:** All equestrian activities

TERSKY

The Tersky's story starts with the Streletsky horse, bred as a Russian cavalry officer's mount in the nineteenth century. Streletskys were never numerous, but had a loyal, devoted following. Russia's devastating civil war (1917–21) left only a handful of Streletsky mares and two stallions alive, too few to resuscitate the breed unaided. Crossing these with Don, Kabardin, Arabian

Tersky

Good humoured – even laid-back – with a highly trainable disposition, the Russian Tersky is a word-class, all-round sport horse, and its unique metal-sheened coat gives it unmatched good looks.

and Lipizzaner horses resulted, after 20 years' intensive work, in the Tersky. A Tersky looks not unlike an Arabian, but is larger, sturdier and more muscular, with a unique silver-sheened grey coat. Terskys are agile and surefooted horses and have passed numerous demanding endurance tests. The greatest of these was a forced march of the foundation herd to escape advancing Nazi forces in 1941, when 900km (560 miles) were traversed in 21 days in temperatures as low as -20°C (4°F), with the loss of only a few foals. Terskys are economical to keep, and are long-lived. These qualities and a talent for jumping have made them favourite circus horses. They have also won top international honours in dressage. Terskys are noted for their cheerful, alert but relaxed nature and are easily trained.

- **Colours:** Metallic grey; some bay and golden chestnut
- **Height:** 14.1-15.2 hands (145-157cm/57-62in)
- **Gaits:** Walk, trot, canter, gallop
- **Recommended for:** Endurance, dressage, steeplechasing, showjumping

THOROUGHBRED

The Thoroughbred is the world's fastest horse, and is often acclaimed as the most elegant. It is certainly one of the most popular breeds of all time. This last is somewhat mysterious. Thoroughbreds are hotblooded horses, and their tremendous energy and determination can power them along at 70km/h (45mph) or so. That energy, and their inbreeding (the stud book closed in 1791; all Thoroughbreds now share more genes than two human half-siblings) have produced a horse that is often supersensitive, and often neither particularly cooperative nor friendly, let alone cheerful. Some of these qualities in individual horses are undeniably the results of keeping these highly strung creatures unnaturally boxed

choosing a horse

into solitary confinement most of the time, together with being raced too young and harshly trained. The consequent explosion of temperament makes for a difficult horse, which traditionally then receives peremptory treatment, storing up more difficulties for the future. If you want a Thoroughbred, then buy a foal and bring it on sensitively and compassionately, being sure to put it under saddle only once it has reached adulthood; your reward will be a big-hearted, courageous, athletic horse with huge potential in any equestrian sport.

- **Colours:** Most solid colours; roans rare
- **Height:** 14.2-18 hands (147-183cm/58-72in)
- **Gaits:** Walk, trot, canter, gallop
- **Recommended for:** Racing, showjumping, cross-country, eventing, hunting, polo

TRAKEHNER

The Trakehner has two histories: the first began in 1732, when Friedrich Wilhelm I of Prussia gathered his finest horses at the Trakehnen stud in order to breed a new, light cavalry horse. Prussian horses, Arabians and Thoroughbreds went into the mix, and by 1940 there were some 80,000 Trakehners in existence, with a string of Olympic gold medals and steeplechase records to their name. Then in 1945 East Prussia was invaded by the Red Army; many of the breed died, and many others disappeared into Soviet Russia and Poland. Some 800 animals of the foundation stock and their handlers set out for western Germany, a trek that involved crossing the frozen Baltic sea while being strafed by Soviet fighter planes; only 100 of these horses survived. Altogether, through various evacuation attempts, about 1000 Trakehners managed to reach the safety of western Germany, and over the next decade the breed was slowly rebuilt. Trakehners are the most pure-bred of all warmblood breeds, and undergo rigorous testing and evaluation before being admitted into the stud book. The resulting 'performance horse' is free-moving with a magical floating trot, athletic, balanced and elegant, alert, spirited but level-headed, and so amiable and patient as to have been called 'charming'. Trakehners are strong enough mentally and physically to take intensive work, and this has brought them great success as dressage horses, as well as in showjumping.

Trakehner

One of the world's toughest breeds, the Trakehner is also one of the most graceful, bringing it renown in the dressage arena.

- **Colours:** Chestnut, bay, black, grey
- **Height:** 15.3-17 hands (160-173cm/63-68in)
- **Gaits:** Walk, trot, canter, gallop
- **Recommended for:** Dressage, endurance; too sharp for beginners

UKRAINIAN SADDLE HORSE

The Ukrainian Saddle horse is a new breed of large, heavy animal with a relatively short back, making it relatively simple for a rider to sit on the centre of gravity and so bring the horse easily into collection. Ukrainian Saddlers have done well at equestrian events at international level, coming first or second at the Olympics and European championships during the Soviet era. The Ukrainian was developed as a war horse after World War II, when the Red Army still maintained an establishment of mounted soldiers. Hungarian mares were crossed with Hanoverians, Thoroughbreds and looted Trakehner horses from Prussia, to produce a classic warmblood: equable and friendly, with a controlled spirit that would explode on request, and the muscle and bone to match intention to demand. When the Soviet cavalry regiments were disbanded in 1954, the Ukrainian breeding programme shifted towards producing sport horses.

- **Colours:** Bay, chestnut, brown most common
- **Height:** 15.3-16.1 hands (160-165cm/63-65in)
- **Gaits:** Walk, trot, canter, gallop
- **Recommended for:** Dressage, showjumping

VIETNAMESE HMONG

There are about 50,000 Hmong horses living in Ha Giang province of northern Vietnam, where they are used as pack animals and for personal transport. The Hmong people live in the mountains, more than 800m (2625ft) above sea level, where they settled some 500 years ago, having migrated from China. Their horses are probably derived from Mongolian or other Asian horses, with a smattering of Arab blood from French colonial times, but with very little other outside influence, because the province was so isolated. Over the centuries, Hmong horses have become surefooted, nimble creatures of huge endurance. Although small – almost with the proportions of a donkey – and distinctly slim, they are reported to be able to carry several hundred pounds of cargo (often rice) at a time without effort. Their thick manes are kept cropped (hogged) so that they form a crest. The horses have been classified as a distinct breed only since 1999, having been largely ignored by Western equine experts until then. Hmongs have intelligent eyes, a good-natured outlook and great patience. Tourists to Vietnam can, with some ingenuity, ride these animals themselves, as they are used on trekking expeditions into the mountains.

- **Colours:** Bay, sorrel, buckskin dun, pewter dun with eel-stripe, palomino, paint, grey
- **Height:** 10–11 hands (102–112cm/40–44in)
- **Gaits:** Walk, trot, canter, gallop
- **Recommended for:** Pack work, trekking, mountain riding

WALER AND AUSTRALIAN STOCK HORSE

The Waler and the Australian Stock Horse are not quite the same, but their history is inextricably linked. Horses first arrived in Australia in 1788, from South Africa; imports of Thoroughbreds, Arabians and other breeds continued from Britain, India and the Cape Colony. By 1844 the distinctive Waler type had emerged and been named after New South Wales. Despite its light and wiry appearance, this was a stout, frugal, affable horse well suited to working on sheep and cattle stations: it also had tough feet and was virtually immune to disease. Australia ended the nineteenth century exporting 5000 Walers a year to mount the British Indian Army. Walers gained universal admiration in the desert campaigns of the Boer War and World War I, when they would carry 135kg (300lb) of soldier and kit on a three-week patrol, on half rations of barley and one drink every 36 hours – and not return in a state of collapse, as British Army horses did. In 1971 a society was founded to establish a breed from the Waler type. Until 1988 any horse resembling a Waler could be registered; the Australian Stock Horse Society is now refining the Waler's astonishing ruggedness, endurance, lightning reflexes, agility and loyalty into a true breed. (A separate society, the Waler Horse Society of Australia, with its own stud book, is dedicated to preserving the original Waler.)

- **Colours:** All solid colours; bay most common
- **Height:** 14.2–16 hands (147–163cm/58–64in)
- **Gaits:** Walk, trot, canter, gallop
- **Recommended for:** Most equestrian disciplines, polo, polocrosse, camp-drafting; an excellent family horse

WARMBLOODS

The terms 'hotblooded', 'warmblooded' and 'coldblooded' refer not to temperatures – all horses are warmblooded mammals, after all – but to temperament. The more docile, heavy draught breeds like Shires, Clydesdales and Percherons are considered coldblooded, while Thoroughbreds, Akhal-Tekes and Andalusians are among the hotblooded breeds. Most, but not all, warmbloods are the result of crossing draught breeds with Thoroughbreds; many have Arab blood too – but there is some disagreement as to whether Arabians are really hot- or warmblooded. Within the general type, there

choosing a horse

Waler/Australian Stock Horse

These two breeds are closely related, but now considered distinct. Very sturdy, with tremendous agility, they make great family horses.

only to misery for mount and rider alike. And bear in mind that American and Russian Warmbloods generally come from much larger gene pools than European ones – so they are both more variable in capacity and temperament within a breed, and at the same time less liable to be quirky.

- **Colours:** All solid colours
- **Height:** 15–17 hands (152–173cm/60–68in)
- **Gaits:** Walk, trot, canter, gallop; some are natural pacers
- **Recommended for:** All equestrian pursuits; not all are suitable for novices

are also a number of breeds known by the specific name of Warmblood. Germany has probably produced more Warmblood breeds (originally as military or carriage horses) than any other country, but these breeds are no more identical in temperament than the sharpish, even slightly scatty, Danish Warmblood is like the soft-hearted but self-confident Dutch Warmblood. Nonetheless these are far more malleable and genial animals than the hotbloods, and much more tolerant of the conditions most people impose on horses (if often from human necessity). All are now bred as sport horses, and bear investigation if you want to go in for serious riding (they are not that cheap to buy); Warmbloods have excelled at dressage and driving, for example. Some Warmbloods are very powerful animals; it is important not to fall into the common trap of over-horsing yourself, which leads

WELSH COB

The Welsh Cob's antecedents are mostly lost in the mists of time. It is known that as far back as the eleventh century Welsh mountain ponies were crossed with Spanish Horses to produce the Powys Cob, and in the eighteenth century these had Arabian blood added, as well as Yorkshire Coach Horse and Norfolk Roadster blood. The Welsh Cob is somewhat more, then, than a large Welsh pony. It is also a merry breed, which means that Welsh Cobs' temperaments can range from the inventively uncooperative to the fall-into-your-arms affectionate – and sometimes you can find both extremes in a single horse. Histrionics aside, Welsh Cobs are doughty steeds, and even the more diminutive ones can be seen carrying farmers across hedges and up mountain tracks on twice-weekly hunts, trekking tourists over treacherous terrain, carrying disabled people in therapeutic programmes, and floating along apace in trotting races. On a few Welsh mountain farms they are still used for sheep herding. Choose carefully, and you will have a fine mount, and bags of entertainment.

- **Colours:** Black, grey, bay, chestnut
- **Height:** 13.2-16 hands (137-163cm/54-64in)
- **Gaits:** Walk, trot, canter, gallop; can be trained to pace
- **Recommended for:** Trekking, trail riding, hunting, driving; child's second pony

WESTPHALIAN

After the Hanoverian, the Westphalian is the second most numerous German warmblood. With breeders based near the German Olympic equestrian centre, they have had the benefit of much useful advice and guidance from riders in producing a world-class sport horse. Like all German horses, Westphalians undergo a battery of tests and assessments before being entered in the stud book. The breed was founded in 1826, appearing initially as a development of the Oldenburg, and then from the 1920s as a heavier version of the Hanoverian; in the 1960s, when the market for military and farm animals had entirely vanished, Thoroughbreds and some Trakehners were brought in to lighten the line. Westphalians have won gold medals in Olympic dressage and eventing, and the World Championships in dressage and showjumping. They are kind and co-operative animals; the breed association's explicit aim was to produce 'a character-wise flawless, large riding horse with quiet temper, usable for shows as well as for pleasure riding'. They seem to have come near to that, and it is surprising that the Westphalian is not better known.

- **Colours:** All solid colours
- **Height:** 15.2-17.2 hands (157-178cm/62-70in)
- **Gaits:** Walk, trot, canter, gallop
- **Recommended for:** Dressage, showjumping, eventing

Welsh Cob

Welsh cobs can range in temperament from quirky to cuddly – but they're never dull. Great fun, hugely willing, but probably not for complete beginners.

Glossary

Action: the movement of the horse's legs and feet.
Aids: signals or cues through which the rider communicates his wishes to the horse. 'Natural' aids include the voice, the legs, the hands and the weight. 'Artifical' aids include the whip and spurs.
Airs above the ground: Haute Ecole movements performed by highly trained horses, in which either the forelegs or all four legs are off the ground. See also: Ballotade, Capriole, Courbette, Levade.
At grass: a horse that has been turned out in a paddock or field.
Back-breed: breeding back to a certain stallion (to preserve a particular trait) means mating the stallion with one of its descendants.
Ballotade: an 'Air above the ground': the horse half rears and then lands with all four feet together in a collected stance.
Barrel: the area of the horse's body between the forelegs and the loins.
Bars of the mouth: the fleshy area between the horse's front and back teeth, where the bit rests.
Bit: mouthpiece, usually made of made of stainless steel but may be rubber or some synthetic material, and attached to the reins in order to guide the horse's head.
Blaze: elongated white marking down the front of the horse's face. Also called a stripe.
Bloodline: the descendants, male or female, of a particular stallion or series of related stallions.
Bone: measurement around the leg, just below the knee or hock, which determines the horse's ability to carry weight. Thus, a 'light-boned' horse will have limited weight-carrying capacity.
Breaking, or breaking-in: taming of the young horse, traditionally conducted with some degree of force, to make it accept tack and a rider. See: Starting

Brushing: the hoof or shoe hits the inside of the opposite leg, at or near the fetlock. Also known as Interfering. Brushing boots are guards used to protect the horse's legs from injury from brushing.
Buck: a kick with both hindlegs in the air, with the head lowered, and the back arched.
Cantle: back ridge of an English saddle.
Capriole: one of the 'Airs above the ground': the horse leaps high into the air from all four legs and strikes out with the hind legs in mid-leap.
Cast: a horse that rolls and gets stuck, either up against the wall of his stable, or near a fence, is said to be cast. Also: a horse that has 'cast' a shoe, has lost his shoe accidentally.
Cavesson: noseband fitted to a bridle. Also, leather or nylon headgear, with attachments for side reins and lunge line, worn by the horse when it is being lunged.
Check rein: see Draw rein.
Cinch: secures a Western saddle to the horse. May be single or double. See Girth.
Clench: end of nail driven through the wall of the hoof when shoeing. This is then bent over and hammered flat to secure the shoe.
Close-coupled: having a relatively short back, which makes for good balance and agility.
Coldblood: heavy European breeds of horse, mostly used for draft purposes, which are deemed to have a placid, unflappable temperament.
Collection: a horse is called 'collected' when the hindlegs are under the horse (not trailing), the croup is lowered, the shoulder is raised and the head is held on the vertical.
Conformation: the way in which a horse is put together (as one speaks of a person's 'build'). Also, its proportions.
Contact: the 'feel', through the reins, of the bit by a rider's hands.

Courbette: an 'Air above the ground': after performing the levade, the horse bounds or hops forward on bent hind legs.
Crop: short, flexible whip used to emphasize the natural aids of seat and legs. Should never be used to punish a horse.
Croupade: an 'Air above the ground': the horse springs from the levade and keeps his legs under him.
Diagonals: horses' legs move together in pairs at the trot, called diagonals. On the left diagonal, the left foreleg and right hindleg move; on the right diagonal, the right foreleg and the left hindleg move.
Dished face: concave head profile seen in breeds such as the Arabian and Welsh pony.
Dishing: faulty action, in which the toe of the foreleg is thrown outward in a circular movement with each stride. Also called Paddling.
Docking: amputation of the dock for cosmetic reasons. Illegal in the UK.
Draw reins: reins, attached to the girth at one end, that pass through the rings of the bit and back to the rider's hands. Used to increase control and keep the horse's head down. Difficult to use correctly, very easy to abuse, and can cause rigidity in the neck. Also known as a Check rein. Avoid them.
Dressage: the art of training the horse so that he is totally obedient and responsive to the rider, as well as supple and agile in his performance. Also, the competitive sport that tests the horse's natural movement and level of training against an ideal.
Easy keeper: see Good doer.
Entire: uncastrated adult male horse; a stallion.
Farrier: skilled craftsman who shoes horses.
Feathering: long hair on lower legs and fetlocks that helps to drain water away from the hoof.
Footing: see Going.
Forehand: the horse's head, neck, shoulder, withers and forelegs.
Frog: triangular pad on the sole of the foot that acts as a shock absorber; viewed from the heel, it looks like the outline of a sitting frog.
Gait: the paces at which horses move, usually the walk, trot, canter and gallop. But a 'gaited' horse is one that either naturally or through training also performs specific gaits such as the rack or the running walk.
Gentling: see Starting a horse.
Girth: circumference of the body measured from behind the withers around the barrel. Also, the band or strap by which an English saddle is secured to the horse, which attaches to the saddle on one side, running under the barrel just behind the legs to the other side. Called a cinch in Western riding.
Going: the nature of the ground, i.e. deep, good, rough. Also known as Footing.
Good doer: a horse that stays in good condition on small rations. Also known as a Thrifty horse, or an Easy keeper.
Green horse: usually young, inexperienced horse that is in the early stages of their training.
Gray: coat colour ranging from bright white to dark gray. Seemingly pure white horses are always called grays, as there is always a percentage of dark hair in their coats.
Hack: to go for a ride on horseback for pleasure or exercise.
Halter-broken: a horse that has been accustomed to wearing a halter.
Hand: unit used to measure a horse's height from the withers to the ground. One hand = 4 inches (10 cm); part measures are 14.1, 14.2, 14.3.
Haute Ecole: the classical art of advanced riding. See also Airs above the ground.
Heavy horse: any large draft horse, such as the Shire, Percheron or Clydesdale; synonymous with a coldblooded horse.
High School: see Haute Ecole.
Hind quarters: the part of the horse's body from the rear of the flank to the top of the tail down to the top of the gaskin. Also called simply the quarters.
Hogged mane: mane that has been shaved close for its entire length. Also known as a Roached mane.
Horn: the hard, insensitive outer covering of the hoof. Also, the prominent pommel at the front of a Western saddle, around which the rider loops or twists the lariat when a steer has been roped to secure the animal.
Hotblood: term used to describe horses generally reckoned to have a 'hot' or highly strung temperament, such as Arabians or Thoroughbreds.
Impulsion: strong but controlled forward movement in the horse. Not to be confused with speed.
In hand: a horse controlled from the ground.
Inside leg: the legs of horse and rider that are on the inside of a circle or turn being ridden.
Interfering: see Brushing
Jog: Western riding term for trot. Also, in English riding, an awkward, uncomfortable pace between walk and trot.
Letting down: see Roughing off.
Levade: an 'Air above the ground': a controlled half-rear, in which the horse remains immmobile.

glossary

Light horse: a horse, or breed of horse, other than a heavy horse or pony, that is suitable for riding or carriage work.

Lunge (or Longe) rein: a long, single rein attached to the horse on the cavesson, while its free end is held by a trainer on the ground. The horse is schooled by working it in various paces on a circle using the lunge rein to control it. Novice riders may be taught on the lunge, so that they do not have to concern themselves initially with controlling the horse.

Manège: rectangular enclosure used for training and schooling horses. Also called a school or an arena. May be open, fenced, or roofed.

Native ponies: the mountain and moorland ponies of the UK – New Forest, Exmoor, Dartmoor, Highland, Fell, Dale, Shetland, Connemara and Welsh.

Nearside: left hand side of the horse.

Offside: right hand side of the horse.

On the bit: a horse is 'on the bit' when he carries his head in a near vertical position and is calmly accepting the rider's contact on the reins.

Overface: to ask a horse to perform beyond his level of training or his physical capability, e.g. to jump a fence too high for him.

Overreaching: the toe of the horse's hind foot catches and injures the back of the pastern or heel of the fore foot.

Pacer: a horse that moves his legs in lateral pairs, rather than the more usual diagonal pairs.

Paddling: see Dishing

Paddock: small enclosure in which horses are turned out for grazing.

Piebald: English term for body colour of white with black patches.

Points: external features of the horse making up its conformation.

Pommel: the centre front of an English saddle. In some designs the pommel is cut back.

Pony: a small horse, standing 14.2 hands or lower; usually has legs shorter in proportion to its body than a full-size horse.

Quarters: see Hind quarters.

Roached mane: see Hogged mane.

Roughing off: gradually reducing the amount of hard feed given to a horse, and increasing forage feeds, preparatory to turning him out. Also called Letting down.

School: to train a horse, usually in an arena, to understand and respond to the aids.

Seat: the rider's position in the saddle.

Skewbald: English term for a horse with irregular white and coloured (not black – see Piebald) patches on its coat. Called pinto in the USA.

Skip or skep: bucket used to gather droppings; hence 'skip out'.

Sock: white marking on any or all of a horse's lower legs. Markings extending higher than the knee or hock are called stockings.

Sound: a 'sound' horse is one free from lameness or any other injury that affects its performance.

Spook: to shy at something that is perceived as a potential threat.

Star: small white marking on the horse's forehead.

Starting a horse: taming the horse by non-violent means, and teaching him without coercion to accept tack and to be ridden. This is also known as 'gentling'.

Stocking: white marking on any or all of a horse's legs which extends beyond the knee or hock.

Strapping: a very thorough grooming to clean right through the horse's coat. The horse is first brushed all over in small circular motions with a rubber curry comb to bring scurf in the coat to the surface. A body brush (cleaned with a metal curry comb) is then used to take the scurf off the coat. As the technique disturbs deep-seated layers of protective oil, it must not be used on a horse kept out, even part-time, at pasture.

Tack: the equipment of a riding horse: saddle, bridle, etc. Short for 'tackle'. To 'tack up' is to put the tack on the horse in preparation for riding.

Thrifty horse: see Good doer.

Transition: changing from one gait to another. Walk to trot, and trot to canter, are 'upward' transitions ('up' from slower to faster). Canter to trot, and trot to walk, are 'downward' transitions.

Turn out: let horses loose in a field or pasture for all or part of the day.

Unsoundness: any condition, or fault in the horse's con-formation, that limits the horse's ability to perform properly.

Warmbloods: breeds of horse created by crossing hotblood and coldblood horses to produce a more refined, but athletically strong and capable horse, for example the Swedish Warmblood, Dutch Warmblood, etc.

Weedy: horse of poor conformation, usually weak in the quarters and shoulders, with long legs.

Well-sprung ribs: long, rounded ribcage with ample room for the lungs to expand.

Directory of resources

BOOKS

Lesley Bayley & Richard Maxwell: **Understanding Your Horse** *David & Charles 1997*

Joni Bentley: **Riding Success Without Stress** *J.A. Allen 1999*

Stephen Budiansky: **The Nature of Horses: Their Evolution, Intelligence and Behavior** *Free Press/Wiedenfeld & Nicolson 1997*

Barbara Cooper (ed.): **The Manual of Horsemanship** *Pony Club 1993*

Elwyn Hartley Edwards & Candida Geddes (eds): **The Complete Book of the Horse** *Ward Lock 1973*

Horace Hayes: **Points of the Horse** *Stanley Paul 1969*

Jane Holderness-Roddam (ed.): **The Life of Horses** *Mitchell Beazley 1999*

Klaus Ferdinand Hempfling: **Dancing with Horses: Communication by Body Language** *Trafalgar Square 2001*

John Kohnke: **Feeding and Nutrition: the Making of a Champion** *Birubi Pacific 1992*

Marthe Kiley-Worthington: **Equine Welfare** *J.A. Allen 1997*

Sylvia Loch: **Dressage in Lightness** *J.A. Allen 2000*

Susan McVane: **How Your Horse Works** *David & Charles 1999*

Heather Moffett: **Enlightened Equitation** *David & Charles 1999*

Eleanor F. Prince & Gaydell M. Collier: **Basic Horsemanship – English and Western** *Doubleday Equestrian Library 1974*

Monty Roberts: **The Man Who Listens to Horses** *Random House 1996*

Mary Rose: **The Horsemaster's Notebook** *Kenilworth 1993*

Moyra Williams: **Understanding Nervousness in Horse and Rider (Revised edition)** *J.A. Allen 1999*

WORLD WIDE WEB

One may spend many happy hours digging up information and advice on horses on the Web. Apart from their own considerable resources, the following sites have links to all manner of highly specialized information on breeds and breed societies, sports, training, and the nature of the horse:

British Horse Society: http://www.bhs.org.uk

Central Pets: http://centralpets.com/pages/mammals/horses.shtml

Cybersteed: http://www.cybersteed.com

Conquistador magazine (Spanish and Spanish-American horses): http://www.conquistador.com

Cowboy Heaven: http://www.cowboyheaven.com

Equine Estates: http://equineestates.com/library

Equisearch (links to everything equine): http://www.equisearch.com

Horse Directory Australia: http://www.horsedirectory.com.au

Horse Previews Magazine (excellent veterinary resource): www.horse-previews.com

Horse Wizard (vast resource on all aspects of horses): http://www.horsewizard.com

Mr Horse: (useful information and some really weird facts about horses, in English and Italian): www.mrhorse.com

International Museum of the Horse (brilliant all-round resource for breeds, sports, history) http://www.imh.org

Oklahoma State University (another brilliant all-round resource on horse breeds, sports and evolution): http://www.ansi.okstate.edu

The following specific URLs deserve special mention:

Kathleen Hunt: 'Horse Evolution' http://www.talkorigins.org/faqs/horses.html

Troika (the best Web resource on Russian horses, run by people who have a passion for them): http://www.horses.ru

International Veterinary Information Service (huge resource available from home page [http://www.ivis.org]: the following URL gives critical information on 'stable vices'): http://www.ivis.org/advances/Behavior_Houpt/nicol/chapter_frm.asp?LA=1

Jackson Arenas: the Lincoln Stable Mirror http://www.jacksonarenas.co.uk

USA Equestrian: http://www.equestrian.org

White Horse Equine Ethology Project (equine psychology, behaviour and senses): http://www.equine-behavior.com

Horsemarwari (everything you ever wanted to know about the marwari): http://www.horsemarwari.com

Index

Page numbers in *italics* refer to illustration captions.

accidents, eventing 45
aggression 54, 56
   snorting and 51
ailments, common *110*, 111-15
Akhal-Tekes 17, 43, 82, *152*, 153
American horses, 'western' 29
anatomy *10-11*, *121*
Andalusians 153
Appaloosas *154*
approaching horses 69, *70*
Arabians 29, 79, 92, 154-5
Australian Stock Horses *183*, 184
azoturia 111
Aztecas 155-6

Barbs 156-7
Basutos *157*
beating 58, 75
beds and bedding 91-2
   eating 65
biting
   rugs 67
   see also cribbing
bits 120, *122*
blankets, saddle 123
blind spots 55, 63
blowing 51
bombproof horses *17*, *43*
boots, riding 118
boredom 18, 68, 100-1
   see also vices
box walking 62
'breaking' horses 77, 85
breeds 151-85

bridles 120, 123, 128, *129*
broken wind 111
brushes 117, 118
bucking 146
Budennys 28-9, 157-9
Budiansky, Stephen 25-6, 48, 52
bullfighters 25

campdrafting *40*
   see also 'cutting' horses
Canadian horses *158*, 159
Caspians 159, *160*
casting 88
catching horses 69-72
choosing a horse 151-85
clipping and rugging 92-8
clubs, riding 44
colic 101, 111
colts 48, 50
communication, horse-to-horse 52
Connemara Ponies 44, 159-60
coolers 94
COPD 111
cribbing 60-2, 66
Criollos 41, 160-1
cross-country, in eventing *42*, *43*, 45
'cutting' horses 36-8
   see also campdrafting

dams 48
Dartmoor and Exmoor ponies 79
domestication 49
Don horses 161-2
draughts 89
dressage 23-6
   in eventing 41, *42*
   Haute Ecole 23, *26*, *27*

   and the Spanish Riding School 26, *27*
droppings 49, 92
   eating 65-6

ears 55
endurance riding *27-30*
   vet checks 29, 31
entires 48
Estonian native horses 163

facial expressions, horse 52
family life, horse 50-4
farriers 145
fears, horses' 16-17, 53, 54-6, *69*
feet
   laminitis *110*
   lifting the 117, 146
   picking out 148
   see also hooves
fences *104*, 105-7
fence walking *64*, 66-7
fighting, avoidance 56
   over food *114-15*
fillies 48
fitness plan 137
Fjords *174-5*
Fleetwood, Sir William 8
flehmen 61
flies *103*
foals 48, 51
   eating mother's droppings 65-6
food and feeding 54, 98-102, *114-15*
   see also pasture
founder *see* laminitis
foxhunting 35-6
friendships, between horses 52-4, 65

Friesans *162*, 163
frightening horses 69

games
   horse play 59, 78
   mounted 18, *19*, *20*
gear, riding 118
geldings 48
gestures, horse 52
girths 120, 123
grass *see* pasture
grooming 117-18, *119*, 127
   horse nibbling your clothes 149
   mutual 52-4, *58*
gymkhanas 18-20
Gypsy Horses (Irish Cobs) 166-7

habits, harmless 65-6
hacking (riding out) 14-18
Haflingers 163-4
halters, pressure 72
handling, horse 68-9
   approaching 69, *70*
   catching 69-72
   leading 72-5
   loading and unloading *74*, 75-7
   'natural' 77-9
   praise 72
   putting on a head collar *70*, *71*
Hanoverians 164
happy horses 8-9
hay, soaking 100
haynets *99*
head-butting 66
head collars, putting on *70*, *71*
hearing 55
heels, cracked 112-13

index

herbs 109
herds 48, 50-4
  exile from 49
  wild 83
hierarchies 50, 52
Hmongs 183-4
Hokkaidos 165
hooves 148, 149
  ailments and 112-13
horseboxes and trailers 74, 75-7
horse whisperers 77-8
Huaso 22, 23
humans
  association with 48-9
  trust of 56-8
hunting 35-6
  drag 37

Icelandic horses 41, 165-6
illnesses see ailments
influenza 111
instinct, horses' 16-17
Irish Cobs (Irish Tinkers; Gypsy Horses) 166-7
Irish Draughts 167-8

jumping 22
  high jump record 22, 23

Kabardins 168
kicking, door and wall 63-5
Kisber Felvers 168, 169
Kustanais 169-70

lameness 111-12
laminitis (founder) 101, 109, 110
leading the horse 72-5
learning (horse), and work 59
learning to ride 125-30, 132
legs
  lameness and 112
  and standing 57
lessons, on the lunge rein 132
levade 26
Lipizzaners 170-1
litter race 19-20
livery 85
loading and unloading horses 74, 75-7
loneliness 60, 64, 66, 100-1
  see also solitude

long-distance rides see endurance riding

mane, hogging the 120
Mangalarga Marchadors 171
mangers 89
mares 48, 50
martingales 125
Marwaris 171-2
mineral supplements 100
mirrors, horse 61, 67
misbehaving 18
  see also problems
Missouri Fox Trotters 172
Morgans 44, 172-3
mounted games 18, 19, 20
muck heaps 91
mucking out 91, 92
mud fever (scratches) 86, 112-13
muscles 121
mustangs 173-4

names, horse 48
napping 148-9
nature, of the horse
  aggression 51, 54, 56
  association with man 48-9
  cooperation 103
  factors for survival 54-6
  family life 50-4
  fears 16-17, 53, 54-6, 69
  feeding 54
  gestures 52
  harmless habits 65-6
  head-butting 66
  mutual grooming 58
  play 59, 78
  problems of stabled horses 59-65
  senses 55
  solitude 49, 50, 64
  standing 57
  time budgets 68
  trust 56-8
  work and play 58-9
  world according to the horse 47-8
Nature of Horses, The (Budiansky) 25-6, 48, 52
navicular disease 113
nickering 51
noises, equine 51

Norwegian Fjords 174-5
numnahs 120, 123

Oldenburgs 175
Olympic Games (2000) 45
outside, keeping horses 81-4, 86, 112

Palaminos 151
Palm, Llynn 23-4
parasites 113
Paso Finos 175-6
pasture 104-9
  care of fields 109-11
  the grass to grow 109
  poisonous plants 108, 109, 113
photosensitivity 113
plants, poisonous 108, 109, 113
play, horse 59, 78
point-to-point racing 36, 37
polo 30-5
polocrosse 32, 33
ponies 152
Pony Clubs 18, 44-5
  and gymkhanas 18-20
praise 72
Prince Philip Cup 18
problems 18
  riding awkward horses 145-8
  of stabled horses 59-65

Quarter Horses 23-4, 41, 44, 176

racehorses, retired 17
racing 48
  point-to-point 36, 37
rainscald 86, 114
rearing 146-8
rearing up 73-5
reining 39-41
reins 120, 123, 125
  holding 132-4
  and leaving your hors tacked up 131
  lunge 132
  and turning 138, 147
riding
  awkward horses 145-8
  cantering 140, 142-4
  galloping 144-5
  inner conflict for the horse 143

learning to ride 125-30, 132
long-distance 27-30
mounting and dismounting 130-1
sitting 131-4, 135, 136, 143
stopping 134-5
trail 27, 28
trotting 138-42
turning 135-8, 147
walking 133, 134-5
riding clubs 44
riding gear 118
riding out see hacking
Riding Ponies 176, 177
riding schools 44
riding terms 9
Roberts, Monty 77, 85-6
rollbacks 41
roller-and-surcingle system 94
rolling 105
roping 38-9
Rugged Lark 23-4
rugging and clipping 92-8
rugs, biting 67
Russian breeds 27, 28, 43, 82-3
  Akhal-Tekes 17, 43, 82, 152, 153

Saddlebreds 176-8
saddles 120-3, 124
  fitting 128, 130
salts 107
sarcoids 113-14
schools, riding 44
scratches see mud fever
Selle Français 43, 178
senses, horse 55
Shetland Ponies 178-9
Shire horses 179
shoeing 145
showing 14, 79
  in hand 15
showjumping 20-3
  in eventing 42-3, 44
sight 55, 63
sires 48
size, horse 29
skeleton 121
sliding stops 38, 39-41
smell(s)
  sense of 55
  sniffing 61

index

snorting 51
solitude *49*, *50*, *64*
   see also loneliness
sounds, horse 51
Spanish Riding School 26, 27
spins 39
sponging down 118
sports and pastimes *12-14*
   campdrafting *40*
   dressage 23-6, 41, *42*
   endurance riding *27-30*
   eventing (horse trials; combined training) 41-4, 45
   getting started 44-5
   hacking 14-18
   hunting *35-6*, *37*
   point-to-point 36, *37*
   polo 30-5
   polocrosse *32*, *33*
   Pony Clubs and gymkhanas 18-20, 44-5
   showing 14, *15*, 79
   showjumping 20-3, *42-3*, 44
   trail riding 27, *28*
   trekking 27
   Western events 36-41
squealing 51
stabled horses 81, 84-6

beds and bedding 91-2
casting *88*, 92
feeding 100-1, 102
part-time 86
problems of 59-65, *84*
salts 107
stable design 86-*90*
time budget *68*
yard and stable kit *93*
stallions 48, 50-2, *83*
standing, legs and 57
steeplechasing 45
steppe horses 82-3
stirrups 120, 123, *126*, 132
strangles 114
straw bedding 91
   eating 65
streams and ponds *106*, 107-9
stroking horses 55
sunburn 113
sweats 107
sweet itch 114

tabuns 82, 109
tack 118-25
   leaving your horse tacked up 131
taste 55
Tennessee Walking Horses 180-1

terms
   for horses of various ages 48
   riding terms 9
Terskys *180*, 181
tetanus 114
Thoroughbreds 17, 43, 92, 181-2
thrush 114
time budgets, horse *68*
touch, sense of 55
   touching companions 61, 68
trail riding 27, *28*
Trakehners 181, *182*
trekking 27
trust 17, 56-8
types 151

Ukrainian Saddle horses 182-3
understanding horses 8

vet checks, for endurance riding 29, 31
vibrissae (whiskers) 55, 79
vices 59-68
   cribbing 60-2, 66
Vietnamese Hmongs 183-4
vision 55, 63

visual signals, horse 52
vitamins 100

Waler Stock Horses 183, *184*
walking 133, 134-5, 136
   box walking 62
   fence walking 64, 66-7
Warmbloods 26, 43, 151, 184-5
washing 118
water 101, 102-3
   streams and ponds *106*, 107-9
water jumps 21
weatherbeat 86, 115
weaving 59-60, 61, 65
   horse mirrors and 61, *67*
weight 109
Welsh Cobs *185*
Welsh ponies 41
Western events 36-41
Westphalians 185
whinnying 50, 51
whiskers (vibrissae) 55, 79
wind sucking 60-2
work, learning and 59
wounds 114, 115

yearlings 48

THANKS AND ACKNOWLEDGEMENTS

Authors and websites that I have found especially useful in writing this book are listed in the Bibliography & References. Use these with care, though: not all of them agree with one another, and not all are written for novices. Individuals who helped me directly include Professor Edwina Cruise, for an invaluable account of the Russian tabun; Raghuvendra Singh Dundlod, who explained the Marwari horse's revaal gait; Luis Gonzales Manso, who translated the account of Huaco's record-breaking high jump from the Spanish for me; Jackson Arenas, for information on the Lincoln Horse Mirror; and Dr Marthe Kiley-Worthington, for various apt and pithy comments on equine welfare. Lizzie Hopkinson did a brilliant job as Technical Contributor in getting me to draw out many finer points of horse maintenance and riding; and, as always, Lesley Riley has done a masterly piece of editing. She is due a special credit besides: for it was her fascination for equines that kindled mine, and has ultimately been the inspiration for this book. Heartfelt thanks to you all. As is traditional among the scribbling classes, the wife has been sorely neglected during its composition: which wasn't fair at all, as it was she who got me on horseback again after a lapse of decades. Special thank you, Rosalind. And, too, to the horses from whom I've learned so much. Any errors that may remain here are, of course, all my own work.

BV - #0021 - 110319 - C0 - 240/189/11 - PB - 9781782745914